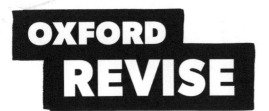

AQA GCSE

RELIGIOUS STUDIES

Christianity and Islam

COMPLETE REVISION AND PRACTICE

Series Editor: Dawn Cox

Dawn Cox

OXFORD
UNIVERSITY PRESS

Great Clarendon Street, Oxford, OX2 6DP, United Kingdom

Oxford University Press is a department of the University of Oxford. It furthers the University's objective of excellence in research, scholarship, and education by publishing worldwide. Oxford is a registered trade mark of Oxford University Press in the UK and in certain other countries.

© Oxford University Press 2023

Written by Dawn Cox

Series Editor: Dawn Cox

The moral rights of the author has been asserted

First published in 2023

British Library Cataloguing in Publication Data
Data available

978-1-382-04038-9

10 9 8 7 6 5 4

The manufacturing process conforms to the environmental regulations of the country of origin.

Printed in the UK by Bell and Bain Ltd, Glasgow

Acknowledgements
The publisher and authors would like to thank the following for permission to use photographs and other copyright material:

Text: p166: Extract from the The Values of Islamic Relief Organization. Reproduced with permission by Islamic Relief Organization.

Scriptures taken from the Holy Bible, New International Version®, NIV®. Copyright © 1973, 1978, 1984, 2011 by Biblica, Inc.™ Used by permission of Zondervan. All rights reserved worldwide. www.zondervan.com The "NIV" and "New International Version" are trademarks registered in the United States Patent and Trademark Office by Biblica, Inc.®

Verses from 'The Qur'an', a new translation by M. A. S. Abdel Haleem, published by Oxford University Press. Used by permission of the translator.

Artworks: QBS Learning, Jason Ramasami

Photos: p8: Damon Ace/Shutterstock; **p11 (L):** rudall30/Shutterstock; **p11(R):** rudall30/Shutterstock; **p12(L):** rudall30/Shutterstock; **p12(R):** AndryDj/Shutterstock; **p13(L):** AndryDj/Shutterstock; **p13(R):** rudall30/ Shutterstock; **p16(L):** AndryDj/Shutterstock; **p16(R):** fizkes/Shutterstock; **p30:** Godong/Alamy Stock Photo; **p31:** Ken Jack/Demotix/Corbis; **p36(T):** Doidam 10/Shutterstock; **p36(B):** Elena Rostunova/Shutterstock; **p40:** Corry Meela; **p41(T):** CAFOD; **p41(M), p209(T):** Christian Aid; **p41(B):** Mark Boulton/Alamy Stock Photo; **p51:** nuttakit/Shutterstock; **p70:** allex wijaya/ Shutterstock; **p84(T):** Mansoreh Motamedi/Shutterstock; **p84(B):** Hasan Hatrash/Shutterstock; **p109:** YANGCHAO/Shutterstock; **p114:** Aphelleon/ Shutterstock; **p115:** Sogno Lucido/Shutterstock; **p116:** Henrik5000/ Getty Images; **p119:** Stokkete/Shutterstock; **p135(T):** Tooykrub/ Shutterstock; **p135(M):** photoJS/Shutterstock; **p135(B):** Wirestock Creators/Shutterstock; **p147(L):** Mario Segovia Guzman/Shutterstock; **p147(R):** MonoLiza/Shutterstock; **p165:** Pacific Press Media Production Corp./Alamy Stock Photo/Shutterstock; **p169:** Universal History Archive/ Contributor/Getty Images; **p203:** Doidam 10/Shutterstock; **p208:** Dragana Gordic/Shutterstock; **p209(B):** Islamic Relief Organisation;

Although we have made every effort to trace and contact all copyright holders before publication this has not been possible in all cases. If notified, the publisher will rectify any errors or omissions at the earliest opportunity.

Links to third party websites are provided by Oxford in good faith and for information only. Oxford disclaims any responsibility for the materials contained in any third party website referenced in this work.

MIX
Paper | Supporting
responsible forestry
FSC
www.fsc.org   FSC® C007785

Contents

 Shade in each level of the circle as you feel more confident and ready for your exam.

Key

✝ Christianity   ☾ Islam

Contents

Contents

How to use this book

This book uses a three-step approach to revision: **Knowledge**, **Retrieval**, and **Practice**.
It is important that you do all three; they work together to make your revision effective.

 **Knowledge**

Knowledge comes first. Each chapter starts with a **Knowledge Organiser**. These are clear easy-to-understand, concise summaries of the content that you need to know for your exam. The information is organised to show how one idea flows into the next so you can learn how everything is tied together, rather than lots of disconnected facts.

Answers and Glossary

You can scan the QR code at any time to access sample answers, mark schemes for all the exam-style questions, a glossary containing definitions of the key terms, as well as further revision support go.oup.com/OR/GCSE/AA/RS/ChristianityIslam

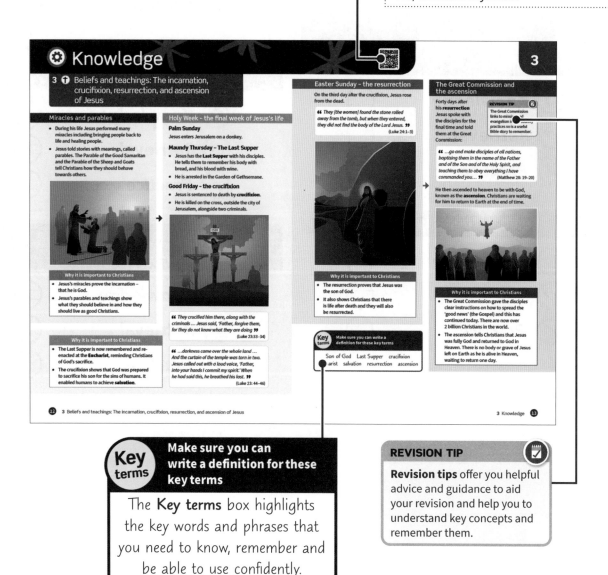

Key terms
Make sure you can write a definition for these key terms

The **Key terms** box highlights the key words and phrases that you need to know, remember and be able to use confidently.

REVISION TIP

Revision tips offer you helpful advice and guidance to aid your revision and help you to understand key concepts and remember them.

Retrieval

The **Retrieval questions** help you learn and quickly recall the information you've acquired. These are short questions and answers about the content in the Knowledge Organiser you have just reviewed. Cover up the answers with some paper and write down as many answers as you can from memory. Check back to the Knowledge Organiser for any you got wrong, then cover the answers and attempt all the questions again until you can answer *all* the questions correctly.

Make sure you revisit the Retrieval questions on different days to help them stick in your memory. You need to write down the answers each time, or say them out loud, otherwise it won't work.

Previous questions

Each chapter also has some **Retrieval questions** from **previous chapters**. Answer these to see if you can remember the content from the earlier chapters. If you get the answers wrong, go back and do the Retrieval questions for the earlier chapters again.

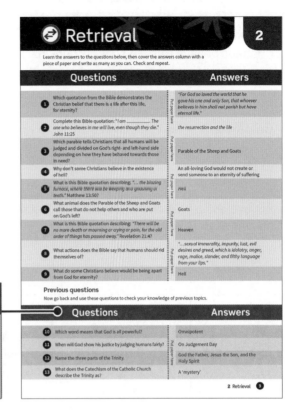

Practice

Once you think you know the Knowledge Organiser and Retrieval answers really well, you can move on to the final stage: **Practice**.

Each chapter has **Exam-style Questions**, including some questions from previous chapters, to help you apply all the knowledge you have learnt and can retrieve.

EXAM TIP

Exam tips show you how to interpret the questions, provide guidance on how to answer them, and advice on how to secure as many marks as possible. Guidance is also offered on how to approach different command words.

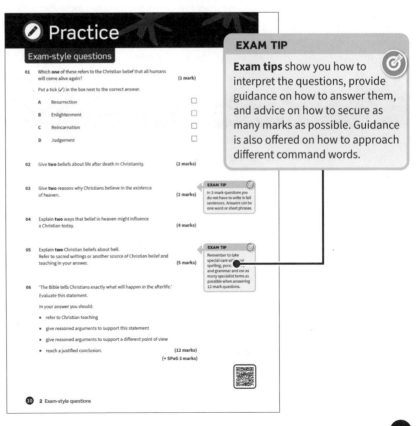

⚙ Knowledge

1 ✝ Beliefs and teachings: The nature of God and beliefs about creation

The nature of God

Christians believe that God has certain characteristics that make him unique. They find these characteristics in the Bible.

Belief	Meaning	Example in the Bible
Omnipotent	God is all powerful.	God created the universe and everything in it: ❝ *In the beginning God created the heavens and the earth.* ❞ (Genesis 1:1)
Benevolent (loving)	God loves his **creation** including all humans.	God sacrificed Jesus to enable humans to achieve salvation: ❝ *For God so loved the world that he gave his one and only Son, that whoever believes in him shall not perish but have eternal life.* ❞ (John 3:16)
Just	God is fair and treats humans fairly.	God will judge people fairly on Judgement Day, as described in the Bible: ❝ *For he has set a day when he will judge the world with justice by the man he has appointed. He has given proof of this to everyone by raising him from the dead.* ❞ (Acts 17:31)

↓

The problem of evil and suffering

Atheists believe there is no God. One of the reasons they give for this is because there is so much evil and suffering in the world, for example, floods, diseases, and war. They argue that if God exists then he is not omnipotent, loving, or all-knowing (**omniscient**).

Theists believe that God exists, but evil and suffering present them with a problem because if God exists, and if they believe he is omnipotent, loving, just, and all-knowing, then why is there still evil and suffering in the world? This is known as the problem of evil and suffering.

An atheist might say...	A Christian might say...
• If God is omnipotent, he would be powerful enough to stop the evil and suffering.	• Evil and suffering (e.g., war) is caused by humans and not God, and God won't interfere with our free will.
• If he is loving, he would not want humans to suffer so he would stop it.	• Suffering can be a test, and we should follow the teachings of Christianity to pass the test. • The way humans respond to suffering can allow them to develop in moral character, for example, showing compassion to others, and therefore grow closer to the likeness of God.
• If he is just, he wouldn't allow innocent people to suffer.	• We don't know why God allows evil and suffering. We should help those who suffer, and we will find out God's purpose of suffering at the end of time.
• If he is all-knowing, he would know that the suffering is happening and want to stop it.	

The oneness of God and the Trinity: Father, Son, and Holy Spirit

Christians believe that God is one. However he is three 'persons': God the Father, Jesus who is 'God the Son', and the Holy Spirit.

The **Trinity** describes all three at once:

- There is only one God.
- Each person of the Trinity is fully God.
- The persons of the Trinity are experienced in different ways.
- God the Father is the omnipotent creator, who is **omnipresent** (everywhere), omniscient (knows everything), and benevolent (loving).
- Jesus the Son, is the human incarnation of God sent to Earth to save humans from their sins. He is fully God and fully human.
- The Holy Spirit is God being present on Earth today, who guides and supports Christians.

The Bible doesn't ever refer to the 'Trinity' – however, all three are present at the baptism of Jesus.

The Trinity is a complex belief to try to understand – the Catholic Catechism calls the Trinity a 'mystery'.

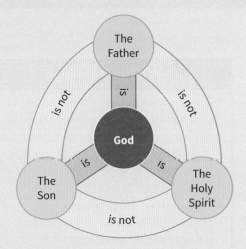

Creation: Genesis 1:1–3

The book of Genesis in the Old Testament of the Bible describes seven days of creation.

 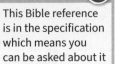
Day 1: light and darkness

Day 2: the sky

Day 3: land, sea, and plants

Day 4: the sun, moon, and stars

Day 5: fish and sea creatures, and birds

Day 6: animals and humans

Day 7: God was pleased and rested

> ❝ *In the beginning God created the heavens and the earth.* ❞ (Genesis 1:1)

→ This tells Christians that God is omnipotent (to be able to create the heavens and the earth).

> ❝ *Now the earth was formless and empty, darkness was over the surface of the deep, and the Spirit of God was hovering over the waters.* ❞ (Genesis 1:2)

→ This tells Christians that there was 'nothing', except for God, before creation, and the (Holy) Spirit of God was present.

> ❝ *And God said, 'Let there be light,' and there was light.* ❞ (Genesis 1:3)

→ This tells Christians that there was a moment that 'light' came into the world which shows God's omnipotence and omniscience. God can create simply by 'saying', and he knows what light is before it is created.

Knowledge

1 ✝ Beliefs and teachings: The nature of God and beliefs about creation

Different Christian beliefs about creation

Different Christians interpret the Genesis creation account in different ways. Two interpretations are:

Literal creation	Theistic evolution
• The universe was made in six days by God, and he rested on the seventh day (Some Christians believe that the original text for 'day' also means 'age' so this could have been over a long period of time rather than six periods of 24 hours). • On each day God created something different. • Happened approximately 6000 years ago using Biblical chronology.	• Creation started with a 'Big Bang'. • Uses evidence from the Bible and science. • The universe was formed over a long period of time. • God the omnipotent creator started it. • Happened approximately 13.8 billion years ago.

REVISION TIP

'Literal' creation means the belief that the story in Genesis 1 of the Bible is literally true. Read Genesis 1 to make sure you are familiar with what it says.

Creation: John 1:1–3

John 1:1–3 in the New Testament says:

> ❝ *In the beginning was the Word, and the Word was with God, and the Word was God. He was with God in the beginning. Through him all things were made; without him nothing was made that has been made.* ❞ (John 1:1–3)

The Word in this passage means Jesus the Son. This tells Christians that Jesus was present in the beginning of time, and they read it alongside Genesis 1. This means that God, Jesus, and the (Holy) Spirit (the Trinity) were present at the beginning of time.

 Key terms Make sure you can write a definition for these key terms

omnipotent   creation   just   atheist
omniscient   theist
Trinity   omnipresent   the Word

Learn the answers to the questions below, then cover the answers column with a piece of paper and write as many as you can. Check and repeat.

Questions | Answers

#	Questions	Answers
1	Which word means that God is all powerful?	Omnipotent
2	When will God show his justice by judging humans fairly?	On Judgement Day
3	Approximately how many years ago did the Big Bang happen?	13.8 billion
4	Name the three parts of the Trinity.	God the Father, Jesus the Son, and the Holy Spirit
5	Which part of the Trinity is present on Earth today, guiding and supporting humans?	The Holy Spirit
6	What does the Catechism of the Catholic Church describe the Trinity as?	A 'mystery'
7	Which part of the Trinity is the human incarnation of God?	Jesus the Son
8	Complete the Bible quotation: "_____ created the heavens and the earth." Genesis 1:1	*In the beginning God*
9	How many days does Genesis say that it took God to complete creation?	Six (he rested on the seventh)
10	What did God create in Genesis 1:3?	Light
11	The theory of theistic evolution uses which sources?	The Bible and science
12	What might 'day' be used to mean in the seven days of creation?	Twenty-four hours, or an 'age' or long period of time
13	According to theistic evolution, what caused the Big Bang?	God
14	Who do Genesis 1:1–3 and John 1:1–3 say was present at the beginning of time?	God, Jesus (the Word), and the (Holy) Spirit
15	What does 'the Word' mean in John 1?	Jesus

(Put paper here)

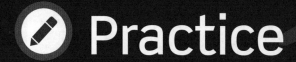

Practice

Exam-style questions

01 Which **one** of the following describes the meaning of the word 'benevolent'?

Put a tick (✓) in the box next to the correct answer.   **(1 mark)**

A   Loving   ☐

B   Powerful   ☐

C   Just   ☐

D   Creator   ☐

02 Which **one** of these is the key term which means that God is fair and treats humans fairly?   **(1 mark)**

Put a tick (✓) in the box next to the correct answer.

A   Just   ☐

B   Loving   ☐

C   Omnipotent   ☐

D   Omniscient   ☐

03 Name **two** of the Trinity.   **(2 marks)**

04 Give **two** examples of suffering in the world.   **(2 marks)**

05 Explain **two** ways that belief in the Trinity may influence Christians today.   **(4 marks)**

06 Explain **two** Christian beliefs about the nature of God.

Refer to sacred writings or another source of Christian belief and teaching in your answer.   **(5 marks)**

> **EXAM TIP**
>
> Remember, you don't have to state the exact verse but you must name a sacred writing or source of authority in your answer, for example 'The Bible says…'.

07 'The world was created exactly as described in the book of Genesis in the Bible.'

Evaluate this statement.

In your answer you should:

- refer to Christian teaching
- give reasoned arguments to support this statement
- give reasoned arguments to support a different point of view
- reach a justified conclusion.   **(12 marks)**

            (+ SPaG 3 marks)

> **EXAM TIP**
>
> Use the bullet points to help ensure that you include everything needed in a 12-mark question.

2 ✝ Beliefs and teachings: Different Christian beliefs about the afterlife

The Bible has many references to death and the **afterlife**, and this helps Christians to consider what happens after death. However, there are different interpretations of the Bible which lead to different views on the afterlife.

Resurrection and life after death

Christians think that if people believe in God and his son Jesus, they will have a life after this life, for **eternity**:

> 66 *For God so loved the world that he gave his one and only Son, that whoever believes in him shall not perish but have eternal life.* 99   (John 3:16)

This shows that humans will be resurrected from death and then will have a life after death. Some Christians believe that it will be a full-body **resurrection**.

Others believe that it will be just our souls that will live on:

> 66 *Jesus said to her, 'I am the resurrection and the life. The one who believes in me will live, even though they die.'* 99   (John 11:25)

Judgement

The **Parable** of the Sheep and Goats (Matthew 25:31–46) is a story told by Jesus. Some Christians interpret it to mean people will all be judged on how they treated other people, for example how they dealt with those who are hungry or ill, etc.

> If we haven't helped others, then we will be on God's left-hand side (goats) and will 'go away to eternal punishment'.

> If we have helped other people as though we were helping Jesus, we will be on God's right-hand side (sheep) and will have a right to eternal life.

This could be interpreted as hell.   This could be interpreted as heaven.

REVISION TIP

This parable is useful when answering exam questions about life after death, but also in some of the Theme topics on how humans should behave. Find it in the Bible and read the parable, so you can use it in your answers.

Knowledge

2 ✝ Beliefs and teachings: Different Christian beliefs about the afterlife

Heaven and hell

Some Christians believe that certain actions will lead us to be apart from God after we die.

> 66 *Put to death, therefore, whatever belongs to your earthly nature: sexual immorality, impurity, lust, evil desires and greed, which is idolatry. Because of these, the wrath of God is coming. You used to walk in these ways, in the life you once lived. But now you must also rid yourselves of all such things as these: anger, rage, malice, slander, and filthy language from your lips.* 99
>
> (Colossians 3:5–8)

Some interpret this to mean that if you commit these sins, then you will go to **hell**. Others believe that this is just a warning to ensure that humans behave as God wants them to.

Heaven	Hell
In **heaven** there will be no sadness or unhappiness. Most Christians believe that heaven is being with God for eternity and not a literal place: 66 *He will wipe every tear from their eyes. There will be no more death or mourning or crying or pain, for the old order of things has passed away.* 99 (Revelation 21:4)	66 *...and throw them into the blazing furnace, where there will be weeping and gnashing of teeth.* 99 (Matthew 13:50) Some think this is a literal description of hell. It will be a painful and unhappy time. Some believe that a loving God would not create such a place or send anyone there, so it is a **symbolic** description of being 'without God', not a place called hell.

The importance of Christian beliefs about the afterlife

These beliefs will have an impact on Christians' beliefs about the value of human life as it tells them that there is a life after this life.

It emphasises that we should think carefully about how we behave in this life because we will be judged on it, and this will influence what happens to us in the afterlife.

Christians believe that after they die God will judge them on their behaviour and actions, and their faith. So it's important for Christians to follow Jesus' teachings rather than to choose sin, because it won't only have an impact on this life but also on the eternal life that Christians believe will come after death.

 Key terms | **Make sure you can write a definition for these key terms** | afterlife eternity resurrection parable
hell heaven symbolic

Learn the answers to the questions below, then cover the answers column with a piece of paper and write as many as you can. Check and repeat.

Questions

		Answers
1	Which quotation from the Bible demonstrates the Christian belief that there is a life after this life, for eternity?	*"For God so loved the world that he gave his one and only Son, that whoever believes in him shall not perish but have eternal life."*
2	Complete this Bible quotation: "*I am _____. The one who believes in me will live, even though they die.*" John 11:25	*the resurrection and the life*
3	Which parable tells Christians that all humans will be judged and divided on God's right- and left-hand side depending on how they have behaved towards those in need?	Parable of the Sheep and Goats
4	Why don't some Christians believe in the existence of hell?	An all-loving God would not create or send someone to an eternity of suffering
5	What is this Bible quotation describing: "*… the blazing furnace, where there will be weeping and gnashing of teeth.*" Matthew 13:50?	Hell
6	What animal does the Parable of the Sheep and Goats call those that do not help others and who are put on God's left?	Goats
7	What is this Bible quotation describing: "*There will be no more death or mourning or crying or pain, for the old order of things has passed away.*" Revelation 21:4?	Heaven
8	What actions does the Bible say that humans should rid themselves of?	"*…sexual immorality, impurity, lust, evil desires and greed, which is idolatry, anger, rage, malice, slander, and filthy language from your lips.*"
9	What do some Christians believe would be being apart from God for eternity?	Hell

(Put paper here)

Previous questions

Now go back and use these questions to check your knowledge of previous topics.

Questions

		Answers
10	Which word means that God is all powerful?	Omnipotent
11	When will God show his justice by judging humans fairly?	On Judgement Day
12	Name the three parts of the Trinity.	God the Father, Jesus the Son, and the Holy Spirit
13	What does the Catechism of the Catholic Church describe the Trinity as?	A 'mystery'

(Put paper here)

Practice

Exam-style questions

01 Which **one** of these refers to the Christian belief that all humans will come alive again? **(1 mark)**

Put a tick (✓) in the box next to the correct answer.

A	Resurrection	☐
B	Enlightenment	☐
C	Reincarnation	☐
D	Judgement	☐

02 Give **two** beliefs about life after death in Christianity. **(2 marks)**

03 Give **two** reasons why Christians believe in the existence of heaven. **(2 marks)**

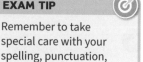

> **EXAM TIP**
>
> In 2-mark questions you do not have to write in full sentences. Answers can be one word or short phrases.

04 Explain **two** ways that belief in heaven might influence a Christian today. **(4 marks)**

05 Explain **two** Christian beliefs about hell.
Refer to sacred writings or another source of Christian belief and teaching in your answer. **(5 marks)**

> **EXAM TIP**
>
> Remember to take special care with your spelling, punctuation, and grammar and use as many specialist terms as possible when answering 12-mark questions.

06 'The Bible tells Christians exactly what will happen in the afterlife.'
Evaluate this statement.

In your answer you should:

- refer to Christian teaching

- give reasoned arguments to support this statement

- give reasoned arguments to support a different point of view

- reach a justified conclusion. **(12 marks)**

(+ SPaG 3 marks)

⚙ Knowledge

3 ✝ Beliefs and teachings: The incarnation, crucifixion, resurrection, and ascension of Jesus

Christians believe that God sent his son Jesus to Earth over 2000 years ago. The story of his life is narrated in the Gospels of Matthew, Mark, Luke, and John in the New Testament of the Bible.

Incarnation – Jesus is born

Jesus was born to his mother, the Virgin Mary, whilst his parents were visiting Bethlehem. The nativity story is described in the books of Matthew and Luke.

> ❝ *His mother Mary was pledged to be married to Joseph, but before they came together, she was found to be pregnant through the Holy Spirit.* ❞
> (Matthew 1:18)

John 1:14 shows that Jesus was incarnate. This means that God took on human form and was on earth.

> ❝ *The Word became flesh and made his dwelling among us.* ❞
> (John 1:14)

REVISION TIP ✅

You don't need to know the whole nativity story – focus on how the incarnation is important to Christians.

Why it is important to Christians

This proves the Old Testament prophet's prophecies to be true. It shows that Jesus is part of the Trinity.

The baptism of Jesus

Approximately 30 years later, Jesus was baptised by his cousin John in the River Jordan. When Jesus was baptised, a voice from Heaven said:

> ❝ *You are my Son* ❞
> (Mark 1:11)

REVISION TIP ✅

Knowing the key events in the life of Jesus will help you answer many different questions. Go through the Christianity practices section and try to match the practices with the events in Jesus's life.

Why it is important to Christians

This shows Christians that Jesus is the **Son of God**, and although he was without sin, provides an example of what they should do to remove sin.

⚙ Knowledge

3 ✝ Beliefs and teachings: The incarnation, crucifixion, resurrection, and ascension of Jesus

Miracles and parables

- During his life Jesus performed many miracles including bringing people back to life and healing people.
- Jesus told stories with meanings, called parables. The Parable of the Good Samaritan and the Parable of the Sheep and Goats tell Christians how they should behave towards others.

Why it is important to Christians

- Jesus's miracles prove the incarnation – that he is God.
- Jesus's parables and teachings show what they should believe in and how they should live as good Christians.

Why it is important to Christians

- The Last Supper is now remembered and re-enacted at the **Eucharist**, reminding Christians of God's sacrifice.
- The crucifixion shows that God was prepared to sacrifice his son for the sins of humans. It enabled humans to achieve salvation.

Holy Week – the final week of Jesus's life

Palm Sunday

Jesus enters Jerusalem on a donkey.

Maundy Thursday – The Last Supper

- Jesus has the **Last Supper** with his disciples. He tells them to remember his body with bread, and his blood with wine.
- He is arrested in the Garden of Gethsemane.

Good Friday – the crucifixion

- Jesus is sentenced to death by **crucifixion**.
- He is killed on the cross, outside the city of Jerusalem, alongside two criminals.

> **"** *They crucified him there, along with the criminals … Jesus said, 'Father, forgive them, for they do not know what they are doing* **"**
> (Luke 23:33–34)

> **"** *…darkness came over the whole land … And the curtain of the temple was torn in two. Jesus called out with a loud voice, 'Father, into your hands I commit my spirit.' When he had said this, he breathed his last.* **"**
> (Luke 23: 44–46)

Easter Sunday – the resurrection

On the third day after the crucifixion, Jesus rose from the dead.

> *They [the women] found the stone rolled away from the tomb, but when they entered, they did not find the body of the Lord Jesus.*
>
> (Luke 24:1–3)

Why it is important to Christians

- The resurrection proves that Jesus was the son of God.
- It also shows Christians that there is life after death and they will also be resurrected.

Key terms — Make sure you can write a definition for these key terms

Son of God   Eucharist
Last Supper   crucifixion   ascension

The Great Commission and the ascension

Forty days after his resurrection Jesus spoke with the disciples for the final time and told them at the Great Commission:

REVISION TIP

The Great Commission links to mission and evangelism in Christianity practices so is a useful Bible story to remember.

> *…go and make disciples of all nations, baptising them in the name of the Father and of the Son and of the Holy Spirit, and teaching them to obey everything I have commanded you…*
>
> (Matthew 28: 19–20)

He then ascended to heaven to be with God, known as the **ascension**. Christians are waiting for him to return to Earth at the end of time.

Why it is important to Christians

- The Great Commission gave the disciples clear instructions on how to spread the 'good news' (the Gospel) and this has continued today. There are now over 2 billion Christians in the world.
- The ascension tells Christians that Jesus was fully God and returned to God in Heaven. There is no body or grave of Jesus left on Earth as he is alive in Heaven, waiting to return one day.

Retrieval

Learn the answers to the questions below, then cover the answers column with a piece of paper and write as many as you can. Check and repeat.

	Questions		Answers
1	In which event in the life of Jesus did God 'become' flesh?	Put paper here	The incarnation
2	In which Gospels is the life of Jesus described?		Matthew, Mark, Luke, and John
3	On which day was Jesus crucified?		Good Friday
4	Who baptised Jesus?	Put paper here	His cousin, John
5	What word is given to the stories with meanings told by Jesus?		Parables
6	Who was crucified alongside Jesus?		Two criminals
7	Why is the resurrection of Jesus important to Christians?	Put paper here	It proves that Jesus was the son of God and it shows Christians that there is life after death and they will also be resurrected
8	What happened at the ascension?		Jesus ascended to heaven
9	What did Jesus tell the disciples to do at the Great Commission?	Put paper here	Make disciples of all nations, baptise them in the name of the Father and of the Son and of the Holy Spirit, teach them to obey everything Jesus commanded

Previous questions

Now go back and use these questions to check your knowledge of previous topics.

	Questions		Answers
10	How many days does Genesis say that it took God to complete creation?	Put paper here	Six (he rested on the seventh)
11	What did God create in Genesis 1:3?		Light
12	Complete this Bible quotation: *"I am _____. The one who believes in me will live, even though they die."* John 11:25	Put paper here	*the resurrection and the life*
13	What is this Bible quotation describing: *"...the blazing furnace, where there will be weeping and gnashing of teeth."* Matthew 13:50?		Hell

✎ Practice

Exam-style questions

01   Which **one** of these is the event in the life of Jesus when he came back to life after dying on a cross?

Put a tick (✓) in the box next to the correct answer.   **(1 mark)**

A	Ascension	☐
B	Incarnation	☐
C	Resurrection	☐
D	Crucifixion	☐

02   Which **one** of these is the belief that 'God became flesh'?

Put a tick (✓) in the box next to the correct answer.   **(1 mark)**

A	Ascension	☐
B	Incarnation	☐
C	Resurrection	☐
D	Crucifixion	☐

> **EXAM TIP**
>
> As these questions are only worth 1 mark, don't spend a long time on them. However, do read the question and answer options carefully so you don't make a silly mistake.

03   Give **two** reasons why the ascension is important to Christians.   **(2 marks)**

04   Give **two** reasons why the resurrection is important to Christians.   **(2 marks)**

05   Explain **two** ways that the incarnation may influence the life of a Christian today.   **(4 marks)**

06   Explain **two** ways that the crucifixion of Jesus may influence the life of a Christian today.   **(4 marks)**

> **EXAM TIP**
>
> When a question asks about 'influence', think about what difference the belief makes to the person's life – what might they do differently because of the belief?

07   Explain **two** Christian beliefs about the incarnation.
Refer to sacred writings or another source of Christian belief and teaching in your answer.   **(5 marks)**

08   'The incarnation is more important than the crucifixion of Jesus.'

Evaluate this statement.

In your answer you should:

- refer to Christian teaching
- give reasoned arguments to support this statement
- give reasoned arguments to support a different point of view
- reach a justified conclusion.   **(12 marks)**

    (+ SPaG 3 marks)

⚙ Knowledge

4 ✝ Beliefs and teachings: Sin and salvation

Sin

- **Sin** means deliberately going against what God wants.
- Christians believe that people sin because God has given humans free will. However, they know what God wants them to do because the Bible tells them.

There are many rules in the Old Testament, including the Ten Commandments. For example, it is wrong to murder, steal, and worship other gods. However, many Christians believe that Jesus summarised the Old Testament rules into two commandments found in the New Testament:

REVISION TIP

Matthew 22:36–40 is useful as it can help when comparing the Old Testament with the New Testament.

> ❝ *'Teacher, which is the greatest commandment in the Law?' Jesus replied: 'Love the Lord your God with all your heart and with all your soul and with all your mind.' This is the first and greatest commandment. And the second is like it: 'Love your neighbour as yourself.' All the Law and the Prophets hang on these two commandments.* ❞
>
> (Matthew 22:36–40)

Original sin and personal sin

Original sin	Personal sin
• Adam and Eve failed to follow God's instruction not to eat the fruit in the Garden of Eden. God punished Adam and Eve and the punishment was to ensure suffering in life. This is known as the Fall. • Some Christians believe that due to the Fall, we have all been born with the inclination to sin. This is called original sin. • Some Christians believe that baptism washes away original sin. 	• This is when humans use their free will to behave in a way that goes against God's wishes. 

Christians believe that due to sin, humans have moved apart from their relationship with God and whilst they have sin, they cannot be with God in Heaven. **Salvation** means being saved from sin and restoring their relationship with God.

REVISION TIP

Remember that as the Fall is a story from the Bible you can use it in an answer to a 5-mark question that requires you to refer to sacred writings or another source of religious belief and teaching.

Getting rid of sin

Different Christians have different beliefs about what can be done to get rid of sin.

How to get rid of sin	Christian belief
Prayer and repentance	Christians believe that humans can pray to God to ask for forgiveness. As he is all-loving, this act of **repentance** means he will forgive them.
Confession	The sacrament of reconciliation – Catholic Christians believe that they can confess their sins to a priest and that God will forgive them through the actions of the priest.

Means of salvation

The means of salvation are the ways that God helps humans to achieve salvation.

Salvation by law

- Also known as salvation by works.
- Shown in the Old Testament:

> *For I command you today to love the Lord your God, to walk in obedience to him, and to keep his commands, decrees and laws; then you will live and increase, and the Lord your God will bless you in the land you are entering to possess.*
> (Deuteronomy 30:16)

- From the Old Testament text, the Pharisees (religious leaders) put together a list of 613 laws that need to be kept to gain salvation.

> *If only you had paid attention to my commands, your peace would have been like a river, your well-being like the waves of the sea.* (Isaiah 48:18)

Salvation by grace

- Christians believe that because God is all-loving and all-merciful, humans can achieve salvation even if they have sinned.
- This is possible as Jesus died on a cross to forgive all sins.
- Grace means that if someone believes in Jesus and asks for forgiveness of their sins, their faith will save them.

> *For it is by grace you have been saved, through faith – and this is not from yourselves, it is the gift of God – not by works, so that no one can boast.*
> (Ephesians 2:8–9)

- Grace does not mean Christians don't have to obey the law and do good works. James 2:26 says, "faith without deeds is dead."
- However, the Christian doctrine of Grace states that Christians do good works because they have salvation and not to earn salvation.

Salvation by Spirit

- Some Christians believe that the Holy Spirit is present around humans today, helping them to achieve salvation.
- The Spirit guides people in day-to-day life, through their conscience, to make the right decisions about how to behave.

- It can help Christians to understand God, including when they are reading the Bible:

> *... the Holy Spirit, whom the Father will send in my name, will teach you all things and will remind you of everything I have said to you.* (John 14:26)

4 ✝ Beliefs and teachings: Sin and salvation

The role of Christ in salvation and the idea of atonement

Christians believe that due to the Fall, humans have become separated from God. However, the Bible says that:

> ❝ *For God so loved the world that he gave his one and only Son.* ❞
>
> (John 3:16)

This shows that God sent Jesus to Earth for humans' sins to be forgiven.

REVISION TIP

Remember these beliefs link to the celebration of Easter in the Christianity practices section. Look at how Christians may celebrate Easter and try to identify which beliefs link to each practice.

Christians believe that Jesus's crucifixion means that his life was sacrificed for all humanity.

This means they can be reconciled (have a restored relationship) with God:

> ❝ *For if, while we were God's enemies, we were reconciled to him through the death of his Son, how much more, having been reconciled, shall we be saved through his life!* ❞
>
> (Romans 5:10)

This is due to **atonement**, restoring the relationship between people and God through the life, death, and resurrection of Jesus. This ensures that all humans can access Heaven and be with God. The Bible says:

> ❝ *… if anybody does sin, we have an advocate with the Father – Jesus Christ, the Righteous One. He is the atoning sacrifice for our sins, and not only for ours but also for the sins of the whole world.* ❞
>
> (1 John 2:1–2)

Key terms — Make sure you can write a definition for these key terms

sin   salvation   repentance   atonement

Learn the answers to the questions below, then cover the answers column with a piece of paper and write as many as you can. Check and repeat.

Questions | Answers

#	Question	Answer
1	What word means humans choosing how they behave?	Free will
2	What type of sin has come from Adam and Eve sinning at the Fall?	Original sin
3	Which means of salvation is following the way of living that God has shown through the Bible?	Salvation by law/salvation by works
4	Which means of salvation is being saved due to God's love by having faith in him?	Salvation by grace
5	Which means of salvation is following the guidance of the Holy Spirit on Earth today?	Salvation by Spirit
6	Give one way that Christians may believe humans can get rid of sin.	One from: prayer / repentance / confession
7	Complete this Bible quotation which shows that God sent Jesus to Earth for humans' sins to be forgiven: "*For God _____.*" John 3:16	*so loved the world that he gave his one and only Son*
8	What is the word for the Christian belief that humans can be saved from their sins?	Salvation
9	Which type of sin comes from when humans use their free will to behave in a way that goes against God's wishes?	Personal sin

Put paper here

Previous questions

Now go back and use these questions to check your knowledge of previous topics.

Questions | Answers

#	Question	Answer
10	What might 'day' be used to mean in the seven days of creation?	Twenty-four hours, or an 'age' or long period of time
11	According to theistic evolution, what caused the Big Bang?	God
12	What does 'the Word' mean in John 1?	Jesus
13	In which event in the life of Jesus did God 'become' flesh?	The incarnation/birth
14	In which Gospels is the life of Jesus described?	Matthew, Mark, Luke, and John
15	On which day was Jesus crucified?	Good Friday

Put paper here

Practice

01   Which **one** of these is a sin humans are born with due to the Fall?

Put a tick (✓) in the box next to the correct answer.   **(1 mark)**

A   Original sin   ☐

B   Personal sin   ☐

C   Deadly sin   ☐

D   Social sin   ☐

02   Which **one** of these is classed as a sin in Christianity?

Put a tick (✓) in the box next to the correct answer.   **(1 mark)**

A   Reconciliation   ☐

B   Charity   ☐

C   Forgiveness   ☐

D   Murder   ☐

03   Name **two** sins in Christianity.   **(2 marks)**

04   Name **two** means of salvation.   **(2 marks)**

> **EXAM TIP**
>
> A 4-mark question requires two developed points. Show the examiner you have done this by writing in two paragraphs.

05   Explain **two** ways that Christians may be influenced by salvation by law in their lives today.   **(4 marks)**

06   Explain **two** ways that belief in sin may influence Christians today.   **(4 marks)**

07   Explain **two** Christian beliefs about the role of Jesus in salvation. Refer to sacred writings or another source of Christian belief and teaching in your answer.   **(5 marks)**

> **EXAM TIP**
>
> Remember to name a sacred writing or source of authority in your answer, for example, the Bible.

08   'You can only achieve salvation by following God's law.'

Evaluate this statement.

In your answer you should:

- refer to Christian teaching
- give reasoned arguments to support this statement
- give reasoned arguments to support a different point of view
- reach a justified conclusion.   **(12 marks)**

   (+ SPaG 3 marks)

5 ✝ Practices: Worship and prayer

Different forms of worship and their significance

Christians believe that they should worship God because:

- it shows how important he is to them
- they should praise him for everything that he has done for them
- they believe he is worthy of worship
- it outwardly shows their belief and trust in him
- they can ask for forgiveness
- it strengthens their belief.

There are different types of worship. Worship varies between individuals and the type of Church (**denomination**) they belong to.

Liturgical worship

Liturgical worship follows a formal set of practices that remains the same, for example, a church service may always have a Bible reading, songs/hymns, Eucharist, **prayers** and a sermon. The specific Bible reading, songs, and sermon are all planned in advance. It is mostly led by a religious leader, for example, a priest.

Most Catholic Church worship is liturgical.

> 66 *Worship the Lord with gladness; come before him with joyful songs.* 99
> (Psalms 100:2)

Why it is important

- It provides a consistent way of worshipping.
- It is traditional and often has been done that way for hundreds of years.
- Worship will always follow the same set pattern anywhere in the world; this gives a sense of community.
- It emphasises the importance of the church leader as part of a Christian's connection with God.

Non-liturgical/informal worship

Non-liturgical worship is informal. It can be spontaneous and unplanned. It can include key elements such as singing, prayers, Bible readings, and Eucharist but as it is **informal worship**, these may vary in length and in who leads them.

It may also include things such as the laying of hands/healing rituals, speaking in tongues, and personal testimonies.

Charismatic worship is often non-liturgical, and can involve the Holy Spirit inspiring and guiding the worship.

Quaker worship is informal as it involves people sitting in silence together, waiting to be inspired to speak by the Spirit. There is no leader and anyone can contribute.

> 66 *When you come together, each of you has a hymn, or a word of instruction, a revelation, a tongue or an interpretation…* 99   (1 Corinthians 14:26)

Why it is important

- Anyone can be involved.
- It is spontaneous so may allow God to speak to or inspire worshippers through the Holy Spirit.

⚙ Knowledge

5 ✝ Practices: Worship and prayer

Private worship

Some Christians may worship by themselves or in a small family/friendship group.

They may read the Bible, pray or meditate to get closer to God.

Why it is important
- A person can choose how they want to worship.
- It develops their personal relationship with God.
- It can be done at any time.

Use of the Bible

The Bible is an important part of worship for Christians. Whilst views differ on how it should be interpreted, it is a central part of liturgical, non-liturgical and private worship.

In some churches they follow a set series of Bible passages throughout the year, often linking to important stories, for example, the nativity story at Christmas.

Other Christians use the Bible in a more spontaneous way and believe that the Holy Spirit guides them to a particular passage that gives a message for that time.

Why it is important
- It keeps the word of God central to worship.
- It reminds Christians of key stories, beliefs, and teachings of Christianity.
- It can inspire Christians and remind them how God wants them to behave.

Prayer and its significance

Prayer is communicating with God, either silently or speaking out loud.

The purposes of prayer

- Praise: worshipping God.
- Thanksgiving: thanking God for everything he has done and does for humans.
- Intercession: praying for others, e.g., praying for their salvation, for someone's health.
- Confession: repenting to God for sinning and asking for forgiveness.
- Petition: praying for yourself, for guidance and support in living the Christian life.

Different Christians pray in different ways – some people:			
	Kneel		Hold their hands outwards or upwards.
	Put their hands together.		Use a rosary to focus on specific prayers.

Why prayer is important to Christians

- Prayer supports a personal relationship with God.
- It is what Jesus did, and he also told Christians how to pray.

- It is what the Bible says Christians should do:

> *I urge, then, first of all, that petitions, prayers, intercession and thanksgiving be made for all people.* (Timothy 2:1)

Set prayers

- **Set prayers** are prayers that have already been written.
- The benefit of using set prayers is that everybody can join in saying the prayer and the prayer can cover key beliefs.
- Examples of set prayers include the Rosary and the **Lord's prayer**.

The Lord's prayer

- Jesus gave the words of the Lord's prayer to his followers in Matthew 6:9–15. Different Christian denominations use different versions of the words.
- It can be said during communal worship or by an individual in private worship.
- It mentions key beliefs for Christians, including the belief in the existence of Heaven and the forgiveness of sins.
- It is sometimes called the 'Our Father'.

REVISION TIP

To help you remember the Lord's prayer try saying it out loud. Start with the first line. Then say the first two lines. Then say the first three lines. Continue doing this until you get to the end. Then try saying it again from memory. Keep going until you have it memorised.

The Lord's prayer

Our Father in heaven,
hallowed be your name,
your Kingdom come,
your will be done, on earth as in heaven.
Give us today our daily bread.
Forgive us our sins as we forgive those who sin against us.
Lead us not into temptation but deliver us from evil.
For the kingdom, the power, and the glory are yours now and for ever.

Amen

Informal prayer

Informal prayers haven't been planned. The words of the prayer are made up by the person saying the prayer. They can be more personal and relate to the situation that someone is in. For example, they may ask God to bless a specific person that they know is struggling. Informal prayers are often part of informal/non-liturgical worship.

Key terms Make sure you can write a definition for these key terms

denomination   liturgical   prayer   non-liturgical
informal worship   set prayer   Lord's prayer   informal prayer

Retrieval

Learn the answers to the questions below, then cover the answers column with a piece of paper and write as many as you can. Check and repeat.

Questions		Answers
1	A Christian might say that worship is important because they can ask God for his _____.	Forgiveness
2	Which type of worship follows a formal set of practices that remains the same?	Liturgical
3	Which type of worship is informal, spontaneous, and unplanned?	Non-liturgical/informal
4	Give one thing that might happen as part of liturgical worship.	One from: a Bible reading / songs / hymns / the Eucharist / prayers / a sermon
5	Which Christian denomination involves people sitting in silence together, waiting to be inspired to speak by the Spirit?	Quakers
6	What is it called when Christians choose to worship by themselves or as part of a small family/friendship group?	Private worship
7	The Bible is an important part of which types of worship?	Liturgical, non-liturgical, and private worship
8	Name five purposes of prayer.	Praise, thanksgiving, intercession, confession, petition
9	Which prayer did Jesus teach the disciples?	The Lord's prayer or Our Father
10	What is another name for the Lord's prayer?	Our Father
11	In which part of the Lord's prayer do Christians ask God to help them avoid sin?	*Lead us not into temptation but deliver us from evil.*
12	Name two examples of set prayer.	The Lord's prayer, the Rosary
13	For what type of prayers have the words already been written?	Set prayers
14	What type of prayers are those which are spontaneous and haven't been planned?	Informal prayers

Put paper here

Exam-style questions

01 Which of these describes a form of worship which follows a formal set of practices that remain the same?

Put a tick (✓) in the box next to the correct answer. **(1 mark)**

A Non-liturgical worship ☐

B Liturgical worship ☐

C Private worship ☐

D Informal prayer ☐

02 Which **one** of these prayers is spontaneous and has not been planned?

Put a tick (✓) in the box next to the correct answer. **(1 mark)**

A Informal ☐

B Formal ☐

C Set ☐

D The Lord's prayer ☐

03 Give **two** reasons why prayer is important to Christians. **(2 marks)**

> **EXAM TIP**
>
> Answers to 2-mark questions can be written as one-word answers, short phrases, or short sentences, depending on the question. Try to keep it short.

04 Give **two** purposes of Christian prayer. **(2 marks)**

05 Explain **two** contrasting ways that Christians may use the Bible in worship. **(4 marks)**

06 Explain **two** ways that Christians pray. Refer to sacred writings or another source of Christian belief and teaching in your answer. **(5 marks)**

> **EXAM TIP**
>
> Remember you must name a sacred writing or source of authority in your answer, for example the Bible. If you use quotes, you don't have to state the exact chapter or verse – you can just write: 'The Bible states…'.

07 'The Lord's prayer is the most important prayer.'

Evaluate this statement.

In your answer you should:

- refer to Christian teaching
- give reasoned arguments to support this statement
- give reasoned arguments to support a different point of view
- reach a justified conclusion. **(12 marks)**

(+ SPaG 3 marks)

⚙ Knowledge

6 ✝ Practices: The role and meaning of the sacraments

The meaning of sacrament

Sacrament comes from the Latin word meaning 'sacred' and the Greek meaning 'mystery'. It is often described as an outer expression of an inner grace. This means it is something that a Christian does to show their belief in God in a spiritual and often symbolic way.

Some Christians don't perform any sacraments at all, for example Quakers. They may argue that every day should be an outer expression of their faith and that these sacraments should not be limited to one day, for example a Sunday. These Christians are also often openly involved in helping the community in different ways, for example, the Salvation Army.

- Catholic Christians have seven sacraments (**baptism**, **confirmation**, Eucharist, **reconciliation**, the anointing of the sick, holy orders, and marriage).

- Other Christian denominations have two main sacraments (baptism and Eucharist).

Baptism and its significance for Christians

Baptism is an initiation rite in which people join the Christian family. Some Christians believe it is a sacrament; for others baptism is just an important ceremony. Some Christian Churches such as Quakers and members of the Salvation Army do not baptise at all.

Reasons for baptism:

- To remember and follow the example of the baptism of Jesus in the River Jordan by his cousin John.
- To follow Jesus's wishes – at the Great Commission, Jesus told the disciples to baptise people.
- As a symbolic demonstration of the washing away of sins.
- To welcome people into the community of the Christian Church.

The baptism of Jesus	The Great Commission
66 *When Jesus was baptised, a voice from Heaven said 'You are my Son.'* 99 (Mark 1:11)	66 *Therefore go and make disciples of all nations, baptising them in the name of the Father and of the Son and of the Holy Spirit.* 99 (Matthew 28:19)

Infant and believer's baptism

Some denominations, including Anglicans and Catholics, baptise babies, others tend to baptise adults only, referring to this as 'believer's baptism'.

Reasons for infant baptism	Reasons for believer's baptism
Symbolises the washing away of original sin.	Symbolises the washing away of personal sin.
Welcomes a baby to the Church community.	Welcomes someone to the Church community.
Part of being brought up in a Christian family.	An individual's decision.

Symbols of baptism

Baptismal rites vary but they usually include common symbols with important beliefs associated with them.

 Water symbolises a washing away of sins and a new life with Jesus Christ.

 Those being baptised often wear white clothing to represent purity and the removal of sin.

 A candle is sometimes used to represent going from 'darkness' (without Jesus Christ/God) to 'light' (with Jesus Christ/God).

Holy Communion/Eucharist

The night before Jesus was crucified, he had a meal with his disciples – this is known as the Last Supper. It is an event that many Christians remember during worship, and they re-enact the meal during a sacrament known as **Holy Communion**/Eucharist.

> 66 *And he took bread, gave thanks and broke it, and gave it to them, saying, 'This is my body given for you; do this in remembrance of me.'*
>
> *In the same way, after the supper he took the cup, saying, 'This cup is the new covenant in my blood, which is poured out for you.* 99 (Luke 22:17–20)

Christians use bread and wine during the Holy Communion/ Eucharist sacrament as Jesus spoke about them.

 Bread – Some Christians use unleavened bread (as Jesus would have); others use leavened bread and others use wafers.

 Wine – Some Christians use red wine; others prefer not to use alcohol and use red grape juice instead.

The significance of the Eucharist and different interpretations of its meaning

Christians interpret the story of the Lord's Supper differently and enact the sacrament in different ways. Some Christians perform the sacrament every Sunday and others do it less frequently. Some Christians do not do it at all.

- Catholic Christians believe that the bread and the wine undergo a special change called transubstantiation. They believe that the bread becomes the body of Jesus, and the wine becomes the blood of Jesus.

- Some Christians take the phrase 'do this in remembrance of me' and believe that the sacrament is about remembering God's sacrifice of Jesus on the cross, leading to the forgiveness of sins.
- Other Christians believe that the bread and wine are symbolic, bringing together the community in sharing them.

 Key terms Make sure you can write a definition for these key terms

sacrament   baptism   confirmation   reconciliation
infant baptism   believer's baptism   Holy Communion

Retrieval

Learn the answers to the questions below, then cover the answers column with a piece of paper and write as many as you can. Check and repeat.

Questions / Answers

#	Questions	Answers
1	How many sacraments do Catholic Christians have?	Seven
2	Name two different types of baptism.	Infant baptism, believer's baptism
3	What does the water symbolise in baptism?	Washing away of sins
4	Name a Christian denomination that does not use baptism.	One from: Quakers / Salvation Army
5	Why do those being baptised often wear white clothes?	To represent purity and the removal of sin
6	Which event in the life of Jesus is remembered at Holy Communion?	The Last Supper
7	Give one other name for Holy Communion.	Eucharist
8	What is the name for the Catholic Christians' belief that during the Mass the bread and the wine become the body and blood of Christ?	Transubstantiation
9	What two things do Christians use during Holy Communion to remember the death of Jesus?	Bread and wine

Put paper here

Previous questions

Now go back and use these questions to check your knowledge of previous topics.

Questions / Answers

#	Questions	Answers
11	Which type of worship follows a formal set of practices that remains the same?	Liturgical
12	Which type of worship is informal, spontaneous, and unplanned?	Non-liturgical
13	Give one thing that might happen as part of liturgical worship.	One from: a Bible reading / songs / hymns / the Eucharist / prayers / a sermon
14	Which Christian group involves people sitting in silence together, waiting to be inspired to speak by the Spirit?	Quakers
15	Name five purposes of prayer.	Praise, thanksgiving, intercession, confession, petition

Put paper here

Exam-style questions

01 Which **one** of these is the event when Jesus told the disciples to 'baptise in the name of the Father, the Son and the Holy Spirit'?

Put a tick (✓) in the box next to the correct answer.   **(1 mark)**

A	The Great Commission	☐
B	The crucifixion	☐
C	The incarnation	☐
D	Pentecost	☐

02 Which **one** of these is the sacrament that remembers Jesus's Last Supper?

Put a tick (✓) in the box next to the correct answer.   **(1 mark)**

A	Baptism	☐
B	Reconciliation	☐
C	Eucharist	☐
D	Marriage	☐

> **EXAM TIP**
> The four options for the multiple-choice questions will include options designed to test you. Read each option carefully to select the correct answer.

03 Name **two** sacraments in Christianity.   **(2 marks)**

04 Give **two** different names for Holy Communion.   **(2 marks)**

05 Explain **two** contrasting beliefs about infant baptism.   **(4 marks)**

06 Explain **two** ways that Christians may carry out Holy Communion.

Refer to sacred writings or another source of Christian belief and teaching in your answer.   **(5 marks)**

> **EXAM TIP**
> Remember that you must name the source of authority when you refer to it, for example the Bible.

07 'The most important sacrament is infant baptism.'

Evaluate this statement.

In your answer you should:

- refer to Christian teaching
- give reasoned arguments to support this statement
- give reasoned arguments to support a different point of view
- reach a justified conclusion.   **(12 marks)**

(+ SPaG 3 marks)

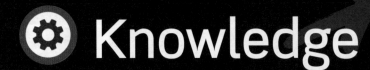

⚙ Knowledge

7 ✝ Practices: The role and importance of pilgrimage and celebrations

Christian pilgrimage

Christians often visit places that are important to Christianity. A **pilgrimage** is a spiritual experience in which the journey and the destination bring them closer to God.

Pilgrimages are important to Christians because:

- they can see where something important in Christianity has happened, for example, Bethlehem and Jerusalem
- it strengthens and renews their belief
- it brings together the Christian community

- it involves prayer and worship in special places
- it brings them closer to God
- they may involve receiving special blessings from God or healing **miracles**.

↓

Lourdes, France

Why Lourdes?

- **Lourdes** is the place where in 1858, a girl called Bernadette had a vision of the Virgin Mary. Mary told Bernadette to dig into the ground and a spring of water appeared.
- Bernadette described her first vision of the Virgin Mary:

> 66 *As I raised my head to look at the grotto, I saw a Lady dressed in white, wearing a white dress, a blue girdle and a yellow rose on each foot, the same colour as the chain of her rosary; the beads of the rosary were white.* 99

▲ *Sick or disabled pilgrims are accompanied by able-bodied helpers at Lourdes, a popular pilgrimage site for Catholics*

FRANCE

📍 Lourdes

What happens at Lourdes?
• Each year millions of Catholic pilgrims visit the grotto where Mary appeared. • They also drink or bathe in the spring water as they believe it has healing powers. Many will take some water home with them to share with others.

Why is Lourdes important?
• Over 67 confirmed miracles and over 6000 other cures have taken place at Lourdes.

Iona, Scotland

Why Iona?

- St Columba, (an Irish missionary) who had brought Christianity to Scotland, set up a monastery on the island of **Iona**. It is now a pilgrimage site, dedicated to the Virgin Mary.

- There is a small community on the island that runs the retreat and looks after the pilgrims.

- Due to its remote location and clear air, Iona has been described as a 'thin place' where the veil between earthly life and the spiritual, heavenly life is thinner than in other places.

- It is a place where pilgrims can become closer to God by being close to nature and his creation.

REVISION TIP

To remember information on pilgrimages, use 'Where?' 'Why?' and 'What?' *Where* is the pilgrimage to? *Why* is it an important place? *What* do pilgrims do there?

▲ *The abbey church on Iona*

What happens at Iona?

- It is a place where Christians of any denomination can visit and stay.
- Whilst there, pilgrims can take part in: daily church services; walks around the island, stopping for prayer and reflection; workshops focusing on Christian teachings; Bible reading, reflection, and prayer in the natural beauty of the island.
- If pilgrims stay in the retreat, they help with daily chores, e.g., preparing food and cleaning the centre.

Why is Iona important?

- It brings Christians together as it is a place where Christians of any denomination can visit and stay.
- It gives pilgrims time and space to reconnect with God.
- It is a place with a 'thin veil' between Earth and the spiritual realm.
- It reminds pilgrims of God's power whilst staying in a place of natural beauty.

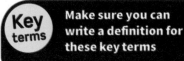

Key terms — Make sure you can write a definition for these key terms

pilgrimage   miracle   Lourdes   Iona   Christmas   Easter

Knowledge

7 ✝ Practices: The role and importance of pilgrimage and celebrations

Celebrations: Christmas

- **Christmas** is a celebration of the birth of Jesus.
- The story is told in the Gospels of Matthew and Luke. Each story gives a different perspective and Christians put them together to tell the nativity story.
- Many Christians celebrate it on 25 December. Most Orthodox Christians celebrate it on 7 January.

> 66 *While they were there, the time came for the baby to be born, and she gave birth to her firstborn, a son. She wrapped him in cloths and placed him in a manger, because there was no guest room available for them.* 99   (Luke 2:6–7)

REVISION TIP

Remember that this is about Christmas in Christianity not as a secular celebration. No need to mention Santa Claus or reindeer!

How is it celebrated?

Christians in Great Britain today celebrate Christmas by:
- performing nativity plays and telling the Christmas story
- giving presents to remember the gifts that Jesus received and the gift of Jesus from God
- putting up lights to represent Jesus being the light of the world
- going to church and singing songs (carols) to celebrate the birth of God's son.

Why is it important?

- It is when the incarnation occurred:

> 66 *The Word became flesh and made his dwelling among us.* 99   (John 1:14)

- It shows that God, in human form, was on Earth.
- The Old Testament prophecies of a messiah coming to Earth came true.

Celebrations: Easter

- **Easter** is the most important Christian festival.
- On Easter Sunday, Christians celebrate the resurrection of Jesus following his crucifixion on Good Friday.
- The story is written in the Gospels of Matthew, Mark, Luke, and John.
- Easter is celebrated on a different date each year. It is calculated from the first Sunday after the full moon that occurs on or after the spring equinox (which is always on 21 March).

> 66 *Christ died for our sins according to the Scriptures, that he was buried, that he was raised on the third day according to the Scriptures, and that he appeared to Cephas, and then to the Twelve.* 99
> (1 Corinthians 15:3–5)

How is it celebrated?

Christians in Great Britain today celebrate Easter by:
- going to church to celebrate the resurrection of Jesus
- singing songs/hymns to thank God for the resurrection
- celebrating new life with eggs including chocolate eggs
- eating hot cross buns (the cross symbolising the cross Jesus died on)
- sharing breakfast at early sunrise to remember his resurrection on Easter Sunday.

Why is it important?

- It proves that God has power over death, which means that all humans will also be resurrected.
- It shows God's sacrifice for humans, which enables their salvation.
- It enables humans to reconcile with God even if they have sinned.
- It enables the forgiveness of sins.
- It enables Christians to achieve atonement and access heaven to be with God.

Learn the answers to the questions below, then cover the answers column with a piece of paper and write as many as you can. Check and repeat.

Questions / Answers

#	Questions	Answers
1	In which country is Lourdes?	France
2	Who did Bernadette see in a vision at Lourdes?	The Virgin Mary
3	Why is the water at Lourdes special?	It is believed to have healing powers
4	In which country is Iona?	Scotland
5	Who founded a monastery on Iona?	St Columba
6	Why is Iona a particularly spiritual place for pilgrims?	It has a 'thin veil' between earthly life and spiritual life
7	Which event in the life of Jesus is celebrated at Christmas?	His birth
8	On which two dates is Christmas celebrated within Christianity?	25 December, 7 January
9	Which event in the life of Jesus is celebrated at Easter?	His resurrection (following his crucifixion)
10	How do Christians celebrate Easter?	Going to church, singing songs/hymns, eggs including chocolate eggs, eating hot cross buns, sharing breakfast

Put paper here

Previous questions

Now go back and use these questions to check your knowledge of previous topics.

Questions / Answers

#	Questions	Answers
11	Which prayer did Jesus teach the disciples?	The Lord's prayer
12	What is another name for the Lord's prayer?	Our Father
13	Give one other name for Holy Communion.	Eucharist
14	Name two different types of baptism.	Infant baptism, believer's baptism
15	What does the water symbolise in baptism?	Washing away of sins

Put paper here

Practice

Exam-style questions

01 Which **one** of the following is when Christians celebrate the resurrection of Jesus?

Put a tick (✓) in the box next to the correct answer. **(1 mark)**

A   Christmas ☐

B   Pilgrimage ☐

C   Spring Equinox ☐

D   Easter ☐

02 Which **one** of the following is when Christians celebrate the birth of Jesus?

Put a tick (✓) in the box next to the correct answer. **(1 mark)**

A   Christmas ☐

B   Pilgrimage ☐

C   Spring Equinox ☐

D   Easter ☐

03 Give **two** Christian beliefs about pilgrimage. **(2 marks)**

04 Give **two** ways that Christians may celebrate Christmas. **(2 marks)**

05 Explain **two** contrasting places a Christian may visit on pilgrimage. **(4 marks)** ◄

> **EXAM TIP**
> Remember that a 4-mark question requires two developed points. Show the examiner you have done this by writing in two paragraphs.

06 Explain **two** reasons why Easter is an important celebration for Christians in Great Britain today.
Refer to sacred writings or another source of Christian belief and teaching in your answer. **(5 marks)**

07 'Christmas is more important than Easter for Christians today.'
Evaluate this statement.

In your answer you should:

- refer to Christian teaching
- give reasoned arguments to support this statement
- give reasoned arguments to support a different point of view
- reach a justified conclusion. **(12 marks)**

(+ SPaG 3 marks)

> **EXAM TIP**
> Make sure you read the question carefully and answer the exact wording in your judgement.

8 ✝ Practices: The church in the community, and mission, evangelism, and growth

The role of the church in the local community

Many Christians believe that the church should be at the centre of the community. They organise events and activities to help to support local people. This is an opportunity for them to show **agape** (selfless, sacrificial, unconditional love for others).

- Some events are for Christians, for example church services and prayer meetings.
- Some events are for all in the community even if they're not Christian, for example, playgroups and coffee mornings.
- These events are not always in the church building itself, for example 'outreach' work in local schools.

The community of Christians are following what the 'sheep' in the Parable of the Sheep and Goat did:

> 66 *For I was hungry and you gave me something to eat, I was thirsty and you gave me something to drink, I was a stranger and you invited me in, I needed clothes and you clothed me, I was sick and you looked after me, I was in prison and you came to visit me.* 99 (Matthew 25:34–36)

Street pastors

Some members of Christian churches volunteer as **street pastors**. Teams of street pastors go out to the local area to help people who might be in need. This is often on Friday and Saturday nights when many people go to town centres and their behaviour is affected by alcohol. The street pastors:

- check if people are OK and help if they are sick
- reunite them with friends they may have become separated from, and help to ensure they get home safely
- may try to calm down people who are upset or violent
- do not have any legal powers but often work alongside the council and local police
- don't aim to convert anyone but to show their faith through action:

> 66 *Faith by itself, if it is not accompanied by action, is dead.* 99 (James 2:17)

> **REVISION TIP** ☑
>
> Try to watch videos online showing what street pastors do. Seeing them in action will help you to remember what they do.

Food banks

Some churches and Christian organisations have set up **food banks** to help people in the community who don't have enough food.

- People donate food items to the food bank, and they are distributed to those who need them.
- The Trussell Trust supports over 1200 food bank centres. They base their work on Christian principles and the values of compassion, justice, community, and dignity.

⚙ Knowledge

8 ✝ Practices: The church in the community, and mission, evangelism, and growth

Mission

- Just before Jesus ascended to heaven, he told his **disciples** to:

  > ❝ ... go and make disciples of all nations, baptising them in the name of the Father and of the Son and of the Holy Spirit. ❞ (Matthew 28:19)

- This event is called 'The Great Commission'.

- A commission is a specific task or job for an individual or group to do.

- It has the word '**mission**' in it – in Christianity this means the vocation or calling of a Christian organisation or individual to go out into the world and spread their faith.

- Many Christians feel that they have an individual mission in life called a vocation, given by God, for them to work for God in a specific way. This may link to something that they already do, for example a surgeon may volunteer to be a surgeon in a place that needs their specialism but would not normally be able to have their expertise.

- Since the Great Commission, many people, known as missionaries, travel to, and often live in, other countries to complete their mission.

- Some Christians believe that they can complete their mission closer to home and work in their local community.

REVISION TIP ✔

Think of a 'mission' like a task or job someone needs to do. Hopefully not a 'Mission Impossible'!

Evangelism

Evangelism is an important part of mission: spreading the Christian gospel by public preaching or personal witness.

The disciples were the first people to evangelise, and St Paul travelled in many areas of the Mediterranean Sea telling communities about Jesus. This can be read in his letters in the New Testament.

Giving out leaflets to passers-by in public places.

Some organisations give away copies of the Bible in the local language of the country, placing them in public spaces such as hotel rooms.

Today, Christians evangelise in different ways

The Alpha course is an 11-week cross-denominational course to help people learn about and potentially convert to Christianity. Millions of people have taken part, in hundreds of countries and different languages.

Evangelism

Some Christians don't agree with some methods of evangelism:

- Some groups have used pressurising tactics or discrimination to try to get others to convert

- There are accounts of missionaries around the world not behaving in a loving way towards non-Christian communities.

REVISION TIP

Have you ever seen someone in the street talking about God and Jesus? Have you ever had someone knock at your door to try and talk about God? This will help you to remember forms of evangelism.

Church growth

The Christian **Church** began at Pentecost, sometimes known as the birth of the Christian Church. (Church with a capital 'C' means the community of Christians.)	After the ascension, the disciples waited in Jerusalem for a sign, as Jesus had told them to.	They then started to spread the word about God and Jesus. After this the Bible says: *"So the word of God spread. The number of disciples in Jerusalem increased rapidly, and a large number of priests became obedient to the faith."* (Acts 6:7)	All but one of the disciples were killed for their beliefs, but the Christian Church began to grow around Europe.

- Today, Christianity is the largest religion in the world with an estimated 2.6 billion followers.

- Roman Catholicism is the biggest denomination.

- Christianity is declining in Europe and the Americas, but it is growing in Africa and in Asia.

- The 2011 England and Wales census reported that 59% of people selected 'Christianity'. By 2021, this figure had fallen to 46%, showing that fewer than half of the population say they are Christian.

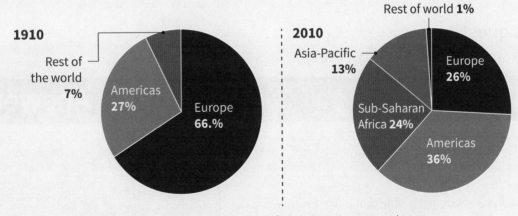

▲ *Approximate regional distribution of Christians in 1910 and 2010*

Key terms — Make sure you can write a definition for these key terms

agape   street pastors   food bank   disciples   mission

evangelism   Church

Retrieval

Learn the answers to the questions below, then cover the answers column with a piece of paper and write as many as you can. Check and repeat.

Questions / Answers

#	Questions	Answers
1	What is the word used in the Bible that describes selfless, sacrificial, unconditional love for others?	Agape
2	Name two types of event that the Christian community might organise for the whole community.	Two from: playgroup / coffee morning / outreach work in local schools
3	Which parable tells Christians to help the hungry, thirsty, and sick, and visit those in prison?	Parable of the Sheep and Goats
4	Name the values that The Trussell Trust bases its work on.	Compassion, justice, community, dignity
5	What is the name of people who volunteer to go out into their local area to help people in need, often at weekends?	Street pastors
6	What did Jesus tell the disciples to do at the Great Commission?	*"... go and make disciples of all nations, baptising them in the name of the Father and of the Son and of the Holy Spirit."*
7	Who travelled around the Mediterranean Sea evangelising to communities and writing them letters about Christianity (now in the New Testament)?	St Paul
8	What is the name of the 11-week course that aims to tell non-Christians about the basics of Christianity?	The Alpha course
9	What does the word Church (with a capital 'C') mean?	The community of Christians
10	Approximately how many Christians are there in the world today?	2.6 billion

Put paper here

Previous questions

Now go back and use these questions to check your knowledge of previous topics.

Questions / Answers

#	Questions	Answers
11	In which part of the Lord's prayer do Christians ask God to help them avoid sin?	*Lead us not into temptation but deliver us from evil.*
12	Why is Iona a particularly spiritual place for pilgrims?	It has a 'thin veil' between earthly life and spiritual life
13	Which event in the life of Jesus is remembered at Holy Communion?	The Last Supper
14	Why is the water at Lourdes special?	It is believed to have healing powers
15	Which event in the life of Jesus is celebrated at Easter?	His resurrection (following his crucifixion)

Put paper here

Exam-style questions

01 Which **one** of the following is the Christian belief in spreading the Christian gospel by public preaching or personal witness?

Put a tick (✓) in the box next to the correct answer. **(1 mark)**

A	Pentecost	☐
B	Agape	☐
C	Evangelism	☐
D	Street pastors	☐

02 Which **one** of these is the event that is known as the birth of the Christian Church?

Put a tick (✓) in the box next to the correct answer. **(1 mark)**

A	Pentecost	☐
B	The Great Commission	☐
C	The Last Supper	☐
D	The resurrection	☐

03 Give **two** Christian beliefs about The Great Commission. **(2 marks)**

> **EXAM TIP**
> Remember – in 2-mark questions answers can be one word or short phrases. You do not have to write in full sentences.

04 Give **two** ways that a Christian may evangelise. **(2 marks)**

05 Explain **two** contrasting ways that a Christian might help others in the local community. **(4 marks)**

06 Explain **two** contrasting ways that a Christian may evangelise. **(4 marks)**

> **EXAM TIP**
> 'Contrasting' just means 'different' in these questions.

07 Explain **two** reasons for Church growth.

Refer to sacred writings or another source of Christian belief and teaching in your answer. **(5 marks)**

08 'All Christians should travel to another country to evangelise.'

Evaluate this statement.

> **EXAM TIP**
> Ensure you include all the parts given in the bullet points in your answer.

In your answer you should:

- refer to Christian teaching
- give reasoned arguments to support this statement
- give reasoned arguments to support a different point of view
- reach a justified conclusion. **(12 marks)**

(+ SPaG 3 marks)

Knowledge

9 ✝ Practices: The importance of the worldwide Church

How Christian churches respond to persecution

Persecution is hostility and ill treatment, especially because of race, or political or religious beliefs. Followers of many religions, including Christianity, are persecuted by being:

- made fun of in public, including unfair or biased media coverage
- banned from meeting with others
- subjected to torture or killed
- removed from their job or not having the same opportunities for work.

The Bible tells Christians to get ready to be persecuted:

> ❝ In fact, everyone who wants to live a godly life in Christ Jesus will be persecuted. ❞ (2 Timothy 3:12)

Christians may find strength in persecution, bringing them together and strengthening their faith:

> ❝ Consider it pure joy … whenever you face trials of many kinds, because you know that the testing of your faith produces perseverance … so that you may be mature and complete … ❞ (James 1:2–4)

Working for reconciliation

- The key message of Christianity is that, due to God's sacrifice, Jesus died on the cross so humans can be reconciled with God.
- Christians around the world work for reconciliation between Christians and non-Christians, and within Christianity, to improve relationships where there has been a breakdown.
- One of the Catholic sacraments is reconciliation where followers confess their sins through a priest to ensure they renew their relationship with God after they have sinned.

- The Bible encourages reconciliation when it says:

> ❝ For if, while we were God's enemies, we were reconciled to him through the death of his Son, how much more, having been reconciled, shall we be saved through his life! ❞ (Romans 5:10)

The Corrymeela Community, Northern Ireland

The Community:

- was started in 1965 by Ray Davey
- is a place where Christians and people of other religions or none can stay and meet to work together on differences
- encourages people to learn how to have difficult conversations on sensitive, potentially divisive issues through workshops, using dialogue, experiential play, art, and storytelling.

▲ Corrymeela gives people from a variety of political and religious backgrounds the opportunity to discuss, and overcome their differences

The work of CAFOD, Christian Aid, Tearfund

There are Christian charities that aim to help people around the world who are in need. They believe that they should follow the Parable of the Good Samaritan and the commandment to 'Love your neighbour', by helping others.

REVISION TIP

You only need to know about the work of one of these charities.

CAFOD

CAFOD is part of Caritas International, one of the largest aid networks in the world. It is the official Catholic aid agency for England and Wales, working with poor communities to end poverty and injustice.

CAFOD aims to:

- reach people in greatest need, save lives, and relieve suffering
- change the conditions and behaviours that lead to poverty, inequality, injustice, and damage to the natural world
- encourage the Catholic community of England and Wales to work together for the common good.

CAF✦D
Catholic Agency for
Overseas Development

REVISION TIP

Remember your charity by thinking 'N-A-R': *Name* (of the charity), *Action* (what they do), *Reason* (why they do it – the link to Christian teaching).

Christian Aid

For over 75 years **Christian Aid** has worked to eradicate poverty around the world by tackling its root causes.

Christian Aid aims to help people:

- uphold their rights and gain access to services such as healthcare and education, and fight discrimination
- deal with disasters such as drought, climate change, and hurricanes, and to develop resilience against them in the future
- improve their situation, for example, by getting a fair price for goods and products.

christian **aid**

Tearfund

Tearfund works with local churches in more than 50 countries to help to tackle and end poverty through sustainable development, by responding to disasters and challenging injustice.

Tearfund works to reduce poverty through:

- rapid response to disasters and conflicts
- working with local churches and organisations, encouraging communities to help themselves
- helping people to speak out against poverty and injustice.

Key terms Make sure you can write a definition for these key terms

persecution   CAFOD   Christian Aid   Tearfund

Retrieval

Learn the answers to the questions below, then cover the answers column with a piece of paper and write as many as you can. Check and repeat.

Questions | Answers

	Questions	Answers
1	What is the key message of Christianity?	Due to God's sacrifice, Jesus died on the cross so humans can be reconciled with God
2	In which sacrament do Catholics confess their sins through a priest?	Reconciliation
3	Which quotation in the Bible encourages reconciliation?	"For if, while we were God's enemies, we were reconciled to him through the death of his Son, how much more, having been reconciled, shall we be saved through his life!"
4	What is meant by persecution?	Persecution is hostility and ill treatment
5	Give one example of how Christians might be persecuted.	One from: being made fun of in public including unfair or biased media coverage / being banned from meeting with others / being subjected to torture or killed / being removed from their job or not having the same opportunities for work
6	Which quotation from the Bible tells Christians that they should be prepared for persecution?	"In fact, everyone who wants to live a godly life in Christ Jesus will be persecuted."
7	Which Catholic charity is part of one of the largest aid agencies in the world?	CAFOD
8	For how long has Christian Aid worked to eradicate poverty?	Over 75 years
9	Which charity works with local churches in more than 50 countries?	Tearfund

Put paper here

Previous questions

Now go back and use these questions to check your knowledge of previous topics.

Questions | Answers

	Questions	Answers
10	For what type of prayers have the words already been written?	Set prayers
11	What two things do Christians use during Holy Communion to remember the death of Jesus?	Bread and wine
12	Which event in the life of Jesus is celebrated at Christmas?	His birth
13	What is the word used in the Bible that describes selfless, sacrificial, unconditional love for others?	Agape

Put paper here

Exam-style questions

01   Which **one** of these means the restoring of harmony after relationships have broken down?

Put a tick (✓) in the box next to the correct answer.   **(1 mark)**

   A   Sacrfice   ☐

   B   Charity   ☐

   C   Persecution   ☐

   D   Reconciliation   ☐

02   Which **one** of these means hostility and ill-treatment, especially because of race, or political, or religious beliefs?

Put a tick (✓) in the box next to the correct answer.   **(1 mark)**

   A   Persecution   ☐

   B   Charity   ☐

   C   Sacrifice   ☐

   D   Reconciliation   ☐

> **EXAM TIP**
> These questions are only worth 1 mark so don't spend a long time on them. But remember to read the question and answer options carefully to avoid making a silly mistake.

03   Give **two** ways that Christians may be persecuted today.   **(2 marks)**

04   Give **two** ways that a Christian charity may help those that are in poverty and are facing injustice.   **(2 marks)**

05   Explain **two** contrasting ways that Christians may respond to persecution.   **(4 marks)**

> **EXAM TIP**
> Contrasting doesn't have to be 'opposite' – it just means 'different'.

06   Explain **two** reasons why reconciliation is important in Christianity.

Refer to sacred writings or another source of Christian belief and teaching in your answer.   **(5 marks)**

07   'Charities can reduce poverty and injustice by themselves.'

Evaluate this statement.

In your answer you should:

- refer to Christian teaching
- give reasoned arguments to support this statement
- give reasoned arguments to support a different point of view
- reach a justified conclusion.   **(12 marks)**

(+ SPaG 3 marks)

10 ☪ Beliefs and teachings: The six articles of faith in Sunni Islam and five roots of Usul ad-Din in Shi'a Islam

- The **six articles of faith** are key beliefs for **Sunni** Muslims.
- The **five roots of Usul ad-Din** are key beliefs for **Shi'a** Muslims.

They are the foundations for a Muslim to be a Muslim, without which their faith (in Arabic 'iman') could be weakened.

> **REVISION TIP** ☑
>
> Try using an acronym or saying that helps you to remember the six articles of faith.

The six articles of faith in Sunni Islam

The six articles can be represented as the foundation stones of a building supported by the five pillars of Islam (see page 69).

#	Article	Description	Quotation
1	Tawhid (the oneness of God)	There is only one God (who is not divided into parts).	❝ Say, 'He is God the One, God the eternal. He begets no one nor was He begotten. No one is comparable to Him.' ❞ (Surah 112)
2	Malaikah (angels)	Angels are spiritual beings, created from light, believed to act as messengers of God.	❝ Praise be to God, Creator of the heavens and earth, who made angels messengers with two, three, four [pairs of] wings. ❞ (Qur'an 35:1)
3	Kutub (books)	Texts that contain the revelations received by some of the prophets.	❝ We sent Jesus, son of Mary, in their footsteps, to confirm the Torah that had been sent before him: We gave him the Gospel with guidance, light, and confirmation of the Torah already revealed – a guide and lesson for those who take heed of God. ❞ (Qur'an 5:46)
4	Risalah (prophets)	• Prophets are an important channel of communication between God and humans. • Each prophet is divinely chosen and has a message to tell the people at that particular time.	❝ Every community is sent a messenger, and when their messenger comes, they will be judged justly; they will not be wronged. ❞ (Qur'an 10:47)
5	Al-Qadr (predestination)	God knows or determines everything that will happen in the universe.	❝ Only what God has decreed will happen to us. He is our Master: let the believers put their trust in God." (Qur'an 9:51) "No soul may die except with God's permission at a predestined time. ❞ (Qur'an 3:145)
6	Akhirah (Day of Judgement)	• A day in the future when God will judge humans according to everything they have done throughout their lives. • Humans will be resurrected and then sent for eternity to Heaven or Hell depending on their deeds.	❝ They ask, 'When is this Judgement Day coming?' On a Day when they will be punished by the Fire, 'Taste the punishment! This is what you wished to hasten.' The righteous will be in Gardens with [flowing] springs. ❞ (Qur'an 51:12–15)

The five roots of Usul ad-Din in Shi'a Islam

For Shi'a Islam, the five roots of Usul ad-Din (in Arabic *Usul* = origins, *Din* = religion) can be represented as a tree (see page 70) with the beliefs being the roots that support the tree and provide its nutrients.

1 Tawhid (the oneness of God) → There is only one God (who is not divided into parts). → 66 Say, 'He is God the One, God the eternal. He begets no one nor was He begotten. No one is comparable to Him.' 99 (Surah 112)

2 Risalah (prophets) → Prophets are an important channel of communication between God and humans. → 66 Every community is sent a messenger, and when their messenger comes, they will be judged justly; they will not be wronged." 99 (Qur'an 10:47)

3 Imamate (divinely appointed leaders) → Divinely appointed leaders, from the descendants of Muhammad, who guard the truth of the religion without error and helped to interpret the Qur'an. → 66 And I am leaving among you two weighty things: There first of which is the Book of Allah… And the members of my household, I remind you of Allah with regards (of your duties) to the members of my family. 99 (Hadith)

4 Adalat (divine justice) →
- God is just and fair.
- When he judges humans, he will base it on how they have behaved and will reward the good and punish the bad.

→ 66 When they see the punishment, they will repent in secret, but they will be judged with justice and will not be wronged. 99 (Qur'an 10:47)

5 Mi'ad (day of resurrection and judgement) →
- Muslims believe they will be resurrected from the dead on the Day of Resurrection and then judged by God on the Day of Judgement.
- This is the start of the afterlife (Akhirah).

→ 66 We [God] will set up scales of justice for the Day of Resurrection so that no one can be wronged in the least, and if there should be even the weight of a mustard seed, We [God] shall bring it out – We take excellent account. 99 (Qur'an 21:47)

REVISION TIP

In a 5-mark question you need to 'Refer to sacred writings or another source of Muslim belief and teaching' so learn these quotes to help you answer questions on the roots.

⚙ Knowledge

10 ☾ Beliefs and teachings: The six articles of faith in Sunni Islam and five roots of Usul ad-Din in Shi'a Islam

Similarities and differences between the six articles and five roots

All Muslims share these core beliefs except for one. The exception is the Imamate, which is a Shi'a Muslim belief only.

THE SIX ARTICLES OF
FAITH IN SUNNI ISLAM

THE FIVE ROOTS OF
USUL AD-DIN IN SHI'A ISLAM

REVISION TIP

To help you remember the similarities and differences, draw this Venn diagram from memory and then check your work.

Books (Kutub)

Angels (Malaikah)

Predestination (Al-Qadr)

The oneness of God
(Shi'a and Sunni = Tawhid)

Prophets
(Shi'a and Sunni = Risalah)

Day of Judgement
(Shi'a = Mi'ad; Sunni = Akhirah)

**Divinely appointed
leaders** (Imamate)
- Shi'a Muslim only

Divine justice (Adalat)

REVISION TIP

You do not need to remember all the Arabic words, as exam questions would include the Arabic and the English translations for: Tawhid, Adalat, Akhirah and Risalah.

Key terms | Make sure you can write a definition for these key terms | six articles of faith   Sunni   five roots of Usul ad-Din   Shi'a
Tawhid   Risalah   Al-Qadr   Akhirah   Imamate   Adalat

Learn the answers to the questions below, then cover the answers column with a piece of paper and write as many as you can. Check and repeat.

Questions

Answers

	Question	Answer
1	What are the five roots of Usul ad-Din?	Key beliefs for Shi'a Muslims
2	What are the five pillars of Islam?	The key practices all Muslims should fulfil throughout their lifetime
3	What is the Muslim belief that there is only one God (who is not divided into parts)?	The Oneness of God (Tawhid)
4	What is the Muslim belief that there are spiritual beings believed to act as messengers of God?	Angels (Malaikah)
5	What is the Muslim belief in texts that contain the revelations received by some of the prophets?	Books (Kutub)
6	What is the Muslim belief that there are messengers between God and humans that give God's message to the people at that particular time?	Prophets (Risalah)
7	What is the Muslim belief that God knows or determines everything that will happen in the universe?	Predestination (Al-Qadr)
8	What is the Muslim belief that one day all humans will face God and he will consider our good and bad actions to determine if we go to heaven or hell?	Day of Judgement
9	What is the Shi'a Muslim belief in the 12 divinely appointed leaders, from the descendants of Muhammad, which guard the truth of the religion?	Imamate
10	What is the Muslim belief that God is just and fair when he judges humans?	Divine justice (Adalat)
11	Which of the five roots of Usul ad-Din are NOT part of the six articles of faith?	Divinely appointed leaders (imamate) and divine justice (adalat)
12	Which quotation from Surah 112 in the Qur'an asserts the oneness of God?	*"He is God the One, God the eternal. He begets no one nor was He begotten. No one is comparable to Him."*
13	Which beliefs are in the six articles of faith (Sunni) AND are part of the five roots of Usul ad-Din (Shi'a)?	Oneness of God, prophets, Day of Judgement
14	Which of the six articles of faith are NOT part of the five roots of Usul ad-Din?	Books, angels, predestination

Put paper here

Practice

Exam-style questions

01 Which of these is **not** one of the six articles of faith?

Put a tick (✓) in the box next to the correct answer. **(1 mark)**

A   Books ☐

B   Imamate ☐

C   Prophethood ☐

D   Tawhid ☐

02 Which **one** of these is one of the five roots of Usul ad-Din?

Put a tick (✓) in the box next to the correct answer. **(1 mark)**

A   Angels ☐

B   Al-Qadr ☐

C   Books ☐

D   Adalat ☐

> **EXAM TIP**
>
> Read each of the answer options carefully. There may be answers that are there to distract you from the correct one!

03 Name **two** of the six articles of faith. **(2 marks)**

> **EXAM TIP**
>
> The examiner will only mark your first two answers on the 2-mark questions so don't waste time writing more than two.

04 Name **two** of the five roots of Usul ad-Din. **(2 marks)**

05 Explain **two** ways in which belief in Tawhid influences Muslims today. **(4 marks)**

06 Explain **two** of the six articles of faith.

Refer to sacred writings or another source of Muslim belief and teaching in your answer. **(5 marks)**

> **EXAM TIP**
>
> Remember to state the source when you are referring to a sacred writing, for example 'The Qur'an says…', (although you don't need to say which chapter or verse the quotation is from).

07 'The Imamate is the most important belief in the five roots of Usul ad-Din.'

Evaluate this statement.

In your answer you should:

- refer to Muslim teaching
- give reasoned arguments to support this statement
- give reasoned arguments to support a different point of view
- reach a justified conclusion. **(12 marks)**

(+ SPaG 3 marks)

11 ☾ Beliefs and teachings: Tawhid, the nature of God, and angels

Tawhid (the Oneness of God), Qur'an Surah 112

- Muslims believe that there is only one God (in Arabic, Allah).
- They believe that God is only one and has not divided into different parts. Surah 112 in the Qur'an helps them to understand what this means.

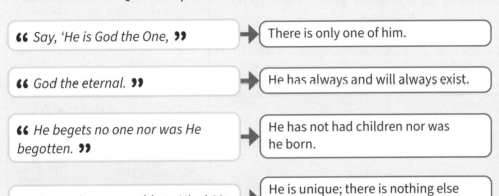

❝ *Say, 'He is God the One,* ❞	➡ There is only one of him.
❝ *God the eternal.* ❞	➡ He has always and will always exist.
❝ *He begets no one nor was He begotten.* ❞	➡ He has not had children nor was he born.
❝ *No one is comparable to Him.'* ❞	➡ He is unique; there is nothing else like him.

> **REVISION TIP**
>
> To help you learn Qur'an Surah 112, write it out 3 times, then wait 3 days, then write it out again. Check that you have remembered it correctly and if not correct it. Wait 3 days, then write it out again. Repeat until you can remember it.

The nature of God

Muslims believe that, whilst God is not fully knowable, the Qur'an tells them about his nature, what he is like. This helps them to understand their religion and their beliefs as a Muslim and helps them to get closer to God.

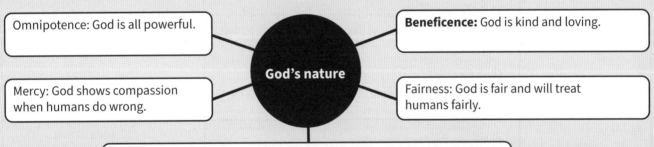

Omnipotence: God is all powerful.

Beneficence: God is kind and loving.

God's nature

Mercy: God shows compassion when humans do wrong.

Fairness: God is fair and will treat humans fairly.

Justice (Adalat In Shi'a Islam): God is just and does not oppress anyone at any time, both in this world and the next. He will ensure that humans will get what they deserve when he judges them.

Knowledge

11 ☾ Beliefs and teachings: Tawhid, the nature of God and angels

The nature of God in the Qur'an

Quality	Qur'an	Example
Omnipotence	*" all power belongs to God. "* (Qur'an 2:165) *" know that God is all powerful and wise. "* (Qur'an 2:260)	God was the only being powerful enough to create the universe.
Beneficence	*" Ask forgiveness from your Lord, and turn to Him in repentance: my Lord is merciful and most loving. "* (Qur'an 11:90)	God sends prophets to Earth to guide them in accordance with God's instructions. **REVISION TIP** To remember the word 'beneficence' think of the word 'benefits' – the good things.
Mercy	*" If you do good, openly or in secret, or if you pardon something bad, then God is most forgiving and powerful. "* (Qur'an 4:149) *" Suffering has truly afflicted me, but you are the Most Merciful of the merciful. "* (Qur'an 21:83) *" ... for God is most compassionate and most merciful towards people. "* (Qur'an 2:143)	God forgave Adam and Eve when they asked for forgiveness.
Fairness	*" On the Day of Resurrection ... the Record of Deeds will be laid open; the prophets and witnesses will be brought in. Fair judgement will be given between them: they will not be wronged and every soul will be repaid in full for what it has done. He knows best what they do. "* (Qur'an 39:67–70)	On the Day of Judgement God will judge humans fairly according to their deeds.
Justice/Adalat	*" We [God] will set up scales of justice for the Day of Resurrection so that no one can be wronged in the least, and if there should be even the weight of a mustard seed, We [God] shall bring it out – We take excellent account. "* (Qur'an 21:47)	On the Day of Judgement there will be justice for all humans. Those with more good deeds will go to Heaven and those with more bad deeds will go to Hell.

The 99 names of God

Some Muslims look to the 99 names of God, many of which come from the Qur'an or Hadith, to help them understand the **nature of God**. These include:

- The Beneficent
- The Merciful
- The Omnipotent One
- The Great Forgiver
- The All-Knowing One

◄ *Many of the 99 names of God come from the Qur'an*

God's relationship with the world

Quality	Qur'an	Example
Immanence God is within and involved in his creation. He knows and has a relationship with humans.	66 *Misfortunes can only happen with God's permission – He will guide the heart of anyone who believes in Him: God knows all things.* 99 (Qur'an 64:11)	God gave humans the Qur'an for them to have a guide to life and for them to understand him more.
Transcendence God exists beyond his creation and is beyond human understanding. He has always existed and will always exist.	66 *God: there is no god but Him, the Ever Living, the Ever Watchful. Neither slumber nor sleep overtakes Him. All that is in the heavens and in the earth belongs to Him. … His throne extends over the heavens and the earth; it does not weary Him to preserve them both. He is the Most High, the Tremendous.* 99 (Qur'an 2:255)	God existed before he created the universe and will exist beyond this universe's existence.

> **REVISION TIP**
>
> To remember the word 'immanence', think of 'im' sounding like 'in' - God is *in* his creation.

Knowledge

11 Beliefs and teachings: Tawhid, the nature of God and angels

The nature and role of angels

Angels (in Arabic, Malaikah) in Islam:

- are God's messengers
- often speak with prophets to give God's revelation
- do not have free will so do as they're instructed by God and cannot sin
- are described in the Qur'an as being made from light, with wings, but they can sometimes take a human form.

> **REVISION TIP**
>
> Angels don't have free will in Islam. Don't confuse them with angels in Christianity that do have free will.

Angels in the Qur'an

The Qur'an mentions several angels and their different roles, including:

- the angel of death (Isra'il)
- Raqib and Atid who write down our good and bad actions, in Arabic they are called *kiraman katibin* meaning honourable scribe
- **Jibril** (Gabriel) and **Mika'il** (Michael).

> **REVISION TIP**
>
> You need to know about Jibril and Mika'il, but knowing about other angels can help you develop your points, including in some Themes topics.

> 66 *If anyone is an enemy of God, His angels and His messengers, of Gabriel and Michael, then God is certainly the enemy of such disbelievers.* 99
>
> (Qur'an 2:98)

Jibril (Gabriel)	Mika'il (Michael)
• Jibril is the angel of revelation. • He brings good news to those he comes to. • He revealed the words of the Qur'an – starting on the night of Power, Qu'ran 96:1–5. • He told Maryam (Mary) she was pregnant with Isa (Jesus).	• Mika'il is the angel of mercy. • He asks God to forgive humans' sins. • He rewards humans for good deeds. • He is in charge of rain, thunder, and lightning.

 Key terms Make sure you can write a definition for these key terms

beneficence   nature of God
immanence   transcendence   Jibril   Mika'il

Learn the answers to the questions below, then cover the answers column with a piece of paper and write as many as you can. Check and repeat.

Questions / Answers

	Questions	Answers
1	Which word means that God is all-powerful?	Omnipotence
2	Which word means God is kind and loving?	Beneficence
3	Which word means God shows compassion when humans do wrong?	Mercy/merciful
4	Name an angel in Islam.	One from: Jibril (Gabriel) / Mika'il (Michael) / Raqib / Atid / Isra'il
5	Which Arabic word means God is just and will ensure that humans will get what they deserve when he judges them?	Adalat
6	How many Muslim names are there for God and where do many of them come from?	99 names; many come from the Qur'an or Hadith
7	Which word means God is within and involved in his creation – he knows and has a relationship with humans?	Immanence
8	Which word means God exists beyond his creation and is beyond human understanding?	Transcendence
9	Give three of Mika'il's roles.	He is the angel of mercy - he asks God to forgive humans' sins, he rewards humans for good deeds, he is in charge of rain, thunder, and lightning
10	At which future event will humans see God's fairness, justice, and mercy?	Day of Judgement

Put paper here

Previous questions

Now go back and use these questions to check your knowledge of previous topics.

Questions / Answers

	Questions	Answers
11	Which quotation from Surah 112 in the Qur'an asserts the oneness of God?	*"He is God the One, God the eternal. He begets no one nor was He begotten. No one is comparable to Him."*
12	What is the Muslim belief that there is only one God (who is not divided into parts)?	The Oneness of God (Tawhid)
13	What is the Muslim belief that there are spiritual beings believed to act as messengers of God?	Angels (Malaikah)
14	What is the Muslim belief in texts that contain the revelations received by some of the prophets'?	Books (Kutub)
15	What is the Muslim belief that there are messengers between God and humans that give God's message to the people at that time'?	Prophethood (Risalah)

Put paper here

Practice

Exam-style questions

01 Which **one** of these angels revealed the Qur'an to Muhammad?

Put a tick (✓) in the box next to the correct answer. **(1 mark)**

A   Mika'il   ☐

B   Isra'il   ☐

C   Jibril   ☐

D   Raqib   ☐

02 Which **one** of these means that God is all-powerful?

Put a tick (✓) in the box next to the correct answer. **(1 mark)**

A   Transcendent   ☐

B   Immanent   ☐

C   Omnipotent   ☐

D   Omniscient   ☐

03 Name **two** angels in Islam. **(2 marks)**

04 Give **two** beliefs about the nature of God in Islam. **(2 marks)**

> **EXAM TIP**
>
> In an 'influence' question think about how the belief might change what a Muslim does/thinks/ believes as an influence.

05 Explain **two** ways that belief in angels may influence Muslims today. **(4 marks)**

> **EXAM TIP**
>
> Remember that the examiner is looking for two detailed explanations of a relevant and accurate belief including a relevant and accurate reference to sacred writing or another source of Muslim belief and teaching. Present them in two paragraphs.

06 Explain **two** Muslim beliefs about Tawhid.

Refer to sacred writings or another source of Muslim belief and teaching in your answer. **(5 marks)**

07 'The most important belief about God is that he is omnipotent.'

Evaluate this statement.

In your answer you should:

- refer to Muslim teaching
- give reasoned arguments to support this statement
- give reasoned arguments to support a different point of view
- reach a justified conclusion. **(12 marks)**

                                            (+ SPaG 3 marks)

Knowledge

12 Beliefs and teachings: Predestination and Akhirah

Predestination and human freedom, and its relationship to the Day of Judgement

Predestination

> *Only what God has decreed will happen to us. He is our Master: let the believers put their trust in God.* (Qur'an 9:51)

- **Predestination** (**al-Qadr**) means that God already knows the future and what will happen in each human being's life.
- This is balanced with the belief that humans have **free will** and make their own decisions.
- Some Muslims believe that God has already determined everything that will happen in humans' lives and in the rest of the universe and it is written in the 'book of decrees'.
- This belief puts emphasis on God's power and knowledge and less on humans' free will but doesn't mean that humans cannot choose how to live.

Human freedom

> *God does not change the condition of a people [for the worse] unless they change what is in themselves.* (Qur'an 13:11)

- Muslims believe that God knows everything that is going to happen because he is **omniscient**.
- However, some Muslims believe he doesn't decide that it will happen. Humans have full free will, but God already knows what decisions and actions they will take.

The day of Judgement

> *Every soul will taste death and you will be paid in full only on the Day of Resurrection. Whoever is kept away from the Fire and admitted to the Garden will have triumphed … you are sure to be tested through your possessions and persons;…. If you are steadfast and mindful of God, that is the best course.* (Qur'an 3:185–186)

- On the **Day of Judgement**, God will hold humans accountable for their actions.
- Life is a test for which humans will be rewarded for good actions by going to heaven and punished for bad actions by going to hell.

⚙ Knowledge

12 ☾ Beliefs and teachings: Predestination and Akhirah

Akhirah (life after death), human responsibility and accountability, resurrection, Heaven and Hell

Muslims believe there is a life after death (akhirah) as described in the Qur'an. When someone dies, Muslims believe that the body should be buried as soon as possible. It is ritually prepared, wrapped in a white cloth, and buried, facing Makkah.

A person's soul is taken by the angel Isra'il to barzakh (barrier) where it waits until the day of judgement. This is known as the intermediary realm, an existence between this life and the hereafter.	❝ … *a barrier stands behind such people until the very Day they are resurrected.* ❞ (Qur'an 23:100)
When the Day of Judgement arrives, the angel Israfil blows a trumpet, and all humans will be resurrected (some Muslims believe in a full body **resurrection** and others believe in the resurrection of only the soul).	❝ *The Trumpet will be sounded and – lo and behold! – they will rush out to their Lord from their graves.* ❞ (Qur'an 36:51)
All humans will face God and will be judged according to their deeds. They will be held to account for what they have done right and wrong.	❝ *Fair judgement will be given between them: they will not be wronged and every soul will be repaid in full for what it has done. He knows best what they do.* ❞ (Qur'an 39:69–70)
Humans will also be responsible for their **intentions** (**niyyah**); what they planned to do but didn't complete.	❝ *Whosoever intended to perform a good deed, but did not do it, then Allah writes it down with Himself as a complete good deed. And if he intended to perform it and then did perform it, then Allah writes it down with Himself as from ten good deeds up to seven hundred times, up to many times multiplied. And if he intended to perform an evil deed, but did not do it, then Allah writes it down with Himself as a complete good deed. And if he intended it [i.e., the evil deed] and then performed it, then Allah writes it down as one evil deed.* ❞ (Hadith)
If a person's good deeds outweigh their bad deeds, then God will reward them and send them to **Heaven (Jannah)**. The Qur'an describes it as:	❝ *Gardens graced with flowing streams; there they will be adorned with golden bracelets and pearls; there they will have silken garments.* ❞ (Qur'an 22:23)
If a person's bad deeds outweigh their good deeds then God may punish them and send them to **Hell (Jahannam)**.	❝ *But those whose scales are light, they will have doomed themselves, staying in Hell forever.* ❞ (Qur'an 23:103–104)

Key terms — Make sure you can write a definition for these key terms

predestination (al-Qadr)   free will   omniscient   Day of Judgement
resurrection   intention (niyyah)   Heaven (Jannah)
Hell (Jahannam)

Retrieval

12

Learn the answers to the questions below, then cover the answers column with a piece of paper and write as many as you can. Check and repeat.

	Questions	Answers
1	What does predestination mean for Muslims?	God already knows the future and what will happen in each human being's life
2	What is the term for humans being able to decide for themselves how to behave?	Free will
3	What is the Arabic name for an afterlife?	Akhirah
4	Where are souls taken to wait until the Day of Judgement?	Barzakh
5	In which direction is a Muslim body buried facing?	Makkah
6	Which angel blows the trumpet to signify the start of the Day of Judgement?	Israfil
7	What does the Qur'an describe as: *"Gardens graced with flowing streams"*?	Heaven
8	What do Muslims believe will happen if a person's good deeds outweigh their bad deeds?	God will reward them and send them to heaven
9	If a person's bad deeds outweigh their good deeds, what do Muslims believe might happen?	God might punish the person and send them to hell
10	Complete the Hadith: *"Whosoever intended to perform a good deed, but did not do it, then Allah writes it down with Himself as _____."*	*a complete good deed*

Put paper here

Previous questions

Now go back and use these questions to check your knowledge of previous topics.

	Questions	Answers
11	What is the Muslim belief that God knows or determines everything that will happen in the universe?	Predestination (al-Qadr)
12	What is the Muslim belief that one day all humans will face God and he will consider our good and bad actions to determine if we go to heaven or hell?	Day of Judgement
13	Which word means God is kind and loving?	Beneficence
14	Which word means God shows compassion when humans do wrong?	Mercy/merciful
15	Which Arabic word means God is just and will ensure that humans will get what they deserve when he judges them?	Adalat

Put paper here

✏ Practice

Exam-style questions

01 Which **one** of these means predestination in Islam?

Put a tick (✓) in the box next to the correct answer.   **(1 mark)**

A   Al–Qadr   ☐

B   Barzakh   ☐

C   Id-ul-Fitr   ☐

D   Akhirah   ☐

02 Which **one** of these is life after death in Islam?

Put a tick (✓) in the box next to the correct answer.   **(1 mark)**

A   Heaven   ☐

B   Hell   ☐

C   Akhirah   ☐

D   Barzakh   ☐

03 Give **two** beliefs about human freedom in Islam.   **(2 marks)**

04 Give **two** ways that humans will be held accountable for their actions.   **(2 marks)**

05 Explain **two** ways that predestination may influence a Muslim today.   **(4 marks)**

> **EXAM TIP**
> Make it clear to the examiner that you have made TWO points by writing in two paragraphs.

06 Explain **two** beliefs about the Day of Judgement in Islam.

Refer to sacred writings or another source of Muslim belief and teaching in your answer.   **(5 marks)**

07 'God has already chosen who will go to Heaven.'

Evaluate this statement.

In your answer you should:

- refer to Muslim teaching
- give reasoned arguments to support this statement
- give reasoned arguments to support a different point of view
- reach a justified conclusion.   **(12 marks)**

(+ SPaG 3 marks)

> **EXAM TIP**
> There is no set way of answering a 12-mark question, but ensure you meet the requirements given in the bullet points.

13 ☾ Beliefs and teachings: Risalah and holy books

Risalah (Prophethood)

- Muslims believe that **prophets** are important people, chosen by God to give out the message of Islam.

- This belief in the importance of prophets is called 'risalah'.

- There are thought to have been 124 000 prophets but only 25 are named in the Qur'an.

- The first prophet was Adam and the final prophet was Muhammad.

- Prophets are important because:
  - they are role models of being a good Muslim
  - they are a method of communication between God and humanity
  - they helped to bring people back onto the straight path

    they are error-free and sinless
  - some received **revelations** that became holy books.

> **❝** *Every community is sent a messenger, and when their messenger comes, they will be judged justly; they will not be wronged.* **❞**   (Qur'an 10:47)

The role and importance of Adam

- Adam was the first human, the first steward on Earth (khalifah) and the first prophet.

- The Qur'an says that he was made from clay and that God breathed life into him.

- Whilst he disobeyed God by eating the fruit in Paradise, he asked for forgiveness and God forgave him; there was no further consequence.

- God then sent Adam and Eve to Earth to look after his creation as stewards.

- Some Muslims say that he first built the Ka'aba. The Ka'aba is in the centre of the Great Mosque in Makkah, and is the most sacred site in Islam.

> **REVISION TIP** ☑
>
> Remember that the story of Adam and Eve in Islam is not exactly the same as that in Christianity. Take note of the differences.

> **❝** *He taught Adam all the names [of things].* **❞**
> (Qur'an 10:47)

> **❝** *But you and your wife, Adam, live in the Garden. Both of you eat whatever you like, but do not go near this tree or you will become wrongdoers.* **❞**
> (Qur'an 7:19)

> **❝** *Adam disobeyed his Lord and was led astray – later his Lord brought him close, accepted his repentance, and guided him.* **❞**
> (Qur'an 20:121–122)

⚙ Knowledge

13 ☾ Beliefs and teachings: Risalah and holy books

The role and importance of Ibrahim

- **Ibrahim** (Abraham) showed his faith to God by standing up to polytheist idol worshippers, even when they tried to kill him.

- He was obedient when he followed God's instructions to leave his wife Hagar and their baby, in the desert. She ran to look for water, and the angel Jibril revealed the spring of Zam Zam to her.

- He showed commitment by being prepared to sacrifice his son, Ishmael, when God asked him to. The devil tempted Ibrahim to reject God, but Ibrahim threw stones at him and continued the sacrifice. At the last moment, God said that he only required Ibrahim's commitment and sent a ram for him to sacrifice instead.

- Some Muslims say that he built (or rebuilt) the Ka'aba with his son Ishmael.

- Most of the rituals completed by Muslims on Hajj are linked to the life of Ibrahim, and the festival of Id-ul-Adha remembers his willingness to sacrifice Ishmael.

> ❝ Who could be better in religion than those who direct themselves wholly to God, do good, and follow the religion of Abraham, who was true in faith? God took Abraham as a friend ❞
> (Qur'an 4:125)

> ❝ Abraham was truly an example: devoutly obedient to God and true in faith. He was not an idolater; he was thankful for the blessings of God who chose him and guided him to a straight path. ❞
> (Qur'an 16:120–121)

> ❝ The first House [of worship] to be established for people was the one at Mecca. It is a blessed place; a source of guidance for all people; there are clear signs in it; it is the place where Abraham stood to pray. Pilgrimage to the House is a duty owed to God by people who are able to undertake it. ❞
> (Qur'an 3:96–97)

The role and importance of Muhammad

> ❝ Muhammad is not the father of any one of you men; he is God's Messenger and the seal of the prophets: God knows everything. ❞
> (Qur'an 33:40)

- Muhammad is the final prophet in Islam, also known as the seal of the prophets.
- He was born in Makkah in 570 CE and died in Medinah in 632 CE.
- He was a role model.
- He restored the Ka'aba to the worship of one God.
- He defended Islam by performing the Lesser Jihad.
- The Islamic calendar started when he fled Makkah to Medinah on the Hijra.
- The way he lived his life is now a guide for Muslims: the Sunnah.
- The things he said are now a guide for Muslims: the Hadith.
- He received the only pure holy book in Islam, the Qur'an.

Muhammad's first revelation of the Qur'an by the angel Jibril, was on the Night of Power:

> ❝ Read! In the name of your Lord who created: He created man from a clinging form. Read! Your Lord is the Most Bountiful One who taught by [means of] the pen, who taught man what he did not know. ❞
> (Qur'an 96:1-5)

REVISION TIP

To help you remember the similarities and differences between Adam, Ibrahim and Muhammad, make a Venn diagram with information about all three.

The holy books

As well as the Qur'an, Muslims believe that there are other holy books that have been revealed by God.

> 66 *We have sent revelation to you [Prophet] as We did to Noah and the prophets after him, to Abraham, Ishmael, Isaac, Jacob, and the Tribes, to Jesus, Job, Jonah, Aaron, and Solomon [.] They were messengers bearing good news and warning, so that mankind would have no excuse before God, once the messengers had been sent.* 99 (Qur'an 14:163 and 165)

REVISION TIP

Write the names of the five holy books on five cards. On another five cards, write the names of the prophets associated with the books. On another five cards write a short description of what is in each of the books. Shuffle all the cards and then try to match them up.

Qur'an

Revealed to the prophet Muhammad.

The Qur'an is the only surviving book that is a complete revelation in its original language that has not been changed. It is the final revelation to the final prophet, Muhammad.

During the Night of Power (Qur'an 96:1–5) the angel Jibril started to reveal the words of the Qur'an to the Prophet Muhammad telling him to 'read'.

These revelations continued over approximately 23 years.

They were collated and compiled as one text after the death of Muhammad.

The Qur'an includes stories, history, and teachings of Islam, which act as a guide for Muslims today.

> 66 *We sent to you [Muhammad] the Scripture with the truth, confirming the Scriptures that came before it, and with final authority over them.* 99 (Qur'an 5:48)

Torah (Tawrat)

Revealed to Musa (Moses).

The **Torah (Tawrat)** contains teachings and laws on how people should live, including the Ten Commandments. It includes the important belief of the judgement of God.

Muslims believe that the Torah that Jews use and the Torah in the first five books of the Bible are not the exact revelation to Moses as it has been changed over time.

> 66 *We sent Jesus, son of Mary, in their footsteps, to confirm the Torah that had been sent before him: We gave him the Gospel with guidance, light, and confirmation of the Torah already revealed – a guide and lesson for those who take heed of God.* 99 (Qur'an 5:46)

13 ☾ Beliefs and teachings: Risalah and holy books

Psalms (Zabur)

Revealed to Dawud (David).

The **Psalms (Zabur)** are prayers and poems used for the worship of God.

Muslims believe that the Psalms in the Jewish Tenakh and those in the Christian Bible are not the exact revelation to David as they have been changed over time.

❝ We gave some prophets more than others: We gave David a book [of Psalms]. ❞ (Qur'an 17:55)

Gospel (Injil)

Revealed to Isa (Jesus).

The revelation to Jesus predicted the coming of the prophet Muhammad.

Muslims believe that the **Gospels (Injil)** in the Christian Bible are not the exact revelations made to Jesus as they have been changed over time.

❝ We sent Jesus, son of Mary, in their footsteps, to confirm the Torah that had been sent before him: We gave him the Gospel with guidance, light, and confirmation of the Torah already revealed – a guide and lesson for those who take heed of God. ❞ (Qur'an 5:46)

Scrolls of Abraham (Sahifah/Suhuf)

Revealed to Ibrahim (Abraham).

The **Scrolls of Abraham (Sahifah/Suhuf)** are known as the first holy book in Islam revealed to Ibrahim (and Moses).

Muslims believe that the full Scrolls have been lost and therefore we cannot be sure of what they contained, although they are referenced in the Qur'an.

❝ Has he not been told what was written in the Scriptures of Moses and of Abraham, who fulfilled his duty: that no soul shall bear the burden of another; that man will only have what he has worked towards; that his labour will be seen and that in the end he will be repaid in full for it; that the final goal is your Lord. ❞ (Qur'an 53:36–42)

Key terms — Make sure you can write a definition for these key terms

Prophets   revelations   Ibrahim   Torah (Tawrat)
Psalms (Zabur)   Gospels (Injil)   Scrolls of Abraham (Sahifah/Suhuf)

Learn the answers to the questions below, then cover the answers column with a piece of paper and write as many as you can. Check and repeat.

Questions | Answers

	Questions		Answers
1	Who was the first prophet in Islam?		Adam
2	Which prophet is associated with most of the actions performed on Hajj?		Ibrahim
3	Which prophet received the Qur'an?		Muhammad
4	Which prophet received the Torah?		Moses
5	Which holy book did David receive?		The Psalms (Zabur)
6	Which holy book did Jesus receive?		The Gospels (Injil)
7	Which holy book is lost and the contents unknown?		The Scrolls of Abraham (Sahifah/Suhuf)
8	Which holy book has prayers, and poems used for the worship of God?		The Psalms (Zabur)
9	Which holy book is the only surviving book that is a complete revelation in its original language that has not been changed?		The Qur'an
10	Which holy book includes the Ten Commandments?		The Torah (Tawrat)

Put paper here

Previous questions

Now go back and use these questions to check your knowledge of previous topics.

Questions | Answers

	Questions		Answers
11	Which Arabic word means God is just and will ensure that humans will get what they deserve when he judges them?		Adalat
12	What do Muslims believe will happen if a person's good deeds outweigh their bad deeds?		God will reward them and send them to heaven
13	Which word means God is within and involved in his creation – he knows and has a relationship with humans?		Immanence
14	Which word means God exists beyond his creation and is beyond human understanding?		Transcendence
15	Where are souls taken to wait until the Day of Judgement?		Barzakh

Put paper here

Practice

Exam-style questions

01   Which **one** of these is the holy book associated with Jesus?

Put a tick (✓) in the box next to the correct answer.   **(1 mark)**

   A   Psalms   ☐

   B   Gospel   ☐

   C   Torah   ☐

   D   Bible   ☐

02   Which **one** of these is the holy book associated with Moses?

Put a tick (✓) in the box next to the correct answer.   **(1 mark)**

   A   Psalms   ☐

   B   Gospel   ☐

   C   Torah   ☐

   D   Bible   ☐

03   Name **two** holy books in Islam.   **(2 marks)**

EXAM TIP

Don't write more than two answers for a 2-mark question. The examiner can only mark the first two that you write.

04   Name **two** prophets in Islam.   **(2 marks)**

05   Explain **two** ways that the Qur'an may influence Muslims today.   **(4 marks)**

06   Explain **two** beliefs about Adam in Islam.

Refer to sacred writings or another source of Muslim belief and teaching in your answer.   **(5 marks)**

EXAM TIP

Remember – you must name a sacred writing or source of authority that is in your answer, for example the Bible, the Qur'an.

07   'The only source of authority a Muslim needs is the Qur'an.'

Evaluate this statement.

In your answer you should:

   • refer to Muslim teaching

   • give reasoned arguments to support this statement

   • give reasoned arguments to support a different point of view

   • reach a justified conclusion.   **(12 marks)**

          (+ SPaG 3 marks)

14 ☾ Beliefs and teachings: The Imamate in Shi'a Islam

The Imamate in Shi'a Islam

- When Muhammad died it wasn't clear who should succeed him and so Muslims split into two groups: Sunni and Shi'a.

- Sunni Muslims believe that Abu Bakr was elected as their first leader (Caliph).

- Shi'a Muslims believe that Muhammad named his cousin and son-in-law Ali as his successor. So Ali was the first Imam for Shi'a Muslims.

- For Shi'a Muslims, it was important that Ali took control because they believed:

  - the prophet had appointed him by divine instruction

  - the leadership should follow Muhammad's family line 'Ahl-ul-Bayt'.

- When Ali died, his son became the Imam. Each Imam that followed was the son of the previous Imam (with the exception of Husayn ibn Ali, who was the brother of Hasan).

- The Imamate is the name given to the divine appointment of the Imams.

- Shi'a Muslims believe the Imams are necessary to give people divine guidance on how to live correctly. Although the final version of God's law was received by Muhammad, the Imams help to preserve and explain this law.

> **REVISION TIP** ☑
>
> Make sure you do not confuse the imamate with imams, who are religious leaders in a mosque.

The Twelver branch of Shi'a Islam

- The Twelver branch of Shi'a Islam teaches there have been twelve Imams in total.

- They believe that in each generation there has always been an Imam who is divinely appointed and part of the Ahl al-Bayt (family of Muhammad).

- They believe that the twelfth Imam has been kept alive by God, hidden on Earth and will return in future.

- All the divinely appointed Imams were poisoned or assassinated, except two:

  - Imam Husayn (3rd) was martyred at the Battle of Karbala, which is commemorated at Ashura.

  - Imam Mahdi (12th) is the final Imam. He didn't die but is hidden from human sight (he is in **occultation**) and will return at the end of the world to join with Isa (Jesus) to bring peace and justice on Earth.

The role of the Imamate for Shi'a Muslims

Shi'a Muslims believe that the **Qur'an** is referencing the Imams as leaders when it says:

> ❝ *I am putting a successor on Earth* ❞
> (Qur'an 2:30)

> ❝ *... obey God and the Messenger, and those in authority among you.* ❞
> (Qur'an 4:59)

⚙ Knowledge

14 ☾ Beliefs and teachings: The Imamate in Shi'a Islam

The significance of the Imamate

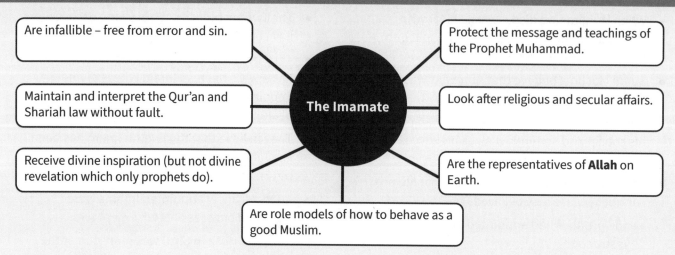

Are infallible – free from error and sin.

Maintain and interpret the Qur'an and Shariah law without fault.

Receive divine inspiration (but not divine revelation which only prophets do).

The Imamate

Protect the message and teachings of the Prophet Muhammad.

Look after religious and secular affairs.

Are the representatives of **Allah** on Earth.

Are role models of how to behave as a good Muslim.

Shi'a Muslims

- Muhammad said:

> ❝ I am leaving among you two weighty things: The first of which is the Book of Allah. In it is guidance and light, so hold fast to the Book of Allah and adhere to it. … And the members of my household, I remind you of Allah with regards (of your duties) to the members of my family. ❞
>
> (Hadith)

Shi'a Muslims believe that Muhammad was telling his followers that his Ahl-ul-Bayt should be followed and are important for the continuation of Islam.

- Belief in the Imamate is one of the five roots of Usul ad-Din.

Sunni Muslims

- Do not believe that the Imamate are divinely appointed leaders.
- Say that the Qur'an, **Hadith**, and **Sunnah** are all that is needed to be a good Muslim.
- Believe that Ali was important as the fourth Rightly Guided Caliph, not the first.

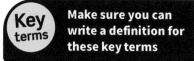

Key terms Make sure you can write a definition for these key terms

occultation   Qur'an   Allah   Hadith   Sunnah

Retrieval

Learn the answers to the questions below, then cover the answers column with a piece of paper and write as many as you can. Check and repeat.

Questions | Answers

#	Question	Answer
1	Which branch of Shi'a Islam teaches there have been twelve Imams in total?	The Twelvers
2	What is the difference between the Imamate and imams?	The Imamate is the divinely appointed 12 Imams, imams are religious leaders in a mosque
3	Who was the first Imam?	Imam Ali
4	Why is Imam Mahdi different from the other Imams?	He didn't die but is hidden from human sight (in occultation) and will return at the end of the world to join with Isa (Jesus) to bring peace and justice on Earth
5	What is the Arabic term for Muhammad's family line?	Ahl-ul-Bayt
6	What does it mean to say the Imams are infallible?	They are free from error and sin
7	Is divine inspiration the same as divine revelation, and why?	No – only prophets receive divine revelation.
8	How do Shi'a Muslims believe that the Imams were chosen?	They were divinely appointed (by God)
9	What do Sunni Muslims believe are all a Muslim needs to lead a good life?	Qur'an, Hadith, and Sunnah

Put paper here

Previous questions

Now go back and use these questions to check your knowledge of previous topics.

Questions | Answers

#	Question	Answer
10	What does the Qur'an describe as *"Gardens graced with flowing streams"*?	Heaven
11	Which holy book did Jesus receive?	The Gospels (Injil)
12	Which holy book is lost and the contents unknown?	The Scrolls of Abraham (Sahifah/Suhuf)
13	Who was the first prophet in Islam?	Adam
14	Which prophet is associated with most of the actions performed on Hajj?	Ibrahim
15	Which prophet received the Torah?	Moses

Put paper here

Exam-style questions

01 Which **one** of these is the first Imam in the Imamate for Shi'a Muslims?

Put a tick (✓) in the box next to the correct answer. **(1 mark)**

A	Muhammad	☐
B	Isa (Jesus)	☐
C	Ali	☐
D	Husayn	☐

02 Which **one** of these is the Imam that was martyred at the Battle of Karbala?

Put a tick (✓) in the box next to the correct answer. **(1 mark)**

A	Ali	☐
B	Hasan	☐
C	Husayn	☐
D	Mahdi	☐

> **EXAM TIP**
>
> Don't spend a long time on 1-mark questions – but do read the question and answer options carefully. You could make a silly mistake if you don't and miss an easy mark.

03 Give **two** Muslim beliefs about the Imamate. **(2 marks)**

04 Give **two** reasons why the Imamate is important to Shi'a Muslims. **(2 marks)**

05 Explain **two** ways that the Imamate may influence Shi'a Muslims today. **(4 marks)**

06 Explain **two** contrasting Muslim beliefs about the Imamate.

Refer to sacred writings or another source of Muslim belief and teaching in your answer. **(5 marks)**

> **EXAM TIP**
>
> In a 12-mark question you don't have to write arguments 'against' the statement. You must present a different view that doesn't have to be the opposite of the statement.

07 'The twelve Imams are important people in Islam.'

Evaluate this statement.

In your answer you should:

- refer to Muslim teaching
- give reasoned arguments to support this statement
- give reasoned arguments to support a different point of view
- reach a justified conclusion. **(12 marks)**

(+ SPaG 3 marks)

15 ☾ Practices: The five pillars of Sunni Islam, the ten obligatory acts of Shi'a Islam, and the Shahadah

- The five pillars of Sunni Islam, and the ten obligatory acts of Shi'a Islam, are key practices for Sunni and Shi'a Muslims.
- They are actions and rituals that a Muslim should perform, without which their faith (Arabic 'iman') could be weakened.

The five pillars of Sunni Islam

All five pillars are mentioned in the prophet Muhammad's final sermon:

> ❝ O People! listen to me in earnest, worship Allah, say your five daily prayers, fast during the month of Ramadan, and give your wealth in Zakat. Perform Hajj if you can afford it. ❞ (Hadith)

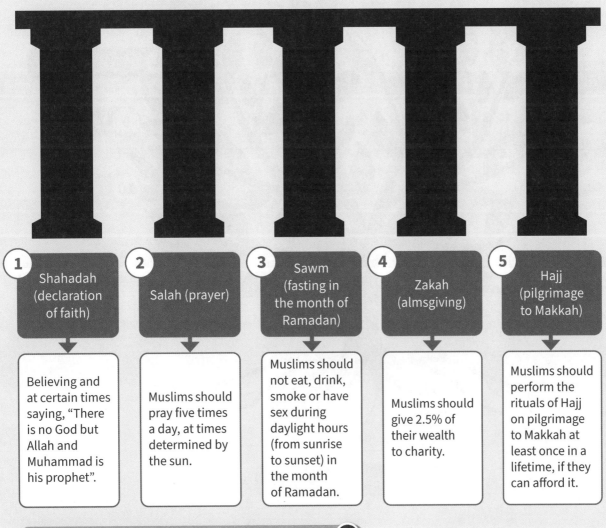

1 Shahadah (declaration of faith)

Believing and at certain times saying, "There is no God but Allah and Muhammad is his prophet".

2 Salah (prayer)

Muslims should pray five times a day, at times determined by the sun.

3 Sawm (fasting in the month of Ramadan)

Muslims should not eat, drink, smoke or have sex during daylight hours (from sunrise to sunset) in the month of Ramadan.

4 Zakah (almsgiving)

Muslims should give 2.5% of their wealth to charity.

5 Hajj (pilgrimage to Makkah)

Muslims should perform the rituals of Hajj on pilgrimage to Makkah at least once in a lifetime, if they can afford it.

REVISION TIP

Remember, whilst the pillars include physical requirements they are also spiritual. To help you remember, for each pillar write down the physical requirements and then the spiritual gains.

15 ☪ Practices: The five pillars of Sunni Islam, the ten obligatory acts of Shi'a Islam, and the Shahadah

The ten obligatory acts of Shi'a Islam

For Shi'a Islam the ten obligatory acts can be represented as a metaphor of a tree with the practices being the branches that are supported by the five roots (beliefs).

REVISION TIP

You could use opposites to remember some of the Ten Obligatory Acts, For example: doing what is right and prohibiting what is bad; following the Prophet and his family and staying away from the enemies of the Prophet and his family.

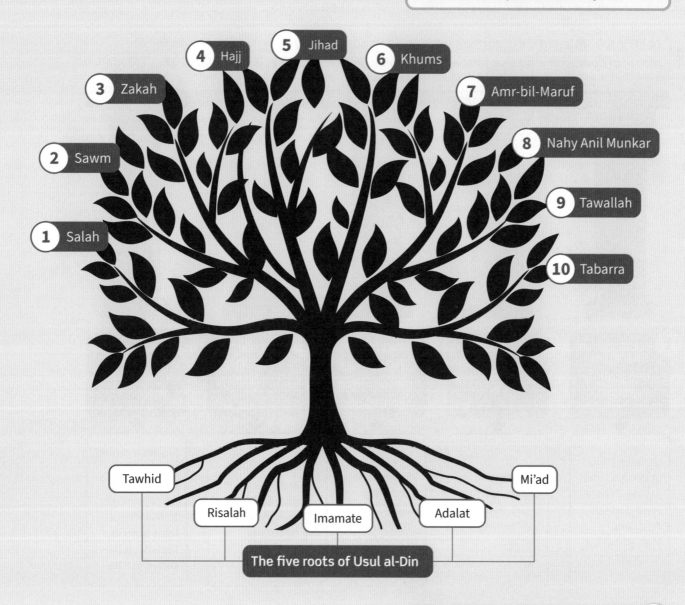

4 Hajj
5 Jihad
6 Khums
3 Zakah
7 Amr-bil-Maruf
8 Nahy Anil Munkar
2 Sawm
9 Tawallah
1 Salah
10 Tabarra

Tawhid
Mi'ad
Risalah
Imamate
Adalat

The five roots of Usul al-Din

REVISION TIP

You don't need to know the Arabic names for all of these, but you will need to remember Salah, Sawm, Zakah, Hajj, Jihad and Khums.

...

1 Salah (prayer) → Saying five prayers a day at times determined by the sun.

These four obligatory acts are mentioned in the prophet Muhammad's final sermon:

2 Sawm (fasting during Ramadan) → Not eat, drink, smoke or have sex during daylight hours in the month of Ramadan.

3 Zakah (almsgiving) → Giving 2.5% of their wealth to charity.

> ❝ O People! listen to me in earnest, worship Allah, say your five daily prayers, fast during the month of Ramadan, and give your wealth in Zakat. Perform Hajj if you can afford it. ❞ (Hadith)

4 Hajj (pilgrimage to Makkah) → Perform Hajj at least once in a lifetime, if they can afford it.

5 Jihad (the 'struggle' for Islam/God) →
- Lesser Jihad – the struggle to defend Islam including physical defence if needed.
- Greater Jihad – the personal struggle to be a good Muslim on a daily basis.

> ❝ Fight in God's cause against those who fight you, but do not overstep the limits: God does not love those who overstep the limits. ❞ (Qur'an 2:190)

6 Khums (almsgiving/tax) → Giving 20% (a fifth) of surplus, income, or profits on:
- war gains
- minerals
- treasure (e.g., gold, silver, jewellery)
- precious items
- land
- business profit.

This purifies the rest of their money.

> ❝ Know that one-fifth of your battle gains belongs to God and the Messenger, to close relatives and orphans, to the needy and travellers. ❞ (Qur'an 8:41)

7 Amr-bil-Maruf (doing what is right) → Following the straight path by doing what is halal (allowed).

8 Nahy Anil Munkar (prohibiting what is bad) → Staying close to Allah, Muhammad, and his family line (Ahl-Bayt) (including the Imams) and those that believe in them.

> ❝ Be a community that calls for what is good, urges what is right, and forbids what is wrong: those who do this are the successful ones. ❞ (Qur'an 3:104)

9 Tawallah (following the Prophet Muhammad and his family) → Avoiding that which is haram (not allowed) and avoiding sin.

> ❝ You who believe, obey God and the Messenger, and those in authority among you. If you are in dispute over any matter, refer it to God and the Messenger, if you truly believe in God and the Last Day: that is better and fairer in the end. ❞ (Qur'an 4:59)

10 Tabarra (dissociating from the enemies of the Prophet Muhammad and his family) → Staying away from those that are against God/the prophet and his family.

> ❝ Do not rely on those who do evil, or the Fire may touch you, and then you will have no one to protect you from God, nor will you be helped. ❞ (Qur'an 11:113)

 # Knowledge

15 ☪ Practices: The five pillars of Sunni Islam, the ten obligatory acts of Shi'a Islam, and the Shahadah

Declaration of faith and its place in Muslim practice

The **Shahadah** is a declaration of faith stating what Muslims believe in. It literally means 'to witness' and is used at certain times in life to show core Muslim beliefs.

Whilst the Qur'an does not state the Shahadah in its full form, it comes from two verses:

> **❝** *... There is no deity but God...* **❞**   (Qur'an 37:35)

> **❝** *Muhammad is the Messenger of God...* **❞**   (Qur'an 48:29)

 REVISION TIP

To remember when the Shahadah is said, think about the 'start' and 'end' of everything: start of the day and end of the day; start of life and end of life; start of prayer; start of becoming a Muslim.

⬇

The Shahadah is said at key moments in a Muslim's life

It is said three times in front of witnesses when someone becomes a Muslim.	It is also said when a Muslim wakes up...	...and when they go to bed.	It is whispered into the ear of a newborn baby as the first words it hears.
It is the last thing a person says before they die...	...and it is said when they are buried.	It is part of the call to prayer (adhan)...	...and it is part of the recitations for prayer.

⬇

The Shahadah in Sunni and Shi'a Islam

The Shahadah is slightly different for Sunni and Shi'a Muslims.

Sunni	Shi'a
There is no God but Allah and Muhammad is his prophet.	There is no God but Allah, Muhammad is his prophet, and Ali is the representative of God.

 Key terms **Make sure you can write a definition for these key terms**

Salah   Sawm   Zakah   Hajj
Jihad   Khums   Shahadah

Learn the answers to the questions below, then cover the answers column with a piece of paper and write as many as you can. Check and repeat.

#	Questions	Answers
1	What are the words of the Shahadah for Shi'a Muslims?	There is no God but Allah, Muhammad is his prophet and Ali is the representative of God
2	What is salah?	Prayer
3	How many prayers should a Muslim say a day?	Five
4	What is sawm?	Fasting (In the month of Ramadan)
5	What is zakah?	Almsgiving – giving 2.5% of wealth
6	What is Hajj?	Pilgrimage to Makkah
7	What is the 'struggle' to defend God and be a good Muslim?	Jihad
8	What is the 20% tax that Shi'a Muslims pay?	Khums
9	What are the two types of Jihad?	Lesser and Greater Jihad
10	How many times should a Muslim perform Hajj?	Once in a lifetime (if they can afford to)
11	What percentage is zakah?	2.5%
12	In which source of authority are all the five pillars mentioned together?	Muhammad's final sermon
13	What should Muslims not do during daylight hours in the month of Ramadan?	Eat, drink, smoke, have sex
14	What are the first words that are whispered into the ear of a newborn Muslim baby?	The Shahadah
15	How many times is the Shahadah recited in front of witnesses when someone becomes a Muslim?	Three times

Put paper here

Practice

Exam-style questions

01 Which **one** of these is the Shi'a practice of giving 20% (a fifth) of surplus, income or profits?

Put a tick (✓) in the box next to the correct answer. **(1 mark)**

A	Zakah	☐
B	Khums	☐
C	Jihad	☐
D	Salah	☐

> **EXAM TIP**
>
> Read all the options carefully. There may be answers that may distract you from the correct answer!

02 Which **one** of these is the place that Muslims perform Hajj?

Put a tick (✓) in the box next to the correct answer. **(1 mark)**

A	Jerusalem	☐
B	Medinah	☐
C	Makkah	☐
D	Jannah	☐

03 Name **two** of the five pillars of Sunni Islam. **(2 marks)**

04 Name **two** of the ten obligatory acts for Shi'a Muslims. **(2 marks)**

05 Give **two** similarities between the five pillars of Sunni Islam and the ten obligatory acts for Shi'a Muslims. **(2 marks)**

06 Explain **two** contrasting ways the Shahadah is used in Islam. **(4 marks)**

07 Explain **two** reasons why the ten obligatory acts are important for Shi'a Muslims.

Refer to sacred writings or another source of Muslim belief and teaching in your answer. **(5 marks)**

> **EXAM TIP**
>
> Remember, you must name the sacred writings or source in your answer to get the fifth mark, for example the Qur'an, Hadith. (Remember too that you don't need to state the chapter or verse.)

08 'Jihad is the most important of the ten obligatory acts for Shi'a Muslims.'

Evaluate this statement.

In your answer you should:

- refer to Muslim teaching
- give reasoned arguments to support this statement
- give reasoned arguments to support a different point of view
- reach a justified conclusion. **(12 marks)**

(+ SPaG 3 marks)

16 ☪ Practices: Salah and its significance

Why Muslims pray

- Salah brings Muslims closer to God.
- Muhammad told Muslims to pray five times a day.
- It is one of the five pillars of Sunni Islam and the ten obligatory acts of Shi'a Islam.
- God rewards those that fulfil their daily prayers.
- It unites the Muslim community (Ummah) when they pray together at the mosque.

- The prostration reminds them of God's greatness and their submission to the will of God.
- The Qur'an says *"bow down in worship and draw close"* (Qur'an 96:19).
- Muhammad said it helps Muslims to get to heaven: *"The key to Paradise is Salah, and the key to Salah is Wudu."* (Hadith).

How Muslims pray

Ablution (wudu)

Before they pray Muslims should find a clean place and perform **ablutions (wudu)**.	This prepares them physically and spiritually for prayer, ready to talk to God and to refocus during a busy day.

Each part of the body is cleaned three times, including the face, hands, arms, head, and feet.

❝ *You who believe, when you are about to pray, wash your faces and your hands up to the elbows, wipe your heads, wash your feet up to the ankles and, if required, wash your whole body.* ❞
(Qur'an 5:6)

Direction and prayer times

- Muslims pray facing the direction of the Ka'aba in **Makkah**, using the mihrab in a mosque (an alcove facing Makkah), a traditional compass or a mobile phone app to work out the direction.
- Sunni Muslims pray at five set times during the day.
- Shi'a Muslims can combine the midday and afternoon prayers, and the sunset and night prayers, so they may pray three times a day.

Arabic prayer time	Time	Sunni rak'ahs	Shi'a rak'ahs
Fajr	Just before sunrise	2	2
Zuhr	Just after midday	4	8
Asr	Afternoon	4	
Maghrib	Just after sunset	3	7
Isha	Night	4	

Prayer movements (rak'ahs)

The set way of performing salah involves prostration and movements called **rak'ah**. In one day Muslims perform a total of 17 rak'ahs.

Recitations

As Muslims perform the rak'ahs, they say **recitations** which include: the first surah (chapter) of the Qur'an; the Shahadah; Allahu Akbar (God is Great).

16 ☪ Practices: Salah and its significance

Jummah prayer – Friday prayer

- Muslim men are expected to go to the mosque to pray for midday prayers on Friday. It is optional for women as they may not be able to leave the house and/or children.

Muhammad said:

> 66 *The best of days on which the sun has risen is Friday. On this day Adam was created, and on this day he was descended to earth.* 99 (Hadith)

- **Jummah** is a communal prayer, promoting the idea of Muslim community (Ummah).

> 66 *The reward of the congregational prayer is twenty-seven times greater (than that of the prayer offered by a person alone).* 99 (Hadith)

Salah in the home, mosque, and elsewhere

	• The whole of the Earth is God's creation so Muslims can perform salah anywhere. • They just need to find a clean place (often using a prayer mat) and also perform wudu.
	• The mosque is important for Jummah prayer and when it is important to pray as a congregation, for example Id prayers. • Men and women usually pray separately.
	• Many Muslim women pray at home to fit in with their other responsibilities. • Families pray together at home to strengthen their relationships with each other and with God. Muslims can pray alone or together. • Muhammad encouraged praying at home: > 66 *Offer some of your prayers in your homes so as not to make these homes like graves.* 99 (Hadith)

Differences between Shi'a and Sunni salah

Shi'a	Sunni
• Use a turbah (piece of clay/natural product) to ensure they are praying on pure earth. • Put their arms by their sides. • Say the five prayers at three times. • Do not use 'Ameen' at the end of prayer.	• Touch the ground as they believe this is what Muhammad did. • Some cross their arms in front of them. • Say the five prayers at five times. • Say 'Ameen' at the end of the prayer.

REVISION TIP

Knowing differences is important for 4-mark questions that ask you about 'contrast' and can also be used for 'different views' in 12-mark questions.

 Key terms — Make sure you can write a definition for these key terms

ablutions (wudu)   Makkah   rak'ah   recitations   Jummah

Retrieval

Learn the answers to the questions below, then cover the answers column with a piece of paper and write as many as you can. Check and repeat.

	Questions	Answers
1	On which day of the week is Jummah prayer?	Friday
2	How many times the rewards does a Muslim receive for completing congregational prayer?	27
3	In which direction do Muslims pray?	Towards the Ka'aba in Makkah (Saudi Arabia)
4	What is the mihrab?	The alcove in the mosque showing the direction to Makkah
5	What is wudu?	Ablution – ritual washing before prayer
6	How many times do Sunni Muslims pray each day?	Five
7	What did Muhammad say about prayer and how it helps Muslims? Add a quotation to support your answer.	Muhammad said that prayer helps Muslims to get to heaven: *"The key to Paradise is Salah, and the key to Salah is Wudu."* (Hadith)
8	How many rak'ahs should Muslims perform a day?	17
9	What do Shi'a Muslims use to ensure they pray on the earth?	A turbah – piece of clay or natural product
10	True or false: Some Sunni Muslims cross their arms during prayer.	True
11	What is the difference between Sunni and Shi'a Muslim prayer times?	Sunni Muslims say the five prayers at five times, Shi'a can say the five prayers at three times

Put paper here

Put paper here

Put paper here

Put paper here

Previous questions

Now go back and use these questions to check your knowledge of previous topics.

	Questions	Answers
12	What are the words of the Shahadah for Shi'a Muslims?	There is no God but Allah, Muhammad is his prophet and Ali is the representative of God
13	What is salah?	Prayer
14	In which source of authority are all the five pillars of Sunni Islam mentioned together?	Muhammad's final sermon
15	What is sawm?	Fasting (in the month of Ramadan)

Put paper here

Practice

Exam-style questions

01 Which **one** of these is the name for one complete movement of prayer in Islam?

Put a tick (✓) in the box next to the correct answer. **(1 mark)**

A   Wudu ☐

B   Rakah ☐

C   Jummah ☐

D   Salah ☐

02 Which of these is the name for ablutions before prayer in Islam?

Put a tick (✓) in the box next to the correct answer. **(1 mark)**

A   Wudu ☐

B   Rakah ☐

C   Jummah ☐

D   Salah ☐

03 Name **two** differences in prayer between Sunni and Shi'a Muslims. **(2 marks)**

> **EXAM TIP**
>
> Don't waste time writing more than two answers as the examiner will only mark your first two answers on the 2-mark questions.

04 Give **two** reasons why prayer is important in Islam. **(2 marks)**

05 Explain **two** contrasting ways that prayer is performed in Islam. **(4 marks)**

06 Explain **two** beliefs about wudu (ablution) in Islam.

Refer to sacred writings or another source of Muslim belief and teaching in your answer. **(5 marks)**

> **EXAM TIP**
>
> Remember you must name a sacred writing or source of authority in your answer, for example, the Qur'an.

07 'It doesn't matter where a Muslim prays.'

Evaluate this statement.

In your answer you should:

- refer to Muslim teaching
- give reasoned arguments to support this statement
- give reasoned arguments to support a different point of view
- reach a justified conclusion. **(12 marks)**

(+ SPaG 3 marks)

17 ☪ Practices: Sawm and Zakah

Sawm (fasting during the month of Ramadan)

The role and significance of sawm

- Sawm is one of the five pillars of Sunni Islam and the ten obligatory acts of Shi'a Islam.
- Ramadan is the ninth month in the Muslim calendar but it is a different date in the Gregorian calendar each year.
- Both the Qur'an and Hadith make it clear that Muslims should fast:

> 66 *You who believe, fasting is prescribed for you, as it was prescribed for those before you, so that you may be mindful of God.* 99   (Qur'an 2:183)

> 66 *Fast in the month of Ramadan.* 99   (Hadith)

Origins of sawm

- Ramadan is the month in which Muhammad first started to receive the revelations of the Qur'an from God, via Jibril.
- During this month, some Muslims will read the Qur'an from start to finish to remind them of the importance of God's message.
- It helps them to focus on God whilst facing the possible challenges of fasting.

> 66 *It was in the month of Ramadan that the Quran was revealed as guidance for mankind, clear messages giving guidance and distinguishing between right and wrong.* 99   (Qur'an 2:185)

Duties during Ramadan
During daylight hours, Muslims should not: • eat • drink • smoke • have sex. When the fast is broken at night (iftar), Muslims often eat together, and start by eating something small such as dates, to line the stomach, ready for the main meal.

Benefits of fasting

- Muslims believe that they are rewarded by God for fasting.
- It reminds them to be thankful to God for the food that they are able to eat.
- It gives them a greater awareness of those who may not have enough food to eat.
- They may invite others to break their fast with them to share food or be especially generous in giving to charity during Ramadan.
- Many Muslims pray, read the Qur'an, and visit the mosque more during Ramadan so it is a particularly spiritual time of the year to focus on their faith and strive to be a better Muslim.

17 ☾ Practices: Sawm and Zakah

Exemptions from fasting

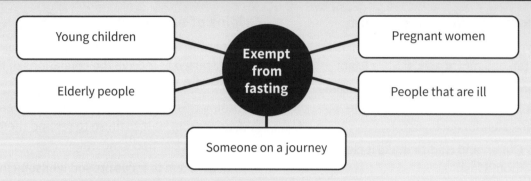

- Fasting is supposed to benefit a Muslim spiritually and not cause any physical issues.
- Some children do a trial fast for shorter periods to get used to not eating and drinking during the day.
- If someone needs to miss a day of fasting for a legitimate reason, they can pay a day's worth of food money to charity and complete that day at a later date (it is forbidden to fast on **Id-ul-Fitr**).

> **❝** *Fast for a specific number of days, but if one of you is ill, or on a journey, on other days later. For those who can fast only with extreme difficulty, there is a way to compensate – feed a needy person.* **❞**
> (Qur'an 2:184)

The Night of Power, Qur'an 96:1-5

The **Night of Power** (Laylat al-Qadr) was the first time that Jibril appeared to Muhammad in a cave to start to reveal the Qur'an. It is described in the Qur'an:

> **❝** *Read! In the name of your Lord who created: He created man from a clinging form. Read! Your Lord is the Most Bountiful One who taught by [means of] the pen, who taught man what he did not know.* **❞**
> (Qur'an 96:1–5)

This event is remembered during the month of Ramadan. This is an especially holy time:

> **❝** *What will explain to you what that Night of Glory is? The Night of Glory is better than a thousand months.* **❞**
> (Qur'an 97:2–3)

During this time Muslims may offer extra prayers (asking God for forgiveness), read and study the Qur'an and pray at the mosque.

> **REVISION TIP** ☑
>
> To remember the name of the Night of Power, think about it being a 'powerful' experience for Muhammad.

Zakah: almsgiving

- Zakah is one of the five pillars of Sunni Islam and the ten obligatory acts of Shi'a Islam.
- It is 2.5% of a Muslim's savings over a certain amount, given as alms each year to help others.
- The Arabic word zakah means 'that which purifies' and it is believed that paying it purifies the rest of a Muslim's money as blessed by God.

How and why zakah is given

- The Qur'an tells Muslims to *"pay the prescribed alms"* (Qur'an 2:83) and Muhammad said in his final sermon to *"pay your wealth in zakah"* (Hadith).
- The percentage amount of zakah is not mentioned in the Qur'an but it is believed that Muslim scholars worked it out at a later date.

REVISION TIP

Remember that you may also be able to use your knowledge of Zakah in one of your Themes, for example, 'wealth and poverty' in Theme F.

The Qur'an lists who should receive zakah:

> *Alms are meant only for the poor, the needy, those who administer them, those whose hearts need winning over, to free slaves and help those in debt, for God's cause, and for travellers in need.* (Qur'an 9:60)

How to pay zakah	Why pay zakah?
• Some Muslims pay zakah monthly, and others pay annually. • Some Muslims give it directly to the mosque for distribution to those that need it, others give to a charity such as Muslim Aid or Islamic relief.	• Muhammad said to pay it in his Hadith. • The Qur'an says to pay alms. • It purifies the rest of a Muslim's money. • It creates equality in society to help reduce poverty for those that receive the money. • It is a reminder that wealth has been given by God, and not to be greedy or selfish.

Khums in Shi'a Islam

Some Shi'a Muslims don't end up paying zakah because they believe that it only applies to gold and silver coins, cattle, and crops. So amongst Shi'a Muslims it may only be paid by farmers and those with gold/silver.

Shi'a Muslims follow the Qur'anic instruction to give a fifth (20%) of their surplus income or profits to those in need, known as khums.

> *Know that one-fifth of your surplus belongs to God and the Messenger, to close relatives and orphans, to the needy and travellers.* (Qur'an 8:41)

Khums is paid from:

war gains	minerals	treasure (e.g., gold, silver, jewellery)	precious items	land	business profit

Khums is usually paid to a Shi'a religious authority or to a charitable cause. Paying khums purifies the rest of a Shi'a Muslim's money.

Sunni Muslims generally don't pay khums because they believe that when the Qur'an says *"Know that one-fifth of your surplus belongs to God."* *(Qur'an 8:41)*, it only applies to war gains.

 Key terms Make sure you can write a definition for these key terms

Id-ul-Fitr   Night of Power

Retrieval

Learn the answers to the questions below, then cover the answers column with a piece of paper and write as many as you can. Check and repeat.

Questions | Answers

	Questions	Answers
1	What should Muslims not do during daylight hours in the month of Ramadan?	Eat, drink, smoke, have sex
2	What is the name of the evening meal that breaks the fast?	Iftar
3	What percentage is khums?	20%
4	What percentage is zakah?	2.5%
5	What does the word 'zakah' mean?	That which purifies
6	What do Sunni Muslims believe that khums should be paid on?	War gains
7	What is sawm?	Fasting in the month of Ramadan
8	Name the five groups of people who are exempt from fasting.	• Young children • Pregnant women • Elderly people • People that are ill • Someone on a journey
9	Which important event in the life of Muhammad is remembered during the month of Ramadan?	The Night of Power
10	Which event is described in Qur'an 96:1–5?	The Night of Power

Put paper here (between columns)

Previous questions

Now go back and use these questions to check your knowledge of previous topics.

Questions | Answers

	Questions	Answers
11	What is wudu?	Ablution – ritual washing before prayer
12	How many times do Sunni Muslims pray each day?	Five
13	What did Muhammad say about prayer and how it helps Muslims? Add a quotation to support your answer.	Muhammad said that prayer helps Muslims to get to heaven: *"The key to Paradise is Salah, and the key to Salah is Wudu."* (Hadith)
14	On which day of the week is Jummah prayer?	Friday
15	In which direction do Muslims pray?	Towards the Ka'aba in Makkah (Saudi Arabia)

Put paper here (between columns)

Exam-style questions

01 Which **one** of these is the name of the event when Muhammad first received the revelation of the Qur'an?

Put a tick (✓) in the box next to the correct answer. **(1 mark)**

A Ramadan ☐

B The First Night ☐

C The Night Journey ☐

D The Night of Power ☐

02 Which of these is **not** something that Shi'a believe that zakah is paid on?

Put a tick (✓) in the box next to the correct answer. **(1 mark)**

A Property ☐

B Crops ☐

C Cattle ☐

D Gold and silver coins ☐

03 Name **two** people that do not have to fast during Ramadan. **(2 marks)**

04 Give **two** reasons why paying zakah is important to Muslims. **(2 marks)**

05 Explain **two** contrasting ways a Muslim may celebrate the Night of Power during Ramadan. **(4 marks)**

> **EXAM TIP**
> 'Contrasting' means 'different' in questions like this.

06 Explain **two** types of almsgiving in Islam.

Refer to sacred writings or another source of Muslim belief and teaching in your answer. **(5 marks)**

07 'All Muslims should fast in the month of Ramadan.'

Evaluate this statement.

In your answer you should:

- refer to Muslim teaching
- give reasoned arguments to support this statement
- give reasoned arguments to support a different point of view
- reach a justified conclusion. **(12 marks)**

(+ SPaG 3 marks)

> **EXAM TIP**
> To ensure that you include everything needed in a 12-mark question, make sure you use the bullet points to help.

18 ☾ Practices: Hajj and Jihad

Hajj: the pilgrimage to Makkah

- Hajj is the pilgrimage to Makkah in Saudi Arabia during the month of the Islamic calendar, Dhul Hijjah (twelfth month).
- It is one of the five pillars of Sunni Islam and the ten obligatory acts of Shi'a Islam.
- It requires Muslims to complete set rituals during the pilgrimage.
- Umrah or lesser pilgrimage is also a pilgrimage to Makkah, but at other times and with different rituals. It doesn't count as Hajj.

> **REVISION TIP**
>
> Try to watch a documentary about Hajj. Seeing pilgrims take part will help you to understand and remember the rituals performed.

Origins of Hajj

Many of the actions performed on Hajj link to the life of Ibrahim or they are sunnah of Muhammad.

Place	Action	Significance
Ka'aba at Makkah	• Muslims walk around the **Ka'aba** seven times in an anti-clockwise direction (tawaf). They complete tawaf at the start and the end of Hajj. • They may try to touch/kiss the black stone which is on one corner.	• Some Muslims believe that Ibrahim (re)built the Ka'aba with his son Ishmael. • Muhammad performed tawaf so it is a sunnah. • The black stone is said to have originally been white and used in the original Ka'aba but has darkened as humanity has sinned. Muhammad is said to have kissed it.
Muzdalifah	• Collecting stones to throw at the large stone pillars (Jamarat) at Mina.	• This reminds Muslims of when Ibrahim threw stones at the devil that tried to tempt him not to complete the sacrifice of Ishmael. • Today, throwing the stones at the Jamarat represents getting rid of temptation and rejecting evil.
Mina	• Throwing small stones at the Jamarat.	
Arafat	• Muslims stand before God and pray to God asking for forgiveness for themselves and all of humanity.	• This reminds Muslims of the Day of Judgement where they will stand before God and answer for their deeds. • Muhammad gave his last sermon on Mount Arafat.

The significance of Hajj

Muhammad said to *"Perform Hajj if you can afford it."* (Hadith) and the Qur'an says Muslims should *"Complete the pilgrimages, major and minor, for the sake of God."* (Qur'an 2:196).

Brings them closer to God.		One of the five pillars of Sunni Islam and the ten obligatory acts of Shi'a Islam.
Shows self-discipline and strength in belief (requires both physical and spiritual strength).	**Why Hajj is important to Muslims**	Reminds them of Ibrahim's importance as a prophet.
Means sins are forgiven and gives a fresh start to life as a Muslim.		Promotes the importance of the Ummah (Muslim community), and the equality and unity within it.

Jihad

- Jihad means 'struggle'.
- It is one of the ten obligatory acts of Shi'a Islam and a key belief for Sunni Muslims.
- It is the struggle against evil as a Muslim and as the Ummah (Muslim community).

The Qur'an says:

> **"** *This is My path, leading straight, so follow it, and do not follow other ways: they will lead you away from it – 'This is what He commands you to do, so that you may refrain from wrongdoing.'* **"**
>
> (Qur'an 6:153)

Greater and lesser jihad

Greater Jihad

Greater Jihad is the personal, daily struggle to be a good Muslim. It means completing religious duties and resisting evil, for example, by:

- completing daily prayers
- fasting during Ramadan
- not sinning by avoiding haram deeds.

Lesser Jihad

Lesser Jihad (Holy war) means physically defending Islam/God. The Qur'an says,

> **"** *Fight in God's cause against those who fight you, but do not overstep the limits: God does not love those who overstep the limits.* **"**
>
> (Qur'an 2:190)

Some may interpret this as a Holy War.

Muhammad performed both:

> **"** *We have finished the Lesser Jihad, let us now focus on the Greater Jihad.* **"**
>
> (Hadith)

Knowledge

18 ☾ Practices: Hajj and Jihad

Different understandings of Jihad

Greater Jihad

Some Muslims believe that this should always be their main focus. It is the struggle to stay on the straight path of Islam and do what is halal (allowed) by:

- looking after others by paying zakah
- giving extra charity (sadaqah) to help those in poverty
- learning the Qur'an off by heart to show devotion to the words of God.

Lesser Jihad

This is interpreted by Muslims in different ways.

- Some believe this is only to be used in defence.
- Some interpret this as meaning to attack anyone who is against Islam.
- Others read the Qur'an in the context of Muhammad and Makkah at the time and say that it doesn't apply to Muslims today as the world is a different place and weapons are very different to those that Muhammad used.

Only a few Muslims will experience the act of physical fighting as the Lesser Jihad in their life. Some religious extremists have justified terrorist actions as Lesser Jihad but have been condemned as misinterpreting the Qur'an and not fulfilling the rules for Lesser Jihad.

> **REVISION TIP**
>
> To help you remember the difference between Greater and Lesser Jihad, remind yoruself that Greater Jihad requires a Muslim to be a 'great' Muslim at all times. Lesser Jihad is 'less' frequently done by Muslims.

Origins, influence, and conditions for the declaration of Lesser Jihad

Muhammad performed the Lesser Jihad when he fought in Makkah to restore the Ka'aba to the worship of God.

There are conditions for Lesser Jihad.

- ☑ Must only be declared by a fair religious leader.
- ☑ Must be in response to a threat to the faith.
- ☑ Must be the last resort – all peaceful methods must have been tried first.
- ☑ Cannot be used to make people convert to Islam.
- ☑ Must not be used to gain territory or wealth.

- ☒ No women, children or elderly should be killed.
- ☒ No crops/fruit-bearing trees should be destroyed.
- ☒ Dead bodies must not be mutilated.

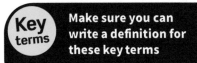 **Key terms** Make sure you can write a definition for these key terms

Ka'aba   Greater Jihad   Lesser Jihad

Learn the answers to the questions below, then cover the answers column with a piece of paper and write as many as you can. Check and repeat.

Questions | Answers

#	Questions		Answers
1	How many times do Muslims go around the Ka'aba during tawaf?	Put paper here	Seven
2	What do Muslims do at Muzdalifah whilst on Hajj?		Collect stones
3	Which type of Jihad is the personal struggle to be a good Muslim?		Greater Jihad
4	When did Muhammad perform the Lesser Jihad?	Put paper here	When he fought in Makkah to restore the Ka'aba to the worship of God
5	During which month of the Islamic calendar is Hajj?		Dhul Hijjah (twelfth month)
6	What does throwing the stones at the Jamarat in Mina symbolise?		Getting rid of temptation and rejecting evil
7	What do Muslim pilgrims do at Arafat during Hajj?	Put paper here	Stand before God on the rocky mount and pray to God asking for forgiveness for themselves and all of humanity
8	What does the word 'Jihad' mean?		Struggle
9	Complete the quotation from the Hadith: *"We have finished the _____ Jihad, let us now focus on the _____ Jihad."*	Put paper here	*Lesser; Greater*
10	Which prophets are remembered when pilgrims throw their stones on Hajj?		Ibrahim and Ishmael

Previous questions

Now go back and use these questions to check your knowledge of previous topics.

Questions | Answers

#	Questions		Answers
11	What is sawm?	Put paper here	Fasting in the month of Ramadan
12	What percentage is khums?		20%
13	Which event is described in Qur'an 96:1–5?		The Night of Power
14	What does the word 'zakah' mean?	Put paper here	That which purifies
15	What is the mihrab?		The alcove in the mosque showing the direction to Makkah

Exam-style questions

01 Which **one** of these is the place where Muslims throw stones at large stone pillars to reject evil on Hajj?

Put a tick (✓) in the box next to the correct answer. **(1 mark)**

A   Ka'aba at Makkah ☐

B   Muzdalifah ☐

C   Mina ☐

D   Arafat ☐

02 Which **one** of these is the personal struggle to be a good Muslim?

Put a tick (✓) in the box next to the correct answer. **(1 mark)**

A   Lesser Jihad ☐

B   Greater Jihad ☐

C   Ummah ☐

D   Ramadan ☐

03 Name **two** places visited on Hajj. **(2 marks)**

04 Name **two** types of Jihad. **(2 marks)**

05 Explain **two** contrasting ways that Muslims perform Hajj. **(4 marks)**

> **EXAM TIP**
>
> 'Contrasting' just means 'different' in this type of question.

06 Explain **two** religious beliefs about Jihad.

Refer to sacred writings or another source of Muslim belief and teaching in your answer. **(5 marks)**

> **EXAM TIP**
>
> Use the words of the statement in your judgement to show you have accurately answered the question.

07 'The Greater Jihad is more important than the Lesser Jihad.'

Evaluate this statement.

In your answer you should:

- refer to Muslim teaching
- give reasoned arguments to support this statement
- give reasoned arguments to support a different point of view
- reach a justified conclusion. **(12 marks)**

(+ SPaG 3 marks)

19 ☪ Practices: Festivals and commemorations

- A festival is a time of happiness and often remembers an important event in a religion that is a reason to come together to celebrate.
- A commemoration is a time to remember something that is important but is often a sad event.

Id-ul-Adha (festival of sacrifice) – Sunni and Shi'a Muslims

- Celebrated on the tenth day of Dhul-Hijjah (12th month of the Islamic calendar) for three days.
- **Id-ul-Adha** celebrates when Ibrahim was prepared to sacrifice his son Ishmael as God told him to in a dream.
- Known as the 'Greater Id'.

> **REVISION TIP** ☑
>
> Both Ids have similar celebrations. To help you remember the similarities and differences, make a Venn diagram to show the common features of the celebrations.

Sacrificing a lamb – to remember God giving Ibrahim a ram to sacrifice instead of Ishmael.

Id prayers at the mosque.

Exchanging cards and presents.

How is it celebrated?

Visiting family and friends.

Listening to the imam's sermon at the mosque to remind them of Ibrahim's devotion to God.

Sharing food with family and friends.

Id-ul-Fitr (festival of the breaking of the fast) – Sunni and Shi'a Muslims

- Celebrated at the end of the month of Ramadan – the first day of Shawwal, the tenth month of the Islamic calendar – for one to three days.
- Id-ul-Fitr celebrates the end of Ramadan.
- Known as the 'Lesser Id'.

> **REVISION TIP** ☑
>
> To help you remember the different Ids remind yourself that 'f' is for 'fast' and Id-ul-Fitr is breaking of the fast.

Giving alms to the poor, known as Zakat al-Fitr.

Sharing food with family and friends.

Id prayers at the mosque – thanking God for the strength that got them through the fast.

Exchanging cards and presents.

How is it celebrated?

Visiting family and friends.

Listening to the imam's sermon at the mosque – reminding them to forgive and to help the poor.

Wearing best or new clothes.

Remembering and praying for loved ones who are deceased.

⚙ Knowledge

19 ☾ Practices: Festival and commemorations

Ashura – Sunni festival (also known as the Day of Atonement)

- Ashura is on the tenth day of Muharram (first month of the Islamic calendar).
- Two events are remembered and celebrated during **Ashura**:
  — Moses rescuing the Israelites from slavery in Egypt
  — Noah leaving the ark for the first time following the flood.

> ❝ We sent Noah out to his people. He lived among them for fifty years short of a thousand but when the Flood overwhelmed them they were still doing evil. We saved him and those with him on the Ark. We made this a sign for all people. ❞
>
> (Qur'an 29:14–15)

Celebrated by Sunni Muslims in the UK by

- Completing a voluntary fast as they believe that Muhammad said to fast on Ashura.
- Going to the mosque.
- Giving to charity and showing kindness to others.
- Praying
- Learning from Islamic scholars.

Ashura – Shi'a commemoration

- Ashura is on the tenth day of Muharram (first month of the Islamic calendar).
- It commemorates the death of Imam Husayn (third in the Imamate) as a martyr in the Battle of Karbala.
- Ashura is a day of great sorrow and mourning.

> ❝ Husayn is from me, and I am from Husayn. Allah loves whosoever loves Husayn. ❞
>
> (Hadith)

REVISION TIP

The specification mentions the importance of these festivals and commemorations for Muslims in Great Britain today, so make sure you know about contemporary celebrations and commemorations.

Commemorated by Shi'a Muslims in the UK by

- Attending Majalis (sermons by Muslim Scholars about the lessons from Ashura).
- Going to a march to join the British Shi'a community.
- Telling children the story of the Battle of Karbala.
- Mourning – wailing, beating of chests.
- Giving blood – to save lives and remind them of the martyrdom of Husayn.

Key terms — Make sure you can write a definition for these key terms

Id-ul-Adha   Ashura

Retrieval

Learn the answers to the questions below, then cover the answers column with a piece of paper and write as many as you can. Check and repeat.

Questions / Answers

	Questions	Answers
1	In which month is Id-ul-Adha?	Dhul-Hijjah (12th month of the Islamic calendar)
2	What is Id-ul-Adha also known as?	The festival of sacrifice
3	What event does Id-ul-Adha remember?	When Ibrahim was prepared to sacrifice his son Ishmael as God told him to in a dream
4	Which animal is sacrificed at Id-ul-Adha and why?	A lamb – to remember God giving Ibrahim a ram to sacrifice instead of Ishmael
5	In which month is Id-ul-Fitr?	Shawwal, the tenth month of the Islamic calendar
6	What does Id-ul-Fitr celebrate?	The end of Ramadan
7	Give three ways that a Muslim may celebrate Id-ul-Fitr.	Three from: sharing food / visiting family and friends / Id prayers at the mosque / listening to the imam's sermon / cards and presents / wearing of best or new clothes / visiting the graves of deceased family members
8	Which event do Shi'a Muslims commemorate at Ashura?	The martyrdom of Imam Husayn
9	Name the two events that Sunni Muslims remember when celebrating Ashura.	• Moses rescuing the Israelites from slavery in Egypt • Noah leaving the ark for the first time following the flood

Put paper here

Previous questions

Now go back and use these questions to check your knowledge of previous topics.

Questions / Answers

	Questions	Answers
10	Which type of Jihad is the personal struggle to be a good Muslim?	Greater Jihad
11	Which prophets are remembered when pilgrims throw their stones on Hajj?	Ibrahim and Ishmael
12	What should Muslims not do during daylight hours in the month of Ramadan?	Eat, drink, smoke, have sex
13	What does throwing the stones at the Jamarat in Mina symbolise?	Getting rid of temptation and rejecting evil
14	What are the first words that are whispered into the ear of a newborn Muslim baby?	The Shahadah

Put paper here

Practice

Exam-style questions

01 Which **one** of these is the commemoration of the martyrdom
of Imam Husayn?

Put a tick (✔) in the box next to the correct answer.   **(1 mark)**

A   Ashura   ☐

B   Id-ul-Fitr   ☐

C   Id-ul-Adha   ☐

D   Battle of Karbala   ☐

02 Which **one** of these is the main prophet remembered at Id-ul-Adha?

Put a tick (✔) in the box next to the correct answer.   **(1 mark)**

A   Muhammad   ☐

B   Isa (Jesus)   ☐

C   Adam   ☐

D   Ibrahim   ☐

03 Give **two** ways that a Sunni Muslim in Great Britain may
celebrate Ashura.   **(2 marks)**

04 Give **two** ways that a Shi'a Muslim in Great Britain may
commemorate Ashura.   **(2 marks)**

05 Explain **two** contrasting ways that Muslims may
celebrate Id-ul-Adha.   **(4 marks)**

> **EXAM TIP**
> Make sure you develop
> each point that you
> make. You could do this
> by adding a teaching, a
> quotation, or an example.

06 Explain **two** ways that Muslims may celebrate Id-ul-Fitr.

Refer to sacred writings or another source of Muslim belief and
teaching in your answer.   **(5 marks)**

> **EXAM TIP**
> Make sure you include
> a 'different view' in a
> 12-mark question. This
> doesn't have to be 'against'
> the statement but an
> alternative view.

07 'Id-ul-Adha is more important than Id-ul-Fitr.'

Evaluate this statement.

In your answer you should:

• refer to Muslim teaching

• give reasoned arguments to support this statement

• give reasoned arguments to support a different point of view

• reach a justified conclusion.   **(12 marks)**

                                                             (+ SPaG 3 marks)

20 A: Sex

Human sexuality

Sexuality can be a controversial topic in society and within religions.

 Heterosexuality – where someone is attracted sexually to people of the opposite sex.

 Homosexuality – where someone is attracted sexually to people of the same sex.

† Christian views on homosexuality

Broadly there are three different views within Christianity about homosexuality, and each one interprets Bible references differently.

Some Christians accept homosexuality	Some Christians accept being homosexual but do not accept homosexual acts	Some Christians do not accept homosexuality
• Homosexual people are part of God's creation and everyone should be treated with respect. • Texts that forbid homosexuality have been misinterpreted. Some Christian churches will marry same-sex couples, and some will bless a **civil marriage**.	• Being **homosexual** is accepted as we are all part of God's creation, but taking part in homosexual acts is not acceptable. • God told humans to procreate ('be fruitful') but homosexual couples are not able to do this naturally so they cannot fulfil God's command. • Catholic teachings say that one of the purposes of sex is **procreation** so homosexuals should remain **chaste**. • Bible texts interpreted as forbidding homosexual acts support their view. These Christian churches will not marry or bless homosexual couples.	• Heterosexuality is part of God's plan for humans and the Bible speaks about a man and a woman as husband and wife (e.g., Adam and Eve). • The Bible speaks about procreation as a command from God ('be fruitful') and only **heterosexual** couples can do this naturally. • There are texts in the Bible that some people interpret as forbidding homosexual acts. These Christian churches will not marry or bless homosexual couples.
❝ So, God created mankind in his own image, in the image of God he created them; male and female he created them. ❞ (Genesis 1:27)	❝ God blessed them and said to them, Be fruitful and increase in number. . . ❞ (Genesis 1:28)	❝ Do not have sexual relations with a man as one does with a woman; that is detestable. ❞ (Leviticus 18:22)

REVISION TIP

Where there are different views you don't need to know the different Christian denominations. You can use 'Some Christians' and 'Other Christians' in your answers.

⚙ Knowledge

20 A: Sex

☾ Muslim views on homosexuality

Muslims who reject homosexuality	Muslims who accept homosexuality
• The majority believe that homosexual acts are against God's will – humans should marry (someone of the opposite sex) and have children, as Muhammad did. • Homosexuality is illegal in many Islamic countries as Islamic teachings forbid it, some with severe punishment for engaging in homosexual acts. • To be convicted under Shari'ah law, a person must confess, or there must be four eyewitnesses. Therefore homosexual acts may not be punished on Earth, but by God on the Day of Judgement.	• Some Muslims believe that homosexuality is not a choice, and that God will judge people's actions. • A few Muslims accept that homosexuality is part of British society and people have the right to make their own choices as society is different from the time of Muhammad and the Qur'an.

> ❝ Must you, unlike [other] people, lust after males and abandon the wives that God has created for you? You are exceeding all bounds. ❞
> (Qur'an 26:165–166)

> ❝ Marry those who are single among you for [God] will develop their moral traits [through marriage]. ❞
> (Hadith)

> ❝ How can you commit this outrage with your eyes wide open? How can you lust after men instead of women? What fools you are! ❞
> (Qur'an 27:54–55)

> ❝ If two men commit a lewd act, punish them both; if they repent and mend their ways, leave them alone – God is always ready to accept repentance, He is full of mercy. ❞
> (Qur'an 4:16)

Sexual relationships before marriage

✝ Christianity	☾ Islam
✘ Many Christians are against sex before marriage as sex has been given by God for married couples to share love, to procreate, and be part of a lifelong union. *"Every sexual act must be within the framework of marriage."* (Pope Pius XI in 1930) ☑ Some allow sex before marriage as part of a loving, committed relationship that will end in marriage.	✘ Islam teaches that sex before marriage is not allowed and is **zinah** (a sexual offence). ✘ Sex is a gift from God, only shared between a married couple and may lead to having children within a family unit. > ❝ *A man should not stay with a woman in seclusion unless he is a relative.* ❞ (Hadith)

Sexual relationships outside of marriage (adultery)

✝ Christianity	☾ Islam
☒ Christianity forbids adultery as it breaks the marriage vows and goes against Biblical teaching.	☒ Islam forbids adultery in the Qur'an and the Hadith. In countries that follow Shari'ah law, adultery needs to be witnessed by four different people, and the punishment for being found guilty is death by stoning.
❝ *You shall not commit adultery.* ❞ (Exodus 20:14)	❝ *And do not go anywhere near adultery: it is an outrage, and an evil path.* ❞ (Qur'an 17:32)

Contraception and family planning

Contraception can be used to:

- prevent unwanted pregnancies
- ensure all children born are wanted and can be cared for
- prevent sexually transmitted diseases (STIs).

Some people use these methods to help with family planning – to control when and how many children they have.

REVISION TIP

Remember that contraception stops conception – 'contra' means 'against' or 'opposite'.

Method	Description	Advantages	Disadvantages
Artificial methods	Stop the sperm from reaching the egg (barrier method), e.g., condom	• Cheap • Widely available in many countries • Helps prevent STIs as well	• Not 100% reliable in preventing pregnancy • Relies on being used correctly
	Change hormones to prevent **conception** (the sperm fertilising the egg), e.g., the pill	• Widely available in many countries	• Not 100% reliable in preventing pregnancy • Relies on being used correctly
	Methods that make it impossible to conceive due to surgery on sexual organs, e.g., sterilisation	• Most reliable way of preventing pregnancy	• Difficult to reverse
The rhythm method	Only having sex at certain times during a woman's menstrual cycle when she is less likely to conceive	• Uses the woman's natural cycle • Free	• Very unreliable at preventing pregnancy • Relies on woman to track her monthly cycle
Withdrawal	Stopping sex just before the male ejaculates	• Can prevent fertilisation • Free	• Very unreliable at preventing pregnancy

⚙ Knowledge

20 A: Sex

† Christian attitudes to family planning and contraception

- In Genesis 1:28 God tells humans to "be fruitful and increase in number" so having children can be part of the role of being a good Christian.

- Children should be born within marriage.
- Children are a gift from God and should be nurtured and guided.

Church of England	The Catholic Church	The Orthodox Church

• Children should be planned for so that they can be cared and provided for, as a blessing.
• Contraception helps to strengthen a relationship before having children and avoid harming the mother's health by spacing out births.
• The Church of England approved the use of artificial contraception in 1930.
	• Does not allow the use of artificial contraception because:
	  – sex is for making new life and expressing love
	  – it goes against **natural law** (the moral principles that are part of human nature) and prevents God's plan for having children.
	• However, the rhythm method can be used to try to ensure children can be cared for, and where the woman's health needs to be considered.
		• God's purpose for marriage is to have children.
		• Artificial contraception goes against natural law.

↓

☾ Muslim attitudes to contraception and family planning

- Muslim couples are expected to have children but can plan when and how many they want to have.

- Children are a gift from God so procreation is a blessing.

- Contraception is generally permitted. Some prefer natural methods and there are Hadith to support the withdrawal method.

- The health of the mother and the well-being of the family is important so contraception can be used to ensure them.

- Some Muslims believe that a lack of money is not a reason to use contraception.

- The Qur'an does not specifically mention contraception, but some Muslims use this quotation from the Qur'an to support the use of contraception:

> **"** *God wishes to lighten your burden; man was created weak* **"**
>
> (Qur'an 4:28)

- Some Muslims do not accept methods where conception has already occurred, and sterilisation is not allowed.

Key terms — Make sure you can write a definition for these key terms

civil marriage   homosexual   procreation   chaste   heterosexual
zinah   contraception   conception   natural law

Learn the answers to the questions below, then cover the answers column with a piece of paper and write down as many as you can. Check and repeat.

Questions	Answers
1 Which quotation from Genesis in the Bible gives Christians the command to procreate?	*"Be fruitful and increase in number…"*
2 Who were the first husband and wife in the Bible?	Adam and Eve
3 How many eyewitnesses must there be to a homosexual act, for a conviction under Shari'ah law?	Four
4 What punishment is sometimes given for adultery in countries that follow Shari'ah law?	Death by stoning
5 What are the moral principles that are part of human nature?	Natural law
6 Give one possible benefit of using contraception.	One from: prevents unwanted pregnancies / ensures all children born are wanted and can be cared for / controls population growth / prevents sexually transmitted diseases
7 Name one type of artificial contraception.	One from: condom / the pill / sterilisation
8 Which method of family planning does the Catholic Church allow to be used?	The rhythm method
9 For which method of family planning is there a supporting Hadith?	The withdrawal method
10 In which year did the Church of England approve the use of artificial contraception?	1930
11 Which quotation from the Qur'an forbids adultery?	*"And do not go anywhere near adultery: it is an outrage, and an evil path."*
12 Which quotation from the Qur'an do some Muslims use to support the use of contraception?	*"God wishes to lighten your burden; man was created weak."*

Put paper here

Exam-style questions

01 Which **one** of these means to be attracted to members of the same sex?

Put a tick (✓) in the box next to the correct answer. **(1 mark)**

    A   Family planning ☐

    B   Heterosexuality ☐

    C   Homosexuality ☐

    D   Procreation ☐

02 Which **one** of these is not a method of artificial contraception?

Put a tick (✓) in the box next to the correct answer. **(1 mark)**

    A   Condom ☐

    B   The pill ☐

    C   Sterilisation ☐

    D   Withdrawal ☐

03 Name **two** types of artificial contraception. **(2 marks)**

04 Give **two** reasons why a couple may use contraception. **(2 marks)**

> **EXAM TIP**
>
> If the question says 'contrasting', make sure your answer gives two different views. They don't have to be the exact opposite.

05 Explain **two** contrasting religious beliefs about sexual relationships outside of marriage.

In your answer you must refer to one or more religious traditions. **(4 marks)**

06 Explain **two** religious beliefs about family planning.

Refer to sacred writings or another source of religious belief and teaching in your answer. **(5 marks)**

> **EXAM TIP**
>
> Remember, you must name the sacred writing or source of authority in your answer, for example, the Bible, the Qur'an.

07 'Sex should only take place between a married couple.'

Evaluate this statement.

In your answer you:

- should give reasoned arguments in support of this statement

- should give reasoned arguments to support a different point of view

- should refer to religious arguments

- may refer to non-religious arguments

- should reach a justified conclusion. **(12 marks)**

(+ SPaG 3 marks)

21 A: Marriage and divorce

Marriage is a legal contract which, in Great Britain, is between two people and provides legal and financial rights to each partner.

In Great Britain, any type of civil marriage cannot involve religion or mention religious beliefs as part of the ceremony.

† The nature and purpose of marriage in Christianity

- Marriage is one of God's gifts to humans at creation.
- It is a **sacrament**: an outward expression of an inner grace.
- Marriage is a lifelong union blessed by God, which reflects the sacrificial love of Jesus, and a covenant (agreement) before God in which the couple vow (promise) to live faithfully together until they die.
- It is a physical and spiritual union which is a loving relationship:

  > ❝ Husbands, love your wives, just as Christ loved the church and gave himself up for her. ❞ (Ephesians 5:25)

- It is the right place for having sex and for having children.
- It provides stability and is a foundation for family life and the wider society.
- The Bible only mentions heterosexual marriage:

  > ❝ That is why a man leaves his father and mother and is united to his wife, and they become one flesh. ❞ (Genesis 2:24)

- The Christian marriage **vows** (promises) show the commitment made between the couple, in front of God.

☾ The nature and purpose of marriage in Islam

- Marriage is an important part of being a Muslim which God permits:

  > ❝ There is no institution in Islam more beloved and dearer [to God] than marriage. ❞ (Hadith)

- It is an important duty in following Islam:

  > ❝ When a person gets married, he has completed half of his religion. ❞ (Hadith)

- It is the right place to have children and bring them up in Islam as a foundation for the wider society.
- Marriage is a social and financial contract that involves both families.
- It is a committed relationship for love to develop and the only place for sexual intercourse.
- The Qur'an encourages single people to marry:

  > ❝ Marry off the single among you. ❞ (Qur'an 24:32)

- A Muslim woman must marry a Muslim man. A Muslim man can marry a Muslim, Christian, or Jew.
- Muslims can choose who they marry; no one should be forced:

  > ❝ If a man gives his daughter in marriage while she is averse to it, then such marriage is invalid. ❞ (Hadith)

⚙ Knowledge

21 A: Marriage and divorce

Same-sex marriage

✝ Christianity	☾ Islam
• Most Christian denominations do not allow same-sex marriage. • The Bible only mentions heterosexual marriage. • One of the main purposes of marriage is to have children, and homosexual couples cannot do this naturally. *"For Christians, marriage – that is the lifelong union between a man and a woman, contracted with the making of vows – remains the proper context for sexual activity. Civil Partnerships – for same sex and opposite sex couples."* (A pastoral statement from the House of Bishops of the Church of England 2019)	• Same-sex marriage is not permitted as homosexual relationships are not allowed. • The Qur'an only mentions heterosexual marriage. • One of the main purposes of marriage is to have children and homosexual couples cannot do this naturally.

Cohabitation

✝ Christianity	☾ Islam
• Most Christian denominations do not permit **cohabitation** of couples as it is likely that pre-marital sex will occur, which is not allowed. • The Catechism of the Catholic Church states: *"The sexual act must take place exclusively within marriage. Outside of marriage it always constitutes a grave sin."* (Catechism of the Catholic Church 2390) • Some Christians accept that although marriage is the ideal, people may live together in a faithful, loving, and committed way without being married, so therefore may accept cohabitation under these conditions.	• Cohabitation is not allowed as sex should only occur in marriage and the assumption is that a cohabiting couple will have sex.

Divorce and remarriage

Divorce is the legal ending of a marriage. There are many different reasons why a marriage may fail and end in divorce:

- people changing, growing apart, and falling out of love
- adultery
- domestic violence or abuse
- illness or disability.

Remarriage is when a person marries again (to a different person) following a divorce. Remarriage is legally allowed in Great Britain. However, different Christian Churches may have restrictions on it.

Ethical arguments related to divorce

Allowing divorce	Against divorce
The most compassionate thing to do if there is unhappiness in the marriage.	Goes against the **sanctity of marriage vows**.
Might be better for children for their parents to be apart.	Can affect children negatively.

† Divorce and remarriage in Christianity

 When divorce and remarriage are accepted in Christianity

- Jesus allows divorce in a specific situation:

  > ❝ But I tell you that anyone who divorces his wife, <u>except for sexual immorality,</u> makes her the victim of adultery, and anyone who marries a divorced woman commits adultery. ❞
  >
  > (Matthew 5:32)

- Some Christians believe that divorce is the lesser of two evils so it is better to divorce than to have an unhappy marriage.
- Some Christian denominations allow divorce and remarriage in certain circumstances.
- The Church of England have allowed remarriage in certain circumstances since 2002, although it is a priest's decision if they want to perform the ceremony.

 When divorce and remarriage are not accepted in Christianity

- Jesus condemns divorce:

  > ❝ Anyone who divorces his wife and marries another woman commits adultery against her. And if she divorces her husband and marries another man, she commits adultery. ❞
  >
  > (Mark 10:11–12)

- **Sanctity of marriage vows** – these are sacred and in front of, and with, God: 'Till death us do part'.
- Marriage is a sacred union between the couple and God:

  > ❝ So they are no longer two, but one flesh. Therefore, what God has joined together, let no one separate. ❞ (Matthew 19:6)

- In the Catholic Church, marriage is a sacrament that cannot be ended by divorce. Couples may separate or get a legal divorce but, within the Church, marriage is permanent and lifelong. However, if the marriage is declared void, it may be annulled in specific circumstances, such as mental incapacity or marriage by force.

 # Knowledge

21 A: Marriage and divorce

☪ Divorce and remarriage in Islam

Sources of wisdom and authority in Islam give Muslims clear teachings about divorce and remarriage.

Source of wisdom and authority	Meaning and explanation
66 *Divorce is the worst thing that Allah permits.* 99 (Hadith)	Divorce is allowed in Islam but should be avoided if at all possible. Muhammad married a divorced woman.
66 *"… when any of you intend to divorce women, do so at a time when their prescribed waiting period can properly start… if you are in doubt, the period of waiting shall be three months…* 99 (Qur'an 65:1 and 4)	There is a system of support for a couple that may wish to divorce, including a period of separation (iddah) which allows time to check if the woman is pregnant. The iddah also offers a chance to restore the relationship.
66 *If you [believers] fear that a couple may break up, appoint one arbiter from his family and one from hers. Then, if the couple want to put things right, God will bring about a reconciliation between them: He is all knowing, all aware.* 99 (Qur'an 4:35)	Family and mosque leaders (Imams) may be involved to try to resolve any issues that may prevent a divorce.
66 *Divorced women shall also have maintenance as is considered fair: this is a duty for those who are mindful of God.* 99 (Qur'an 2:241)	A man must financially support his wife if they divorce.
66 *Divorced women must wait for three monthly periods before remarrying.* 99 (Qur'an 2:228)	Once divorced, Muslims are allowed to remarry after a certain period.

 Key terms Make sure you can write a definition for these key terms

marriage   sacrament   vows
cohabitation   divorce   remarriage
sanctity of marriage vows

REVISION TIP

You don't need to know these quotations word-for-word. As long as you know the source and the key belief then you can use this in your 5-mark answer for your reference to sacred writings.

Learn the answers to the questions below, then cover the answers column with a piece of paper and write down as many as you can. Check and repeat.

Questions | Answers

	Questions		Answers
1	What is the name for the period of separation before divorce in Islam?	Put paper here	Iddah
2	What is the correct term for the promises made during a Christian marriage ceremony?		Vows
3	What religions can a Muslim man marry a woman from?		Islam, Christianity, Judaism
4	What is cohabitation?	Put paper here	Living together as a couple without being married
5	For what reason does Jesus allow divorce in Matthew 5:32?		Sexual immorality
6	Which quotation from Matthew in the Bible supports the Christian belief that marriage is a sacred union between a couple and God?	Put paper here	*"So they are no longer two, but one flesh. Therefore, what God has joined together, let no one separate."*
7	Which Christian denomination does not allow divorce but may annul a marriage if it is void?		The Catholic Church
8	In Islam, who may be involved in trying to resolve issues in a marriage to prevent a divorce?	Put paper here	Family and mosque leaders (imams)
9	Which Hadith demonstrates that divorce is allowed in Islam, but should be avoided if possible?		*"Divorce is the worst thing that Allah permits."*
10	For how many months should a Muslim couple separate (iddah) before a divorce?		Three

Previous questions

Now go back and use these questions to check your knowledge of previous topics.

Questions | Answers

	Questions		Answers
11	Which quotation from Genesis in the Bible gives Christians the command to procreate?	Put paper here	*"Be fruitful and increase in number…"*
12	Who were the first husband and wife in the Bible?		Adam and Eve
13	Which method of family planning does the Catholic Church allow to be used?		The rhythm method
14	For which method of family planning is there a supporting Hadith?	Put paper here	The withdrawal method
15	Which quotation from the Qur'an do some Muslims use to support the use of contraception?		*"God wishes to lighten your burden; man was created weak."*

Practice

Exam-style questions

01 Which **one** of these means living together as a couple without being married?

Put a tick (✓) in the box next to the correct answer.   **(1 mark)**

A	Cohabitation	☐
B	Contraception	☐
C	Annulment	☐
D	Vows	☐

02 Which **one** of these is the Catholic practice of declaring a marriage void?

Put a tick (✓) in the box next to the correct answer.   **(1 mark)**

A	Cohabitation	☐
B	Remarriage	☐
C	Divorce	☐
D	Annulment	☐

03 Name **two** reasons why a couple may divorce.   **(2 marks)**

04 Give **two** purposes of marriage in Christianity.   **(2 marks)**

05 Explain **two** contrasting religious beliefs about same-sex marriage.

In your answer you must refer to one or more religious traditions.   **(4 marks)**

> **EXAM TIP**
>
> Make sure you keep your writing to two clear paragraphs in a 4-mark answer.

06 Explain **two** religious beliefs about cohabitation.

Refer to sacred writings or another source of religious belief and teaching in your answer.   **(5 marks)**

07 'All marriages should last until death.'

Evaluate this statement.

In your answer you:

- should give reasoned arguments in support of this statement
- should give reasoned arguments to support a different point of view
- should refer to religious arguments
- may refer to non-religious arguments
- should reach a justified conclusion.   **(12 marks)**

(+ SPaG 3 marks)

> **EXAM TIP**
>
> Remember to read the statement carefully and use the words from it in your answer to ensure you answer it fully.

22 A: Families

† The role of parents and children in Christianity

- Children should support and look after their parents, including when they get old:

> **"** *Anyone who does not provide for their relatives, and especially for their own household, has denied the faith and is worse than an unbeliever.* **"**
>
> (1 Timothy 5:8)

- Children should respect, love and honour their parents. The Bible says:

> **"** *Honour your father and your mother . . .* **"**   (Exodus 20:12)

- Parents should provide for, love, care for, and protect their children, showing them right and wrong. Catholic parents believe:

> **"** *Here one learns endurance and the joy of work [...] love, generous – and even repeated – forgiveness, and above all divine worship in prayer and the offering of one's life.* **"**
>
> (Catechism 1657)

☾ The role of parents and children in Islam

- It is the parents' role to bring up the children in Islam to be good Muslims and support them in learning the Qur'an and the teachings of Islam.
- Mothers are important in Islam as the Hadith says:

> **"** *Heaven is under the feet of the mothers.* **"**   (Hadith)

- The father's role is to provide for the family – usually by going to work to bring in money for the family.
- Parents often help their children to find a suitable marriage partner.
- Parents are told to:

> **"** *Honour your children and perfect their manners.* **"**   (Hadith)

- Children should respect their parents:

> **"** *It is one of the greatest sins that a man should curse his parents.* **"**
>
> (Hadith)

- Children are expected to look after their parents when they get old:

> **"** *Lower your wing in humility towards [your parents] in kindness and say, 'Lord, have mercy on them, just as they cared for me when I was little.'* **"**
>
> (Qur'an 17:24)

⚙ Knowledge

22 A: Families

The purpose of families

Different views on the purpose of families include:

- procreation (having children)
- providing stability for children
- protecting children
- educating children in a faith.

Different types of families	
Single-parent family	One parent with a child/children.
Extended family	A family that extends beyond just parents and their child/children by including grandparents and other relatives as well.
Nuclear family	A couple and their child/children regarded as a basic social unit.
Same-sex parent family	People of the same sex who are raising a child/children together.
Step-family	A family created when a divorced or widowed person, who has a child/ children, remarries.

- Many people believe that the ideal family types in Islam and Christianity are nuclear and extended families.
- These are spoken about in holy texts – a mother and a father provide a stable foundation for children to grow up and learn about their religion.
- However, many also understand that marriages don't always work out and there may be single-parent and step-families.

Contemporary family issues

- Same-sex marriage is legal in Great Britain, and some Christian groups may believe that same-sex parents can also provide stability, love, and happiness for their children. Islamic teachings on homosexuality mean that same-sex parents are not accepted.

- **Polygamy** (having more than one wife at the same time) is illegal in Great Britain. It is legal in some countries, for example, Iran and Saudi Arabia. Polygamy is generally not permitted in Christianity today. In Islam, men are allowed to have up to four wives under certain conditions. Muhammad had more than one wife, and the Qur'an says:

> **❝** *If you fear that you will not deal fairly with orphan girls, you may marry whichever [other] women seem good to you, two, three, or four. If you fear that you cannot be equitable [to them], then marry only one.* **❞**   (Qur'an 4:3)

This means that if a man has more than one wife then they should be treated fairly.

> **REVISION TIP**
>
> You can use the information about views on homosexuality to support your points on the topic of same-sex parents too.

 Key terms — Make sure you can write a definition for these key terms

extended family   nuclear family   same-sex parent family
step-family   polygamy

Learn the answers to the questions below, then cover the answers column with a piece of paper and write down as many as you can. Check and repeat.

Questions | Answers

	Questions	Answers
1	Which family type consists of a mother, father, and a child/children?	Nuclear family
2	Which family type consists of a mother, father, a child/children, and other family members, for example, grandparents?	Extended family
3	Give one purpose of families.	One from: to procreate (have children) / to provide stability for children / to protect children / to educate children in a faith
4	Complete this quotation from the Bible: "_____ your father and your mother." (Exodus 20:12)	*Honour*
5	How many wives can a Muslim man have, according to Islamic teachings?	Up to four
6	Which Hadith shows the importance of mothers in Islam?	*"Heaven is under the feet of the mothers."*
7	What is the father's role in Islam?	To bring up the children in Islam and to provide for the family
8	What does the Hadith say is one of the greatest sins a person can commit in their behaviour towards their parents?	*"It is one of the greatest sins that a man should curse his parents."*
9	What is polygamy?	Having more than one wife at the same time
10	What does the Qur'an say must happen if a man has more than one wife?	All the wives must be treated fairly

Put paper here

Previous questions

Now go back and use these questions to check your knowledge of previous topics.

Questions | Answers

	Questions	Answers
11	Who were the first husband and wife in the Bible?	Adam and Eve
12	Which Christian denomination does not allow divorce but may annul a marriage if it is void?	The Catholic Church
13	In Islam, who may be involved in trying to resolve issues in a marriage to prevent a divorce?	Family and mosque leaders (imams)
14	For how many months should a Muslim couple separate (iddah) before a divorce?	Three
15	Which quotation from Matthew in the Bible supports the Christian belief that marriage is a sacred union between a couple and God?	*"So they are no longer two, but one flesh. Therefore, what God has joined together, let no one separate."*

Put paper here

✏️ Practice

Exam-style questions

01 Which **one** of these is the practice of having more than one wife or husband?

Put a tick (✓) in the box next to the correct answer. **(1 mark)**

A   Divorce ☐

B   Polygamy ☐

C   Remarriage ☐

D   Adultery ☐

02 Which **one** of these is a family that is formed on the remarriage of a divorced or widowed person which includes a child or children?

Put a tick (✓) in the box next to the correct answer. **(1 mark)**

A   Nuclear family ☐

B   Extended family ☐

C   Same-sex parent family ☐

D   Step-family ☐

03 Give **two** roles of parents. **(2 marks)**

> **EXAM TIP** 🎯
>
> Read the question carefully and answer 2-mark questions as succinctly and as quickly as possible.

04 Give **two** purposes of families. **(2 marks)** ◀

05 Explain **two** similar religious beliefs on same-sex parents.

In your answer you must refer to one or more religious traditions. **(4 marks)** ◀

> **EXAM TIP** 🎯
>
> 'Similar' does not mean that the beliefs have to be exactly the same. Your two points just need to be in agreement with each other.

06 Explain **two** religious beliefs about polygamy.

Refer to sacred writings or another source of religious belief and teaching in your answer. **(5 marks)**

07 'Nuclear families are the ideal type of family.'

Evaluate this statement.

In your answer you:

> **EXAM TIP** 🎯
>
> Remember to name the religion that you are writing about so the examiner is clear if your answer is correct.

- should give reasoned arguments in support of this statement
- should give reasoned arguments to support a different point of view
- should refer to religious arguments
- may refer to non-religious arguments
- should reach a justified conclusion. **(12 marks)**

(+ SPaG 3 marks)

23 A: Gender equality

Gender equality, prejudice and discrimination

- In the past, men and women have been thought of and treated differently.
- **Gender prejudice** meant that people thought that men and women should only do certain things and have certain jobs. For example, the role of a woman was to stay in the home and look after any children, and men would go out to work to provide for their family.
- Women did not have the same rights as men and often faced **discrimination**. For example, they were not allowed to do certain jobs and did not have the right to vote or divorce.
- Laws have made it illegal to discriminate by treating men and women differently in Great Britain. This has promoted gender **equality**.
- However, there is still evidence that women are not fully treated equally to men, for example, in the amount they are paid in work and the job opportunities they get.

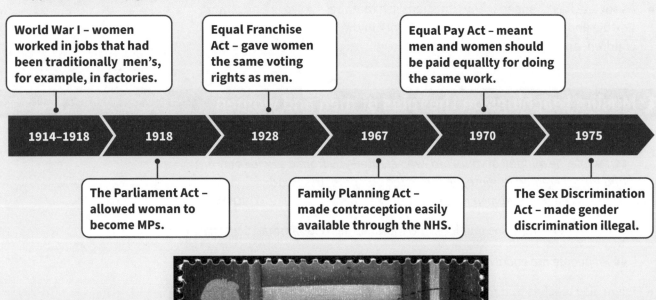

> **World War I** – women worked in jobs that had been traditionally men's, for example, in factories.

> **Equal Franchise Act** – gave women the same voting rights as men.

> **Equal Pay Act** – meant men and women should be paid equallty for doing the same work.

1914–1918 > **1918** > **1928** > **1967** > **1970** > **1975**

> **The Parliament Act** – allowed woman to become MPs.

> **Family Planning Act** – made contraception easily available through the NHS.

> **The Sex Discrimination Act** – made gender discrimination illegal.

▲ *Before the Equal Franchise Act of 1928, women did not have the right to vote in Great Britain*

⚙ Knowledge

23 A: Gender equality

✝ Christian teachings on the roles of men and women

- The Bible says that God made both men and women in his image (Imago Dei):

> ❝ *So God created mankind in his own image, in the image of God he created them; male and female he created them.* ❞ (Genesis 1:27)

- Jesus treated women with respect, and they are often mentioned in the Gospel accounts of his life. In the Bible, St Paul emphasises equality when he says:

> ❝ *There is neither Jew nor Gentile, neither slave nor free, nor is there male and female, for you are all one in Christ Jesus.* ❞ (Galatians 3:28)

- Traditional Christian views were that a woman's role is to work in the home and look after children, and a man's role is to go to work to provide for the family.

- As society has changed many Christians see that these roles are now more flexible and both men and women can work in the home and bring up children, and both can have jobs.

↓

☪ Muslim teachings on the roles of men and women

- The Qur'an says that God created men and women from the same soul:

> ❝ *People, be mindful of your Lord, who created you from a single soul, and from it created its mate, and from the pair of them spread countless men and women far and wide.* ❞ (Qur'an 4:1)

- They both have the same religious and moral duties. Muhammad said that:

> ❝ *All people are equal as the teeth of a comb.* ❞ (Hadith)

- Islam also teaches that men and women are equal but they may have different roles in life:
  - Both the mother and father have the responsibility to raise and look after children in Islam.
  - Some believe that women should look after the home and raise the children as good Muslims. It is then acceptable for a woman to work if her duties as a mother are fulfilled.
  - Some consider that the role of a man is to provide for his family, usually through working to bring in money.

Key terms Make sure you can write a definition for these key terms

gender prejudice   discrimination   equality

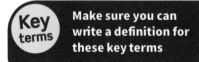

Learn the answers to the questions below, then cover the answers column with a piece of paper and write down as many as you can. Check and repeat.

Questions | Answers

	Questions		Answers
1	Which event in history meant that women had to take on men's jobs, for example, in factories, to keep the country running?	Put paper here	World War I
2	In what year was contraception made easily available via the NHS?	Put paper here	1967
3	What does Imago Dei mean?	Put paper here	In God's image/in the image of God
4	What has helped to promote gender equality in Great Britain?	Put paper here	Laws have been passed that make it illegal to discriminate by treating men and women differently
5	Which quotation from Galatians in the Bible emphasises equality?	Put paper here	*"There is neither Jew nor Gentile, neither slave nor free, nor is there male and female, for you are all one in Christ Jesus."*
6	What is the traditional role of women in Islam?	Put paper here	Look after the home and bring up children as good Muslims
7	Which Hadith tells Muslims that all people are equal?	Put paper here	*"All people are equal as the teeth of a comb."*
8	Give one example of when women have been discriminated against.	Put paper here	One from: access to certain jobs / right to vote / right to divorce
9	What is the role of a man in Islam?	Put paper here	To provide for his family, usually through working to bring in money

Previous questions

Now go back and use these questions to check your knowledge of previous topics.

Questions | Answers

	Questions		Answers
10	What punishment is sometimes given for adultery in countries that follow Shari'ah law?	Put paper here	Death by stoning
11	How many wives can a Muslim man have, according to Islamic teachings?	Put paper here	Up to four
12	In which year did the Church of England approve the use of artificial contraception?	Put paper here	1930
13	What is the correct term for the promises made during a Christian marriage ceremony?	Put paper here	Vows
14	Which Hadith shows the importance of mothers in Islam?	Put paper here	*"Heaven is under the feet of the mothers"*

Practice

Exam-style questions

01 Which **one** of these means giving people the same rights and opportunities regardless of whether they are male or female?

Put a tick (✓) in the box next to the correct answer. **(1 mark)**

A   Gender equality ☐

B   Sexism ☐

C   Gender stereotyping ☐

D   Gender roles ☐

02 Which **one** of these gave women the same voting rights as men?

Put a tick (✓) in the box next to the correct answer. **(1 mark)**

A   The Parliament Act ☐

B   Equal Pay Act ☐

C   The Sex Discrimination Act ☐

D   Equal Franchise Act ☐

EXAM TIP

Remember – don't spend too long on a 1-mark question but DO read the question and options carefully.

03 Give **two** ways that someone may discriminate against a person due to gender. **(2 marks)**

04 Give **two** events in history that have influenced the change in women's rights. **(2 marks)**

05 Explain **two** similar religious beliefs about the roles of men and women.

In your answer you must refer to one or more religious traditions. **(4 marks)**

06 Explain **two** religious beliefs about gender equality.

Refer to sacred writings or another source of religious belief and teaching in your answer. **(5 marks)**

07 'It is the role of both men and women to look after children.'

Evaluate this statement.

In your answer you:

- should give reasoned arguments in support of this statement
- should give reasoned arguments to support a different point of view
- should refer to religious arguments
- may refer to non-religious arguments
- should reach a justified conclusion. **(12 marks)**

(+ SPaG 3 marks)

EXAM TIP

Make sure you include religious teachings in your 12-mark answer, otherwise you will limit your marks.

Knowledge

24

24 B: The origins of the universe and human life

The origins of the universe

- If we look at how the world works, there are many things that exist that seem amazing, for example, the Grand Canyon, the inside of a human eye, or the vastness of the universe. This gives us a sense of **awe** and **wonder**. It may lead us to ask ourselves, 'How was it created?', 'Who created it?' and 'Why?'.

- There are different ideas about the **origins of the universe**, based on the evidence people use to inform their view.
- Even within religions there are many different views, some of which are outlined below, but there are more.

Scientific view: The Big Bang

Source of evidence	Detail
• Red shift theory – the universe is still expanding. • We can detect radiation from the 'bang'.	• Most scientists agree the universe began approximately 13.8 billion years ago with a '**Big Bang**'. • It expanded over time to create what we know as our solar system and planet Earth. • Scientists are unsure of the cause of the Big Bang and cannot explain it.

† Christian views on the origins of the universe

View and source of evidence	Detail	Quotation
Literal creation • The Bible – the book of **Genesis** in the Old Testament	• Some Christians believe that the universe was made in six days by God, and he rested on the seventh. • On each day he created something different: day 1, light and darkness; day 2, the sky; day 3, land, sea, and plants; day 4, the sun, moon, and stars; day 5, fish and sea creatures, and birds; day 6, animals and humans. • Some believe it was approximately 6000 years ago (using Biblical chronology to work it out). • Some Christians believe that the original text for 'day' also means 'age' so this could have been over a long period of time rather than six periods of 24 hours.	❝ In the beginning God created the heavens and the earth. ❞ (Genesis 1:1)
Theistic evolution • The Bible • Scientific evidence (see above)	• Some Christians believe we can look at both the Bible and scientific evidence to see that whilst **creation** started with a 'Big Bang', something must have started it. • They believe this was God as the omnipotent creator. • They agree that this would have been approximately 13.8 billion years ago.	❝ And God said, 'Let there be light,' and there was light. ❞ (Genesis 1:3)

Knowledge

24 B: The origins of the universe and human life

☾ Muslim views on the origins of the universe

View and source of evidence	Detail	Quotation
Literal creation • The Qur'an	• Muslims believe that God created the universe in six days using his divine word. • The Qur'an does describe what God made but not in a particular order. • Some believe that the translation for 'day' also means 'period of time', which isn't defined, so this could have been over a long period of time rather than six periods of 24 hours.	66 *Your Lord is God, who created the heavens and earth in six days, then established Himself on the throne; He makes the night cover the day in swift pursuit; He created the sun, moon, and stars to be subservient to His command.* 99 (Qur'an 7:54)

The relationship between scientific and religious views

• Some Christians and Muslims say that religion gives all the answers to the questions we have about the creation of the universe whereas science doesn't. They believe that God provides the explanation of 'how' and 'why' it happened.

• Others say that science tells us 'how' creation was created but that their holy book tells them 'why', and it answers the questions that science leaves unanswered, for example, what caused the Big Bang?

The origins of human life

- There are different views on how humans came into existence. People base their views on different sources of evidence.
- Even within religions there are different views, some of which are outlined below but there are more.

Scientific view: Evolution

Source of Evidence	Detail
• Evidence of survival of the fittest. • Bones from humans' ancestors. • Genetic similarities between animals and humans.	• Humans have evolved over millions of years from single-celled creatures. • Only creatures that adapted to their environment survived over time (survival of the fittest).

† Christian views on the origins of human life

View and source of evidence	Detail	Quotation
Christian – literal creation • The Bible – Genesis 1–2	• These Christians believe that humans have descended from the first two humans, Adam and Eve. • The Bible says that God created Adam from dust and one version of the story says Eve was made from his rib.	**66** *Then the Lord God formed a man from the dust of the ground and breathed into his nostrils the breath of life, and the man became a living being.* **99** (Genesis 2:7)
Christian – theistic evolution • The Bible • Scientific evidence (see above)	• They use scientific evidence and the Bible. • They believe that God caused evolution to occur. • The Bible account is a story that tells us about God's relationship with humanity but is not a literal account of our origins.	**66** *So, God created mankind in his own image, in the image of God he created them; male and female he created them.* **99** (Genesis 1:27)

Knowledge

24 B: The origins of the universe and human life

☽ Muslim views on the origins of human life

View and source of evidence	Detail	Quotation
Islam – literal creation • The Qur'an and Hadith 	• Some Muslims believe the story in the Qur'an and in the Hadith. • In the Qur'an it says that God created the first human (Adam) from clay and breathed life into him. • All humans descended from Adam and Eve.	❝ *People, We [God] created you all from a single man and a single woman, and made you into races and tribes so that you should recognise one another.* ❞ (Qur'an 49:13)

The relationship between scientific and religious views

- Some Christians and Muslims say that their sources of wisdom and authority tell them everything they need to know about the **origins of life**.

- However, other Christians and Muslims say that the scientific evidence of how humans evolved can work with the teachings in their holy book. The science tells us 'how' it happened, and the holy book tells us 'why'.

 Key terms

Make sure you can write a definition for these key terms

awe   wonder   origins of the universe
Big Bang   literal creation   Genesis
theistic evolution   creation   evolution
origins of life

REVISION TIP

Make sure you know the difference between a question on the 'origins of the universe' and the 'origins of human life' as you can be asked about either.

Learn the answers to the questions below, then cover the answers column with a piece of paper and write down as many as you can. Check and repeat.

Questions

Answers

	Questions	Answers
1	What is the scientific theory of the origins of the universe known as?	The Big Bang
2	How long do Christian literal creationists believe it took for the universe to be created?	Six days/'ages'
3	What evidence do Christian literal creationists use to explain the origins of the universe?	The Bible
4	According to Christian literal creationists, who created the universe?	God
5	When do Christian theistic evolutionists believe the universe was created?	Approximately 13.8 billion years ago
6	What evidence do Christian theistic evolutionists use to explain the origins of the universe?	The Bible and scientific evidence
7	In which Muslim source will you find the stories of God's creation of Adam?	The Qur'an
8	What might the original word for 'day' also mean in some religious texts, rather than 24 hours of time?	An 'age'/a long period of time
9	In a Muslim literal creationist view, how long did it take the universe to be created?	Six days
10	In a Muslim literal creationist view, who created the universe?	God
11	According to the Bible, who was the first human?	Adam
12	What is the process of humans developing from single-celled creatures over millions of years known as?	Evolution
13	According to the Bible, what was Adam made from?	Dust/clay
14	According to the Qur'an, who was the first human to be made by God?	Adam
15	According to the Qur'an, what was the first human made from?	Clay

Put paper here

Practice

Exam-style questions

01 Which **one** of these books in the Bible describes creation?

Put a tick (✓) in the box next to the correct answer.   **(1 mark)**

   A   Matthew ☐

   B   Psalms ☐

   C   Job ☐

   D   Genesis ☐

02 Which **one** of these is the scientific theory of the origins of the universe?

Put a tick (✓) in the box next to the correct answer.   **(1 mark)**

   A   Literal creationism ☐

   B   The Big Bang ☐

   C   Theistic creationism ☐

   D   Genesis ☐

> **EXAM TIP**
> Don't write more than two answers on a 2-mark question as the examiner can only mark the first two.

03 Give **two** religious beliefs about the origins of human life.   **(2 marks)**

04 Name **two** pieces of scientific evidence for evolution.   **(2 marks)**

05 Explain **two** similar religious beliefs about the origins of human life.

In your answer you must refer to one or more religious traditions.   **(4 marks)**

> **EXAM TIP**
> If the exam question asks for 'similar', it requires you to give two answers that are in agreement with each other.

06 Explain **two** views on the origins of human life.

Refer to sacred writings or another source of religious belief and teaching in your answer.   **(5 marks)**

07 'Scientific and religious views on the origins of the universe are not compatible.'

Evaluate this statement.

In your answer you:

- should give reasoned arguments in support of this statement
- should give reasoned arguments to support a different point of view
- should refer to religious arguments
- may refer to non-religious arguments
- should reach a justified conclusion.   **(12 marks)**

(+ SPaG 3 marks)

> **EXAM TIP**
> A 'different view' doesn't have to be opposite but just different from the statement given.

25 B: The value of the universe

The value of the world and duty of human beings to protect it

Our planet is a one-off and is special, so we should look after it.

Many humans believe:

Out of all the species on Earth, humans are the most dominant, and have a duty to protect the other species we live with.

We have a responsibility to protect Earth from harm and should act as stewards of Earth.

The use and abuse of the environment

- We use the planet and its resources in many ways to help us live.
- Nature gives us **natural resources** that come from the earth itself, for example, trees and coal that we use for energy.
- Some energy resources are finite and non-renewable so when we've used them all, there will be no more. They can also pollute the environment when they are used.
- However, we have developed renewable sources of energy which won't run out and are less harmful to the environment.

Non-renewable energy resources
- Coal
- Oil
- Gas

Renewable energy resources
- Solar power
- Wind power
- Wave power

Pollution
We also pollute the environment in other ways:
- Water **pollution**
- Litter, including plastic waste
- Soil pollution (from fertilisers).

Protecting the environment

We can help to protect the environment by:

- reducing the energy we use, for example, using public transport
- reusing items instead of throwing them away
- recycling, for example, plastic, glass, and paper.

⚙ Knowledge

25 B: The value of the universe

✝ Christian views on protecting the environment

- The Bible teaches that creation belongs to God:

> " *The earth is the Lord's, and everything in it, the world, and all who live in it.* "
>
> (Psalm 24:1)

- His creation promotes a sense of awe and wonder:

> " *When I consider your heavens, the work of your fingers, the moon and the stars, which you have set in place, what is mankind that you are mindful of them, human beings that you care for them?* "   (Psalm 8:3–4)

- However, it says that God gave humans **dominion** over creation:

> " *Then God said, 'Let us make mankind in our image, in our likeness, so that they may rule over the fish in the sea and the birds in the sky, over the livestock and all the wild animals, and over all the creatures that move along the ground.'* "   (Genesis 1:26)

- Most Christians believe that it is humans' **responsibility** and **duty** to look after God's creation as stewards, as he gave Adam and Eve this responsibility in the Garden of Eden.

- Christians leaders have said that we should look after creation, including the Pope, the leader of the Orthodox church and the Archbishop of Canterbury.

☪ Muslim views on protecting the environment

- The Qur'an teaches that creation belongs to God:

> " *It is to God that everything in the heavens and earth belongs: God is fully aware of all things.* "   (Qur'an 4:126)

- God's creation brings a sense of awe and wonder to humans who reflect on it:

> " *…it is He who spread out the earth, placed firm mountains and rivers on it, and made two of every kind of fruit; He draws the veil of night over the day. There truly are signs in this for people who reflect.* "   (Qur'an 13:3)

- We are God's '**khalifahs**' (Arabic for 'stewards') so it is our duty to look after his creation:

> " *It is He who has made you successors on the earth.* "   (Qur'an 6:165)

- We should use the earth's resources carefully:

> " *Do not seek from it more than what you need.* "   (Hadith)

- On the **Day of Judgement** humans will be asked how they have looked after the planet. For example, growing plants for food:

> " *Every single Muslim that cultivates or plants anything of which humans, animals or birds may eat from is counted as charity towards them on his behalf.* "   (Hadith)

> **REVISION TIP**
>
> 'Day of Judgement' is an important belief in Islam and can be used in different themes and in religious beliefs and teachings (Paper 1).

The use and abuse of animals

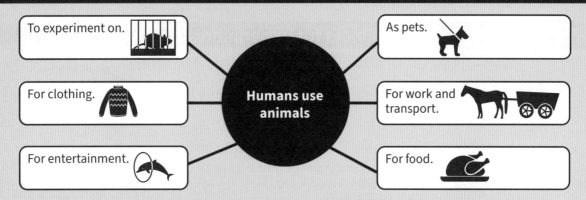

To experiment on.	As pets.
For clothing.	For work and transport.
For entertainment.	For food.

Humans use animals

There are different views about the use of animals for our own benefit:

✗ Animals have their own rights and should not be subject to any pain or killing.

☑ Humans are superior to animals so we can use them to help make our lives better.

Animal experimentation

- Animals are used in experiments to ensure that what we use on humans is safe and works.
- In Great Britain all medicines have to be trialled on animals (for example, mice and rabbits) before they can be used on humans.
- Testing on animals for cosmetics was made illegal in Great Britain in 1998, however it is now legal for some ingredients to be tested on animals.

Views on using animals for food

Using animals for food	Not using animals for food
☑ Humans have always eaten meat.	✗ Animals have the right to be unharmed.
☑ Our bodies need the nutrients from meat to stay healthy.	✗ We can live a healthy life without eating meat.
☑ Animals are not equal to humans and do not have the same rights.	✗ Mass farming of animals contributes to global warming.

REVISION TIP

These are 'non-religious' views so can be used in 12-mark questions.

25 B: The value of the universe

†Christian views on using animals for experimentation and food

- The Bible says animals should be cared for.

> 66 *The righteous care for the needs of their animals.* 99 (Proverbs 12:10)

- However, the Bible says that God gave humans dominion over animals, which they believe means we can use them as we need to:

> 66 *Then God said, 'Let us make mankind in our image, in our likeness, so that they may rule over the fish in the sea and the birds in the sky, over the livestock and all the wild animals, and over all the creatures that move along the ground.* 99 (Genesis 1:26)

- Many Christians will accept **animal experimentation** for medicines only as this is necessary to help humans in curing diseases.

- The Bible is clear that humans can eat animals for food:

> 66 *Everything that lives and moves about will be food for you.* 99
> (Genesis 9:3)

However, the Bible says they can choose if they want to eat meat and shouldn't be judged if they do or do not.

> **REVISION TIP**
>
> Read the whole of Genesis 1-2 in the Bible to help you understand and remember why creation is important in Christianity.

☪ Muslim views on using animals for experimentation and food

- Animals are part of God's creation and the Qur'an highlights their importance.
- Muhammad treated animals well, and there are several stories that show this:
  - He told someone to return a bird's eggs when he saw the bird was distressed by them being removed.
- The Qur'an says that it is acceptable to use animals for food (and other needs):

> 66 *It is God who provides livestock for you, some for riding and some for your food; you have other benefits in them too. You can reach any destination you wish on them: they carry you, as ships carry you [on the sea].* 99
> (Qur'an 40:79-80)

- However, the Qur'an is clear that only some animals should be used for food and that they must be killed by slitting their throat and saying a prayer to make it '**halal**' (allowed). Other animals such as pigs are '**haram**' (not allowed).

- Most Muslims will allow experimentation on animals for medicines because this benefits humans, and we are allowed to use science to help prevent or cure disease to reduce suffering.

> **REVISION TIP**
>
> Read the Islam sections of the revision guide and write a list of things that are allowed (halal) and not allowed (haram) in Islam.

 Key terms **Make sure you can write a definition for these key terms**

natural resource   pollution   dominion   responsibility   duty   khalifah
Day of Judgement   animal experimentation   halal   haram

Learn the answers to the questions below, then cover the answers column with a piece of paper and write down as many as you can. Check and repeat.

Questions — Answers

#	Questions	Answers
1	Give one way that humans can help to protect the environment.	One from: reducing the energy we use / reusing items instead of throwing them away / recycling
2	Name one type of non-renewable energy source.	One from: coal / oil / gas
3	Name one type of renewable energy source.	One from: solar power / wind power / wave power
4	Which word means that humans have power over creation?	Dominion
5	How should an animal be killed to make it halal?	Its throat should be slit whilst a prayer is said
6	Which animal is forbidden (haram) to be eaten in the Qur'an?	Pig
7	Name one way in which humans use animals.	One from: to experiment on / as pets / for clothing / for transport / for entertainment / for food
8	When was animal experimentation for cosmetics made illegal in Great Britain?	1998
9	True or false: all medicines in Great Britain must be tested on animals before they can be used on humans.	True
10	What is the Arabic word meaning that humans have a responsibility to look after God's creation?	Khalifah

Put paper here

Previous questions

Now go back and use these questions to check your knowledge of previous topics.

Questions — Answers

#	Questions	Answers
11	In which Muslim sources will you find the stories of God's creation of Adam and Eve?	The Qur'an and Hadith
12	What is the scientific theory of the origins of the universe known as?	The Big Bang
13	According to the Qur'an, who was the first human to be made by God?	Adam
14	How long do Christian literal creationists believe it took for the universe to be created?	Six days/'ages'
15	What evidence do Christian literal creationists use to explain the origins of the universe?	The Bible

Put paper here

Practice

Exam-style questions

01   Which **one** of these is a renewable source of energy?

Put a tick (✓) in the box next to the correct answer.   **(1 mark)**

A   Coal   ☐

B   Solar power   ☐

C   Oil   ☐

D   Gas   ☐

02   Which **one** of these means that humans have the right to control, and have power over, other living creatures?

Put a tick (✓) in the box next to the correct answer.   **(1 mark)**

A   Dominion   ☐

B   Stewardship   ☐

C   Responsibility   ☐

D   Creation   ☐

03   Name **two** types of natural resource.   **(2 marks)**

04   Give **two** things that animal experimentation is used for.   **(2 marks)**

05   Explain **two** contrasting religious beliefs on animal experimentation.

In your answer you must refer to one or more religious traditions.   **(4 marks)**

> **EXAM TIP**
>
> Remember, you can use 'Some' and 'Other' in contrasting questions, for example, 'Some Christians... Other Christians...'.

06   Explain **two** religious beliefs about the value of the world.

Refer to sacred writings or another source of religious belief and teaching in your answer.   **(5 marks)**

> **EXAM TIP**
>
> Remember to name the religion that you are writing about so the examiner is clear if your answer is correct. You also need to state clearly the source of any quotations you use, for example 'The Bible says...' or 'The Qur'an states...', but you don't need to state the exact chapter/verse.

07   'All religious people should stop using non-renewable sources of energy.'

Evaluate this statement.

In your answer you:

- should give reasoned arguments in support of this statement
- should give reasoned arguments to support a different point of view
- should refer to religious arguments
- may refer to non-religious arguments
- should reach a justified conclusion.   **(12 marks)**

(+ SPaG 3 marks)

26 B: Abortion and euthanasia

Sanctity of life and quality of life

- These are key concepts that people may apply to a situation to decide if they think it is right or wrong.
- We can apply these to important issues such as **abortion** and **euthanasia**.

Sanctity of life	Quality of life
• Life is holy and given by God (so it should not be misused or abused).	• The general well-being of a person, in relation to their health and happiness. • The theory that the value of life depends upon how good or how satisfying it is.

Abortion

Abortion is the removal of a **foetus** from the womb to end a pregnancy. It is controversial because people have different views on when life begins and when a human is alive.

Since 1967 abortion has been legal in Great Britain up to 24 weeks of pregnancy (it is only legal after 24 weeks in exceptional medical circumstances). Two doctors have to confirm one of the legal conditions for abortion:

1. There is a risk to the woman's physical and mental health
2. The woman's life is in danger if the pregnancy continues
3. There is a significant risk that the baby will be born with severe physical or mental disabilities
4. An additional child may affect the physical or mental health of existing children.

REVISION TIP

Note that when we talk about abortion, the words we use can show a bias so think carefully when you write about it.

◀ ·········· This is the most commonly cited condition because it can cover a range of personal reasons for abortion, including:

- being too young to have a child
- not wanting children at that point in life
- contraception failure.

Views on abortion

Arguments about abortion are often based on whether the mother or the foetus has priority.

- Those who believe it is the mother's choice are known as '**pro-choice**'.
- Those who support the rights of the foetus are '**pro-life**'.

REVISION TIP

Keep an eye on the news for current debates about abortion around the world. You can use this information in your 12-mark answers.

👥 Pro-life arguments	👥 Pro-choice arguments
• A foetus is alive from **conception**, and abortion would be killing it (murder). • A foetus has the right to life. • We don't have the right to make decisions about a future human.	• **Quality of life** – the life of the baby and/or the mother may not be a good one if it is an unplanned pregnancy. • Life begins when a foetus can survive once born. • If the mother's life is at risk, the mother is already alive and the foetus isn't, so she takes priority.

Knowledge

26 B: Abortion and euthanasia

† Christian views on abortion

 Some Christians are always against abortion

- Life begins at conception, so abortion is murder. The Bible says:

> 66 *You shall not murder.* 99 (Exodus 20:13)

- **Sanctity of life** – only God has the right to decide when we die so we are 'playing God' when we abort a foetus.

> 66 *Before I formed you in the womb I knew you, before you were born I set you apart.* 99
> (Jeremiah 1:5)

 Some Christians allow abortion in some cases

- **Situation ethics** is a theory where the situation is taken into account first, before deciding what is right and wrong. There are some situations in which abortion might be the most loving thing to do as the Bible says that we should behave in a loving way:

> 66 *As God's chosen people, holy and dearly loved, clothe yourselves with compassion, kindness, gentleness, and patience.* 99
> (Colossians 3:12)

- Lesser of two evils – the quality of life of the foetus/mother is important. An abortion might be better than a life of suffering for the mother or the child.

☾ Muslim views on abortion

 Some Muslims are always against abortion

- Sanctity of life – it should only be God that takes life. It is a great sin to play the role of God by taking life.

> 66 *If anyone kills a person – unless in retribution for murder or spreading corruption in the land – it is as if he kills all mankind, while if any saves a life it is as if he saves the lives of all mankind.* 99 (Qur'an 5:32)

- If someone wants an abortion due to poverty, God will support them – therefore it is forbidden.

> 66 *Do not kill your children for fear of poverty – We [God] shall provide for them and for you – killing them is a great sin.* 99 (Qur'an 17:31)

 Some Muslims allow abortion in some cases

- **Ensoulment** occurs at 120 days so the foetus is not a person until this point, therefore abortion before this time is allowed.

> 66 *One of you [i.e. the human being] is put together in the womb of his mother for forty days, then he becomes in that [period] a clinging clot in a like period of time, then he becomes in that [period] a little lump of flesh in a like period of time, then an angel is sent to him who breathes life into him.* 99 (Hadith)

- If the woman's life is at risk, she takes priority over the foetus.

> 66 *No one should be burdened with more than they can bear: no mother shall be made to suffer harm on account of her child...* 99
> (Qur'an 2:233)

Euthanasia

- The word euthanasia comes from Latin meaning 'good death'.
- It is when someone helps another person who is suffering from an incurable and painful disease to die, in order to put them out of their suffering.
- It is illegal in Great Britain as it is classed as murder.

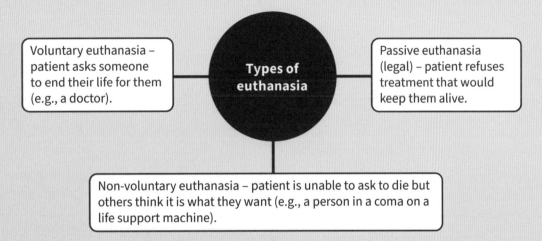

Voluntary euthanasia – patient asks someone to end their life for them (e.g., a doctor).

Types of euthanasia

Passive euthanasia (legal) – patient refuses treatment that would keep them alive.

Non-voluntary euthanasia – patient is unable to ask to die but others think it is what they want (e.g., a person in a coma on a life support machine).

Views on euthanasia

Arguments against euthanasia	Arguments supporting euthanasia
<ul><li>It's killing someone, which is murder and will be punished in law.</li><li>We can manage pain and ensure a person's final days are comfortable, for example, in a hospice.</li><li>People can make decisions when they're ill that they wouldn't normally do. There could be a chance they say they want to die but actually mean they want their pain to end.</li></ul>	<ul><li>It's your life, you can choose when you die.</li><li>It is the most loving thing to do – to put someone out of their suffering.</li><li>It gives someone a dignified and peaceful death – watching someone die when they are in pain and suffering is upsetting and unnecessary.</li></ul>

REVISION TIP

Make sure you don't confuse euthanasia with assisted suicide. Euthanasia is deliberately ending a person's life to relieve suffering. Assisted suicide is deliberately assisting a person to kill themselves.

⚙ Knowledge

26 B: Abortion and euthanasia

✝ Christian views on euthanasia

 Some Christians are always against euthanasia

- It is deliberately taking someone's life, which is a sin against God.

  > ❝ *You shall not murder.* ❞ (Exodus 20:13)

- Sanctity of life – only God has the right to decide when we die. We are 'playing God' when we commit euthanasia.

  > ❝ *Before I formed you in the womb I knew you, before you were born I set you apart.* ❞
  > (Jeremiah 1:5)

- Christian leaders have condemned it.

 Some Christians allow euthanasia in some cases

- Situation ethics – there are some situations in which euthanasia might be the most loving thing to do. The Bible says that we should behave in a loving way:

  > ❝ *As God's chosen people, holy and dearly loved, clothe yourselves with compassion, kindness, gentleness, and patience.* ❞
  > (Colossians 3:12)

- Lesser of two evils – quality of life is important. Helping someone to end their suffering might be the better thing to do. God gave humans the ability to develop life-ending drugs and the free will to use them, so we should.

  > ❝ *Blessed are the merciful.* ❞
  > (Matthew 5:7)

☪ Muslim views on euthanasia

- Most Muslims are against euthanasia as it is taking life, i.e. murder, which the Qur'an forbids:

  > ❝ *Do not kill each other, for God is merciful to you.* ❞ (Qur'an 4:29)

- It is 'playing God', which is the greatest sin (shirk) and goes against God's plan for your life.

  > ❝ *No soul may die except with God's permission at a predestined time.* ❞
  > (Qur'an 3:145)

 Key terms — Make sure you can write a definition for these key terms

> abortion   euthanasia   foetus   pro-choice   pro-life   conception   quality of life   sanctity of life   situation ethics   ensoulment

Learn the answers to the questions below, then cover the answers column with a piece of paper and write down as many as you can. Check and repeat.

Questions | Answers

#	Questions		Answers
1	Up to how many weeks of pregnancy can a woman get an abortion in Great Britain?	Put paper here	24 weeks (except in exceptional medical circumstances)
2	What term is used for people who support the rights of the mother in the abortion debate?		Pro-choice
3	What term is used for people who support the rights of the foetus in the abortion debate?		Pro-life
4	How many doctors must confirm the legal conditions for an abortion in Great Britain?	Put paper here	Two
5	What does this quotation from the Qur'an tell some Muslims about abortion? *"No one should be burdened with more than they can bear: no mother shall be made to suffer harm on account of her child…"* (Qur'an 2:233)	Put paper here	If the woman's life is at risk, she takes priority over the foetus, so abortion is permissible
6	At how many days does the Hadith say that ensoulment happens?		120
7	The word 'euthanasia' comes from Latin – what does it mean?	Put paper here	'Good death'
8	Which type of euthanasia is when the patient is unable to ask to die but those around them think that it would be wanted?		Non-voluntary euthanasia
9	State one quotation from the Qur'an which tells Muslims that euthanasia is wrong.	Put paper here	One from: *"Do not kill each other, for God is merciful to you."* / *"No soul may die except with God's permission at a predestined time."*
10	What way of making a moral decision is following the most loving thing to do?	Put paper here	Situation ethics

Previous questions

Now go back and use these questions to check your knowledge of previous topics.

Questions | Answers

#	Questions		Answers
11	In a Muslim literal creationist view, who created the universe?		God
12	What is the scientific theory of the origins of the universe known as?	Put paper here	The Big Bang
13	True or false: all medicines in the UK must be tested on animals before they can be used on humans.		True
14	What is the Arabic word meaning that humans have a responsibility to look after God's creation.		Khalifah

Practice

Exam-style questions

01 Which **one** of these is the type of euthanasia when the patient asks someone to end their life for them?

Put a tick (✓) in the box next to the correct answer. **(1 mark)**

A	Voluntary euthanasia	☐
B	Non-voluntary euthanasia	☐
C	Passive euthanasia	☐
D	Abortion	☐

02 Which **one** of these describes the concept that life is holy and given by God?

Put a tick (✓) in the box next to the correct answer. **(1 mark)**

A	Sanctity of life	☐
B	Quality of life	☐
C	Shirk	☐
D	Ensoulment	☐

> **EXAM TIP**
> Read all the options carefully. There may be answer options that will distract you from the correct answer!

03 Name **two** types of euthanasia. **(2 marks)**

04 Give **two** reasons people may choose to have an abortion. **(2 marks)**

05 Explain **two** contrasting religious beliefs on euthanasia.

In your answer you must refer to one or more religious traditions. **(4 marks)**

06 Explain **two** religious beliefs on the sanctity of life.

Refer to sacred writings or another source of religious belief and teaching in your answer. **(5 marks)**

> **EXAM TIP**
> You can only achieve the fifth mark if your reference to a sacred writing or source of authority includes where it has come from, for example, the Bible.

07 'Only God should decide when we die.'

Evaluate this statement.

In your answer you:

- should give reasoned arguments in support of this statement
- should give reasoned arguments to support a different point of view
- should refer to religious arguments
- may refer to non-religious arguments
- should reach a justified conclusion. **(12 marks)**

(+ SPaG 3 marks)

27 B: Death and the afterlife

✝ Christian beliefs on the afterlife

Bible text	Belief
66 *For God so loved the world that he gave his one and only Son, that whoever believes in him shall not perish but have eternal life.* 99 (John 3:16)	Some Christians think that if we believe in God and his son Jesus, we will have a life after this life, for eternity.
66 *Jesus said to her, 'I am the **resurrection** and the life. The one who believes in me will live, even though they die.'* 99 (John 11:25)	This shows that humans will be resurrected from death and then will have a life after death.
The Parable of the Sheep and Goats told by Jesus (Matthew 25:31–46)	Christians may interpret this story to mean: • if we helped other people as though we were helping Jesus, we will be on God's right-hand side (sheep) and will be the 'righteous [that go] to eternal life'. Some may interpret this as **heaven**. • if we haven't helped others, then we will be on God's left-hand side (goats) and will 'go away to eternal punishment'. Some may interpret this as **hell**.
66 *Put to death, therefore, whatever belongs to your earthly nature: sexual immorality, impurity, lust, evil desires and greed, which is idolatry. Because of these, the wrath of God is coming. You used to walk in these ways, in the life you once lived. But now you must also rid yourselves of all such things as these: anger, rage, malice, slander, and filthy language from your lips.* 99 (Colossians 3:5–8)	Some Christians believe that certain actions will lead us to be apart from God after we die.
66 *He will wipe every tear from their eyes. There will be no more death or mourning or crying or pain, for the old order of things has passed away.* 99 (Revelation 21:4)	In heaven there will be no sadness or unhappiness.
66 *…and throw them into the blazing furnace, where there will be weeping and gnashing of teeth.* 99 (Matthew 13:50)	• Some think this is a literal description of hell. It will be a painful and unhappy time. • Some believe that a loving God would not create such a place, so it is a symbolic description of being 'without God', not a place called hell.

- These beliefs impact Christians' beliefs about the value of human life as it tells them that there is a life after this life.
- Christians believe that we should think carefully about how we behave in this life because we will be judged on it, and this will influence what happens to us in the afterlife. For example, it will help Christians consider the importance of the sanctity of life alongside the idea of quality of life.

⚙ Knowledge

27 B: Death and the afterlife

☪ Muslim beliefs on the afterlife

Muslim beliefs about life after death are based on what the Qur'an and Hadith tell them. Most Muslims agree that this is based on the existence of heaven and hell.

Qur'an text	Belief
❝ *When death comes to one of them, he cries, 'My Lord, let me return so as to make amends for the things I neglected.' Never! This will not go beyond his words: a barrier stands behind such people until the very day they are resurrected.* ❞ (Qur'an 23:99–100)	• This shows that how we behave in this life matters for our afterlife. • The barrier between this life and the afterlife is called '**barzakh**' and it is where human souls wait for the Day of Judgement to arrive.
❝ *Those whose good deeds weigh heavy will be successful, but those whose balance is light will have lost their souls for ever and will stay in Hell.* ❞ (Qur'an 23:102–103)	• This shows that our actions in this life matter. We will be judged by God, on the Day of Judgement, on how we have behaved. • Our good behaviour will be rewarded; however, our sins may lead to an existence in hell.
❝ *But those who are mindful of their Lord will have lofty dwellings built for them, one above the other, graced with flowing streams.* ❞ (Qur'an 39:20)	The Qur'an describes heaven (**Jannah**) as a paradise and an eternal beautiful garden of physical and spiritual pleasures and delights.
❝ *We have also prepared the torment of a blazing fire. For those who defy their Lord We have prepared the torment of Hell: an evil destination.* ❞ (Qur'an 67:5–6)	The Qur'an describes hell (**Jahannam**) as a blazing fire where there will be pain and suffering.

- These teachings have an impact on Muslims' beliefs about the value of human life as they guide them on how we should treat others, because we will be judged on our actions.

- They also give guidance on issues of life and death, such as abortion and euthanasia, as the teachings emphasise the importance of the sanctity of life, because life is given by God.

> **REVISION TIP**
> Remember, you don't have to use the Arabic terms in your answers.

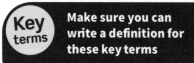

Key terms **Make sure you can write a definition for these key terms**

resurrection   heaven   hell   barzakh   Jannah   Jahannam

Retrieval

Learn the answers to the questions below, then cover the answers column with a piece of paper and write down as many as you can. Check and repeat.

	Questions	Answers
1	What did Jesus say that tells Christians they will be resurrected from death and have a life after death?	*"I am the resurrection and the life. The one who believes in me will live, even though they die."*
2	In which parable is the judgement of humans described?	The Parable of the Sheep and Goats
3	Why don't some Christians believe in the existence of hell?	They believe a loving God wouldn't create something that causes pain and suffering to his people
4	How is heaven described in the Qur'an?	A paradise, a garden of eternal pleasure
5	How is hell described in the Qur'an?	An eternal, blazing fire
6	What is the name of the place that souls will wait for the Day of Judgement, in Islam?	Barzakh – the barrier
7	According to Islam, who judges us on Judgement Day?	God
8	What is the Arabic word for heaven?	Jannah
9	What is the Arabic word for hell?	Jahannam
10	How might a Christian interpret Bible references to heaven and hell?	Literally or symbolically

Put paper here

Previous questions

Now go back and use these questions to check your knowledge of previous topics.

	Questions	Answers
11	In a Muslim literal creationist view, how long did it take the universe to be created?	Six days
12	What evidence do theistic evolutionists use to explain the origins of the universe?	The Bible and scientific evidence
13	Which word means that humans have power over creation?	Dominion
14	What does this quotation from the Qur'an tell some Muslims about abortion? *"No one should be burdened with more than they can bear: no mother shall be made to suffer harm on account of her child…"* (Qur'an 2:233)	If the woman's life is at risk, she takes priority over the foetus, so abortion is permissible
15	Up to how many weeks of pregnancy can a woman get an abortion in Great Britain?	24 weeks (except in exceptional medical circumstances)

Put paper here

✏️ Practice

01 Which **one** of these is the name of the parable that describes the judgement of humans?

Put a tick (✓) in the box next to the correct answer. **(1 mark)**

A   The Parable of the Talents ☐

B   The Parable of the Lost Son ☐

C   The Parable of the Good Samaritan ☐

D   The Parable of the Sheep and Goats ☐

02 Which **one** of these does the Bible class as a sin?

Put a tick (✓) in the box next to the correct answer. **(1 mark)**

A   Charity ☐

B   Noise ☐

C   Anger ☐

D   Prayer ☐

03 Name **two** places in the afterlife in Islam. **(2 marks)**

04 Give **two** religious beliefs about life after death. **(2 marks)**

05 Explain **two** similar religious beliefs on life after death.

In your answer you must refer to one or more religious traditions. **(4 marks)**

> **EXAM TIP** 🎯
> To be sure the examiner is clear if your answer is correct, remember to name the religion that you are writing about.

06 Explain **two** religious beliefs about life after death.

Refer to sacred writings or another source of religious belief and teaching in your answer. **(5 marks)**

07 'This life is our only life.'

Evaluate this statement.

In your answer you:

- should give reasoned arguments in support of this statement
- should give reasoned arguments to support a different point of view
- should refer to religious arguments
- may refer to non-religious arguments
- should reach a justified conclusion. **(12 marks)**

(+ SPaG 3 marks)

> **EXAM TIP** 🎯
> Remember to take special care with your spelling, punctuation, and grammar, and use as many specialist terms as possible when answering 12-mark questions.

28 C: Arguments for the existence of God

People have tried to prove that God exists through logical reasoning, using evidence to create arguments for the existence of God.

The Design argument

The **Design argument** looks to our universe to help prove the existence of God. Christians may support this view as Genesis 1 in the Bible describes the designer God, creating things each day over six days.

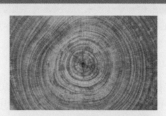

Many things in the universe are intricately made and specifically designed to function in a certain way.

⬇

For example, the rings in a tree trunk, the human eye, and human fingerprints, which are unique.

⬇

There must be a designer intelligent and powerful enough to have done this.

⬇

God is the only being with these powers.

⬇

Therefore, the designer must be God.

Variations to the Design argument	
William Paley	Paley uses a watch analogy to compare the complexity of a watch and its designer to the complexity of the universe and its designer, God.
Isaac Newton	Newton used the design of the thumb and its unique print, and how it functions, as evidence of a designer. He said, 'In the absence of any other proof, the thumb alone would convince me of God's existence'.
Thomas Aquinas	Aquinas looked at things being in order in the universe as evidence of a designer. For example, the way the planets, sun, moons, and stars rotate within the solar system must be down to an **omnipotent**, intelligent designer – God.
A modern argument	F.R. Tennant said that everything in the universe works in just the right way for it to survive; everything is balanced to work. For example, the strength of gravity is just enough to keep us stable or the exact size of protons and neutrons to function correctly. These must be deliberately designed by the designer, God.
A Muslim argument	Everything in the universe is perfectly balanced, designed with purpose and beautifully complex. The Qur'an teaches that God is omnipotent and therefore he is the designer of the universe.

⚙ Knowledge

28 C: Arguments for the existence of God

Strengths and weaknesses of the Design argument

😐 Strengths	⚖ Weaknesses
• Many examples of things on Earth only work if balanced correctly, for example, the human body. • Humans lack the ability to have created many of these things so it must be due to an omnipotent being (God).	• **Atheists** argue that we don't need an omnipotent being to explain the complexity of the universe. Evolution can explain this. • Why would such an **omnibenevolent** designer design things such as cancer? • Humans look for meaning in life and have interpreted the order of the universe to try to justify things that cannot be explained. • Who/what designed God?

The First Cause argument

The **First Cause argument** or Cosmological argument, uses a logical chain of reasoning to try to prove the existence of God. Christians may believe the First Cause argument as the Bible supports the idea that God was the first cause in Genesis 1.

Everything in the universe has a cause. → There must be a first cause – the cause of the universe's existence. → The first cause must be something that is eternal and does not need to be caused (an 'unmoved mover'). → This first cause can only be God. → Therefore, God exists.

Variations to the First Cause argument	
Thomas Aquinas	Aquinas argued that everything in the universe has been caused and that only God can be the uncaused causer of the universe.
The Kalam Cosmological (First Cause) argument	Muslim philosophers argued that God does not have a beginning (or end), but the universe does. There must be something that caused the beginning of the universe. As God is **transcendent** and eternal, he doesn't need a cause and therefore he caused the universe to exist. ❝ *We built the skies with Our power and made them vast...* ❞ (Qur'an 51:47)

Strengths and weaknesses of the First Cause argument

Strengths	Weaknesses
• We can see that everything that exists within the universe has a cause. • Whilst science has found that the Big Bang was the cause of the existence of the universe, something must have caused it, and it was God.	• Who/What caused God? • Scientists have discovered that the cause of the existence of the universe is the Big Bang. • Just because things within the universe have a cause, this doesn't mean that the universe itself needed a cause.

The argument from miracles

Some events do not have a scientific explanation (**miracles**). → These events must be **supernatural** – outside of nature. → Only God is outside of nature (transcendent). → As he is outside of nature, God must be responsible for miracles. → Therefore, God exists.

† Christian responses to miracles

- Miracles are proof of the existence of God.
- The Bible includes examples of many miracles including the most important ones of the incarnation and resurrection of Jesus.
- Jesus performed miracles such as walking on water, bringing people back from the dead, and making the blind see.
- At Pentecost, the Holy Spirit blessed the disciples so they could perform miracles.
- Some Christians believe that they can also perform miracles through the Holy Spirit.
- Catholic Christians believe that Lourdes in France is an important place of pilgrimage where miracles have happened, and still happen today.

> **REVISION TIP**
>
> Read in the Bible in the New Testament gospels about the different types of miracles that Jesus performed.

☪ Muslim responses to miracles

- The supreme miracle within Islam is the revelation of the Qur'an to Muhammad. Muslims believe no human could write such a book without divine intervention.
- Miracles can be required as a sign that someone is a prophet and are evidence of their status.
- Apart from the giving of the Qur'an to Muhammad, miracles are not seen by Muslims to be particularly important.
- Some events might be seen as miracles but these are individual cases, for example some Muslims believe that Muhammad's ascent to heaven on the Night Journey (Al-Isra'wal-Mi'raj) was a miracle.

Knowledge

28 C: Arguments for the existence of God

Strengths and weaknesses of the argument from miracles

Strengths – why miracles prove the existence of God	Weaknesses – why miracles don't prove the existence of God
• Miracles have no scientific explanation so they must be caused by something outside of nature, which can only be God. • There are some events that we cannot explain. Sometimes God can work in mysterious ways, and we should accept that he knows why these happen. • Miracles occur in holy texts.	• Non-religious views of miracles often explain them without the need for God to have been responsible for them. • 'Miracles' may be unusual, coincidental, and very lucky but they are possible according to the laws of nature. They aren't the work of God. • Some things could not be explained with science in the past but they can be now. There may be things that we cannot explain with science yet, but we potentially will. In the meantime, we cannot attribute them to God as miracles. • Some people make up stories of miracles for attention or to make money. • Some people believe there is not enough evidence for miracles, and that witnesses to these events are unreliable. • Why do miracles only happen to some people? Surely an omnibenevolent God would want to help all of his people?

† Examples of miracles in Christianity

From the Bible – Jesus heals the paralysed man

> ❝ *Some men brought to him [Jesus] a paralyzed man, lying on a mat. When Jesus saw their faith, he said to the man, 'Take heart, son; your sins are forgiven.' … he said to the paralyzed man, 'Get up, take your mat and go home.' Then the man got up and went home.* ❞
>
> (Matthew 9:1–8)

Marie Bailly, Lourdes, France 1902

Aged 22, Marie Bailly was diagnosed with tuberculosis peritonitis. She wanted to visit Lourdes but was so ill when she arrived that she was taken to hospital. She was told she was going to die so she asked to be taken to the baths where holy water was poured over her. She prayed to Mary and said, 'I am cured'. She then recovered and returned to good health.

REVISION TIP

Lourdes is an important place of pilgrimage for some Christians. Read more about why it is important in the Christian Practices section.

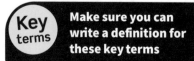 **Make sure you can write a definition for these key terms**

Design argument   omnipotent   atheist   omnibenevolent
First Cause argument   transcendent   miracle   supernatural

Learn the answers to the questions below, then cover the answers column with a piece of paper and write down as many as you can. Check and repeat.

Questions | Answers

#	Question	Answer
1	What analogy does William Paley use to compare with the design of the universe?	A watch
2	In which book of the Bible does God create the universe?	Genesis
3	What might a Muslim say about the Design argument?	Everything in the universe is perfectly balanced, designed with purpose, and beautifully complex, the Qur'an teaches that God is omnipotent, and therefore he is the designer of the universe
4	What is another name for the First Cause argument?	The Cosmological argument
5	What word means that God is beyond nature, the earth, and the universe?	Transcendent
6	What is the name of the event when Muhammad ascended to heaven?	The Night Journey (Al-Isra' wal-Mi'raj)
7	At which event in the Bible were the disciples given the power to perform miracles?	Pentecost
8	At which town in France do Catholic Christians believe that healing miracles occur?	Lourdes
9	What are the most important examples of miracles in the Bible?	The incarnation and resurrection of Jesus
10	Which argument for the existence of God is Thomas Aquinas associated with?	The First Cause argument/Cosmological argument
11	What is the strongest evidence for the existence of God in Islam?	The revelation of the Qur'an to Muhammad
12	True or false: in the Kalam Cosmological argument Muslim philosophers argued that God does not have a beginning (or end), but the universe does.	True
13	What did Jesus say when he healed the paralysed man?	*"Take heart, son; your sins are forgiven."*
14	What is the miracle of the incarnation for Christians?	When God's son came to Earth – Jesus was born

Put paper here

Practice

Exam-style questions

01   Which **one** of these did William Paley use as an analogy for the design of the universe?

Put a tick (✓) in the box next to the correct answer.   **(1 mark)**

A	A tree	☐
B	A fingerprint	☐
C	A watch	☐
D	A thumb	☐

02   Which **one** of these argues that God is the 'unmoved mover'?

Put a tick (✓) in the box next to the correct answer.   **(1 mark)**

A	The Design argument	☐
B	The First Cause argument	☐
C	The argument from miracles	☐
D	Science	☐

03   Give **two** weaknesses of the Design argument.   **(2 marks)**

04   Give **two** examples of miracles in the Bible.   **(2 marks)**

> **EXAM TIP**
>
> Two-mark questions require two answers.

05   Explain **two** contrasting beliefs in modern British society about miracles.

In your answer you should refer to the main religious tradition of Great Britain and non-religious beliefs.   **(4 marks)**

> **EXAM TIP**
>
> Make sure that you develop your points to make two clear paragraphs.

06   Explain **two** strengths of the First Cause argument.

Refer to sacred writings or another source of religious belief and teaching in your answer.   **(5 marks)**

07   'The Design argument is a strong argument for the existence of God.'

Evaluate this statement.

In your answer you:

- should give reasoned arguments in support of this statement
- should give reasoned arguments to support a different point of view
- should refer to religious arguments
- may refer to non-religious arguments
- should reach a justified conclusion.   **(12 marks)**

(+ SPaG 3 marks)

> **EXAM TIP**
>
> You can use non-religious views in your answer but you must include religious views as well.

29 C: Arguments against the existence of God

People have tried to prove that God does not exist using logical reasoning and evidence as arguments against the existence of God.

Evil and suffering as an argument against the existence of God

Atheists may argue that the existence of **evil and suffering** in the world proves that God does not exist.

| There are many examples of evil and suffering in the world. | → | For example, people have painful illnesses and people are fighting and killing each other. | → | God is supposed to be:
• all-knowing (**omniscient**) so he knows it is happening
• all-loving (omnibenevolent) so he would want to stop it
• all-powerful (omnipotent) so he should be able to stop it. |

REVISION TIP

How can you remember the 'omnis'?

• omni*potent* – *powerful*
• omnibene*vol*ent – '*love*' backwards
• omni*sci*ent – '*science*' brings knowledge

However, he doesn't do this, so he clearly doesn't exist.

Responses to the argument of evil and suffering

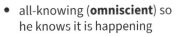

† Christian responses	☪ Muslim responses
• God can stop evil and suffering but he has given humans free will (as with Adam in Genesis 3) to behave how they want. They choose to cause evil and suffering themselves (e.g., war), so God will not interfere with **free will**. • We may not understand why God does not intervene, but we should behave in the most loving way to those that are suffering and we will be rewarded by him in the **afterlife**. • Life is a test and God wants to see how humans respond to such events. We will be rewarded for our positive actions in the afterlife. • Allowing evil and suffering means that humans can learn from mistakes and work together to make the world a better place, instead of thinking it's all God's job.	• The Qur'an says: ❝ *God does not burden any soul with more than it can bear.* ❞ (Qur'an 2:286) This shows that we have the ability to handle the suffering that we may have in life. • Shaytan (the source of evil) tries to tempt humans to sin but we should put our trust in God. ❝ *Beware of Shaytan, he is desperate to divert you from the worship of Allah, so beware of him in matters of religion.* ❞ (Hadith) • Life is a test and God wants to see if humans stay on the straight path of Islam. We will be rewarded if we resist evil. • We may not understand why God does not intervene but we should behave in the most loving way ourselves and we will be rewarded by him in the afterlife. God is just and wise and knows best when and why certain things happen.

29 C: Arguments against the existence of God

Arguments against the existence of God based on science

In the past people have used the existence of God to help answer big questions such as:

- How did the universe get here?
- How did humans get here?
- What happens when we die?

↓

Scientific knowledge has advanced so now we have the answers to many of these questions.

↓

While science doesn't have the answers to everything yet, it has shown so far that none of them rely on the existence of God.

↓

We no longer need to believe in the existence of God to answer these questions – science will answer them.

REVISION TIP

Draw a table with two columns. Label the first column 'Arguments for the existence of God' and the second column 'Arguments against the existence of God'. See if you can write 3 arguments in each column.

Responses to the arguments based on science

† Christian	†☾ Both Christian and Muslim	☾ Muslim
Some Christians reject the scientific argument as they believe the Genesis version of creation is literally true: ❝ *In the beginning God created the heavens and the earth* ❞ (Genesis 1:1)	• Scientific accounts do not necessarily conflict with the holy book. • God created science for humans to use to their advantage and it reveals his creation to us. • Science cannot disprove the existence of God. • Science can tell us 'how' things work and religion (God) can tell us 'why'.	Some Muslims reject the scientific argument as the Qur'an gives humans what they need to know about the **creation** of the universe: ❝ *Are the disbelievers not aware that the heavens and the earth used to be joined together and that We [God] ripped them apart, that We [God] made every living thing from water?* ❞ (Qur'an 21:30)

 Key terms — Make sure you can write a definition for these key terms

evil and suffering   omniscient   free will   afterlife   creation

Retrieval

29

Learn the answers to the questions below, then cover the answers column with a piece of paper and write down as many as you can. Check and repeat.

Questions / Answers

#	Questions	Answers
1	What word means that God is all-powerful?	Omnipotent
2	What word means that God is all-knowing?	Omniscient
3	What does omnibenevolent mean?	All-loving
4	Who do Muslims believe tries to tempt humans to come off the straight path and to sin?	Shaytan (the source of evil)
5	Give a quotation from the Qur'an which demonstrates to Muslims that humans have the ability to deal with any suffering they might have in life.	*"God does not burden any soul with more than it can bear."*
6	What term means that humans can choose how they behave (without interference from God)?	Free will
7	In which book of the Bible is the account of creation?	Genesis
8	Give one argument that Christians and Muslims might use to disagree with the scientific belief that there is no God.	One from: scientific accounts do not necessarily conflict with the holy book / God created science for humans to use to their advantage, and it reveals his creation to us / science cannot disprove the existence of God / science can tell us 'how' things work and religion (God) can tell us 'why'

(Put paper here)

Previous questions

Now go back and use these questions to check your knowledge of previous topics.

Questions / Answers

#	Questions	Answers
9	What are the most important examples of miracles in the Bible?	The incarnation and resurrection of Jesus
10	What might a Muslim say about the Design argument?	Everything in the universe is perfectly balanced, designed with purpose, and beautifully complex, the Qur'an teaches that God is omnipotent, and therefore he is the designer of the universe
11	What is another name for the First Cause argument?	The Cosmological argument
12	What word means that God is beyond nature, the earth, and the universe?	Transcendent
13	What is the name of the event when Muhammad ascended to heaven?	The Night Journey (Al-Isra' wal-Mi'raj)

(Put paper here)

Practice

Exam-style questions

01 Which **one** of these means that God is all-loving?

Put a tick (✓) in the box next to the correct answer. **(1 mark)**

A   Omnipotent ☐

B   Omniscient ☐

C   Omnibenevolent ☐

D   Omnipresent ☐

02 Which **one** of these is the belief that humans can choose how they behave without interference from God?

Put a tick (✓) in the box next to the correct answer. **(1 mark)**

A   Free will ☐

B   Creation ☐

C   Sin ☐

D   Natural selection ☐

> **EXAM TIP**
> Check all four possible answers carefully before you select the correct answer.

03 Give **two** Christian responses to evil and suffering. **(2 marks)**

04 Give **two** reasons why science may challenge the existence of God. **(2 marks)**

05 Explain **two** similar beliefs about evil and suffering as an argument against the existence of God.

In your answer you must refer to one or more religious traditions. **(4 marks)**

06 Explain **two** religious responses to the arguments against the existence of God based on science.

Refer to sacred writings or another source of religious belief and teaching in your answer. **(5 marks)**

> **EXAM TIP**
> Remember – you must name the sacred writing or source of authority that is in your answer, e.g., 'The Bible says…', 'The Qur'an says…'. If you use a quotation, you don't need to state the chapter or verse.

07 'Science gives all the answers to questions we have about the universe.'

Evaluate this statement.

In your answer you:

- should give reasoned arguments in support of this statement
- should give reasoned arguments to support a different point of view
- should refer to religious arguments
- may refer to non-religious arguments
- should reach a justified conclusion. **(12 marks)**

(+ SPaG 3 marks)

30 C: The nature of the divine and revelation

Revelation means the way that God can show himself to humans. Whilst not all religions have a God or gods, they have an ultimate reality which does not change. These can be called the 'divine', and there are different ways that humans can experience the divine.

Special revelation

- **Special revelation** is when a person directly experiences God in an extraordinary event.
- This is often life changing and sometimes convinvces a person to convert to a religion.
- However, Christians believe these experiences are rare, and many people are committed Christians without experiencing a special revelation.

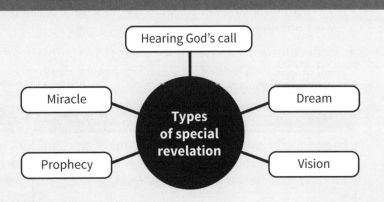

✝ Special revelation in Christianity

- In the Bible, the angel Gabriel visited Mary to tell her she would become pregnant with God's son, Jesus:

> **❝** *You will conceive and give birth to a son, and you are to call him Jesus.* **❞**
> (Luke 1:31)

- Jesus performed miracles:

> **❝** *Jesus reached out his hand and touched the man. 'I am willing,' he said. 'Be clean!' Immediately he was cleansed of his leprosy.* **❞**   (Matthew 8:3)

- God told Aaron and Miriam:

> **❝** *Hear my words: If there is a prophet among you, I the LORD make myself known to him in a vision, I speak with him in a dream.* **❞**   (Numbers 12:6)

☪ Special revelation in Islam

- Muslims say it was a special revelation when Muhammad received the Qur'an from God via the angel Jibril (Qur'an 96:1-5) and because he is a prophet and God's messenger it can also be called divine revelation.
- Muslims may feel that they are nearer to God through dreams, **visions**, or miracles but they will never experience a divine revelation as these ended with Muhammad as the final prophet.

Knowledge

30 C: The nature of the divine and revelation

Visions

- A vision is a supernatural experience when a person sees something in a dream or a trance that shows them something about God or life after death. In this special revelation, they may see a special person, an angel, or even hear the voice of God.
- Some atheists attribute people's visions to lack of sleep or the effects of mind-altering intoxicants, for example, drugs.
- Both Christianity and Islam see visions as a spiritual experience but will only accept them if they don't go against the key beliefs as given in the Bible/Qur'an.

† Visions in Christianity	☪ Visions in Islam
An example of a vision in Christianity is the conversion of St Paul. Before his conversion, St Paul was known as Saul and he persecuted followers of Jesus. ❝ *As he [Saul] neared Damascus … a light from heaven flashed around him. He fell to the ground and heard a voice say to him, 'Saul, Saul, why do you persecute me?' 'Who are you, Lord?' Saul asked. 'I am Jesus, whom you are persecuting,' he replied. 'Now get up and go into the city, and you will be told what you must do.' Saul got up from the ground, but when he opened his eyes he could see nothing.* ❞ (Acts 9:1–8)	Visions in Islam are not special revelations, rather they are a spiritual experience that a person may have. Seeing an angel, for example, Muhammad seeing Jibril on the Night of Power, is not classed as a vision but is a divine revelation as God revealed the Qur'an to Muhammad.

Enlightenment as a source of knowledge of the divine

- **Enlightenment** is a concept often associated with religions such as Buddhism.
- As most Buddhists do not believe in one divine being such as God, there is no special revelation.
- However, they believe humans can achieve a state of 'enlightenment' where they understand the ultimate reality (the divine) by gaining true knowledge of life and suffering.
- Some Buddhists believe this can be achieved through meditation and self-discipline.

General revelation

- **General (or indirect) revelation** is when God shows himself through everyday, ordinary life experiences. This can happen to anybody at any time.

Examples of general revelation

> Looking at nature and feeling God's presence

> A person's conscience telling them right and wrong

> Reading a holy text and being inspired by God

> Worshipping God

> The lives of religious leaders that reflect God's purpose in life

Nature as a way of understanding the divine

- Nature can provide us with many special experiences.

- Christians and Muslims believe that these are down to God and can create a sense of awe and wonder.

- God's creation helps humans to understand him more, for example, the stars in the sky on a clear night or a powerful storm can remind us of God's omnipotence.

† The Bible:

> 66 *The heavens declare the glory of God; the skies proclaim the work of his hands.* 99
>
> (Psalm 19:1)

☾ The Qur'an:

> 66 *Among His signs, too, are that He shows you the lightning that terrifies and inspires hope; that He sends water down from the sky to restore the earth to life after death.* 99
>
> (Qur'an 30:24)

- However, some atheists would say that nature is not evidence of God but proof that science is complex and powerful in itself.

Scripture as a way of understanding the divine

- Both Christians and Muslims believe their holy books help them to understand God.

- Whilst he may be ineffable (too great or extreme to be expressed or described in words) the stories and teachings in the holy books can give a sense of what God wants for his creation and how he expects humans to behave.

- Some atheists say that religious texts were written by humans and therefore aren't inspired by a God, nor do they tell them anything about God.

✝ Reading the Bible helps Christians understand God's nature:

> 66 *The God who made the world and everything in it is the Lord of heaven and earth and does not live in temples built by human hands. And he is not served by human hands, as if he needed anything. Rather, he himself gives everyone life and breath and everything else.* 99
>
> (Acts 17:24–25)

However, Christians can read and interpret the Bible in different ways:

- Some take it literally as God's words and as an exact account of what has happened and will happen, so the words shouldn't be changed

- Others believe the Bible is inspired by God but is often symbolic and has a spiritual rather than literal meaning to inspire humans to how they might live.

☪ Reciting the Qur'an helps Muslims to feel God's presence:

> 66 *This is the **Scripture** in which there is no doubt, containing guidance for those who are mindful of God.* 99
>
> (Qur'an 2:2)

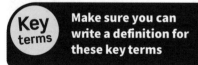

Key terms	Make sure you can write a definition for these key terms	revelation special revelation visions enlightenment general (or indirect) revelation scripture

Learn the answers to the questions below, then cover the answers column with a piece of paper and write down as many as you can. Check and repeat.

Questions | Answers

	Questions		Answers
1	Name one type of special revelation.	Put paper here	One from: dream / miracle / prophecy / vision
2	How might some atheists interpret special revelation?		As a result of lack of sleep, the effects of intoxicants (e.g., drugs)
3	Give an example of a general revelation.	Put paper here	One from: looking at nature and feeling God's presence / reading a holy text and being inspired by God / worshipping God / a person's conscience telling them right and wrong / the lives of religious leaders that reflect God's purpose in life
4	Which type of revelation is when God shows himself through everyday, ordinary life experiences?		General revelation
5	Which holy book do Christians use to help them understand God?	Put paper here	The Bible
6	Which holy book do Muslims use to help them understand God?		The Qur'an
7	Who, in the Bible, experienced a vision of Jesus whilst walking on the road to Damascus?	Put paper here	Saul/St Paul
8	Name one way in which the Bible can be interpreted.		One from: literally / symbolically / spiritually
9	Which word means that God is too great or extreme to be expressed or described in words?	Put paper here	Ineffable
10	What word means understanding the ultimate reality (the divine) by gaining true knowledge of life and suffering?		Enlightenment

Previous questions

Now go back and use these questions to check your knowledge of previous topics.

Questions | Answers

	Questions		Answers
11	At which town in France do Catholic Christians believe that healing miracles occur?	Put paper here	Lourdes
12	What word means that God is all-powerful?		Omnipotent
13	What word means that God is all-knowing?		Omniscient
14	What does omnibenevolent mean?		All-loving

Exam-style questions

01 Which **one** of these is when a person directly experiences God in an extraordinary event?

Put a tick (✓) in the box next to the correct answer. **(1 mark)**

A Special revelation ☐

B Scriptural revelation ☐

C Nature ☐

D Enlightenment ☐

02 Which **one** of these is a supernatural experience when a person sees something in a dream or a trance that shows them something about God or life after death?

Put a tick (✓) in the box next to the correct answer. **(1 mark)**

A Miracle ☐

B Vision ☐

C Enlightenment ☐

D General Revelation ☐

03 Give **two** different ideas about the divine. **(2 marks)**

04 Explain **two** contrasting beliefs about nature as general revelation.

In your answer you must refer to one or more religious traditions. **(4 marks)**

05 Explain **two** contrasting beliefs about visions.

In your answer you must refer to one or more religious traditions. **(4 marks)**

> **EXAM TIP** ◎
> Write your answer in two clear paragraphs.

06 Explain **two** religious beliefs about scripture as a way of understanding the divine.

Refer to sacred writings or another source of religious belief and teaching in your answer. **(5 marks)**

> **EXAM TIP** ◎
> Be clear what religious views you are writing about so the examiner knows if your answer is correct.

07 'We can see the divine through the natural world around us.'

Evaluate this statement.

In your answer you:

- should give reasoned arguments in support of this statement
- should give reasoned arguments to support a different point of view
- should refer to religious arguments
- may refer to non-religious arguments
- should reach a justified conclusion. **(12 marks)**

(+ SPaG 3 marks)

31 C: Ideas about the divine and the value of revelation and enlightenment

Ideas about the divine

For Christians and Muslims, God has certain qualities that may help them to understand his nature.

† For Christians, the Bible gives them examples of how God works and his relationship with humans.

☾ For Muslims these are exemplified in the 99 names of God and in the Qur'an. However, the belief in Tawhid (the oneness of God) means that these can only ever be superficial in understanding God's nature.

Ideas about the divine from scripture

Quality	Meaning	Example from holy books
Omnipotent	God is all-powerful and almighty; he can do anything.	" *God has power to do everything.* " (Qur'an 2:148)
Omniscient	God is all-knowing. He knows everything that has happened and will happen.	" *Great is our Lord and mighty in power; his understanding has no limit.* " (Psalm 147:5)
Personal	God is close to humans and has a relationship with them due to his human characteristics.	" *We [God] created man – We [God] know what his soul whispers to him: We [God] are closer to him than his jugular vein.* " (Qur'an 50:16)
Impersonal	God is not like humans and is unknowable.	" *How great is God – beyond our understanding!* " (Job 36:26)
Immanent	God is within and involved in his creation (the universe). Humans can experience God in their lives.	" *So praise be to God, Lord of the heavens and earth, Lord of the worlds. True greatness in the heavens and the earth is rightfully His: He is the Mighty, the Wise.* " (Qur'an 45:36–37)
Transcendent	God is beyond and outside of his creation (the universe). He is not limited by the world, time, or space.	" *As the heavens are higher than the earth, so are my ways higher than your ways and my thoughts than your thoughts.* " (Isaiah 55:9)

> **REVISION TIP**
>
> Make a set of 18 cards: six with words that describe the divine, six with the definitions, and six with an example from a holy book. Mix them up and match them. Check to see if you have matched them correctly.

 # Knowledge

31 C: Ideas about the divine and the value of revelation and enlightenment

The value of general and special revelation, and enlightenment

- For some it strengthens their belief in the divine as it proves its existence.
- For others it brings them closer to the divine.
- Some types of revelation can help people to understand the divine more.
- For theists, it can show them how God wants them to live their lives.

Problems arising from these experiences

- Some people will question these experiences and ask if they actually happened or if they were really caused by the divine.
- If the person did experience something, then maybe it was an illusion?
- Many of these experiences lack scientific evidence and therefore are difficult to prove.

How can someone know if an experience is real?

We could ask:

- Does it support or contradict the main beliefs and teachings of the religion?
- Does it match previously reported experiences within the religion?
- Does it change a person's beliefs or outlook on life?

- Does it have the power to make someone join a religion?
- Is it something that seems possible within the real world or within the limits of what a religion says can happen?

> **REVISION TIP**
>
> Research real life examples and write down questions that you could ask the person or people involved to help you understand the event. Think about what answers you think they might give.
>
> This will help you to remember the kinds of questions we can ask about these experiences.

Alternative explanations for these experiences

- Some say that general revelation, special revelation, and enlightenment are not actual experiences of the divine.
- Some atheists would say that God is not responsible and that there are alternative explanations for these experiences.

Some experiences can be associated with mental or physical illnesses.

The effects of taking intoxicants, such as drugs or alcohol.

Alternative explanations

People mistake the cause, for example, a healing miracle could be medicine having an unexpected impact on an ill person, not God healing them.

Wishful thinking – some people really want to have an experience.

People lie about their experiences to gain popularity, fame, or money.

Key terms Make sure you can write a definition for these key terms

personal   impersonal   immanent

Learn the answers to the questions below, then cover the answers column with a piece of paper and write down as many as you can. Check and repeat.

Questions / Answers

	Questions		Answers
1	Which belief in Islam means that the names of God can only ever be superficial in understanding God's nature.	Put paper here	Tawhid (the oneness of God)
2	What quotation from the Qur'an demonstrates to Muslims that God is all-powerful?		*"God has power to do everything."*
3	Which quotation from the Bible shows that God is all-knowing?		*"Great is our Lord and mighty in power; his understanding has no limit."*
4	Which word means that God is close to humans and has a relationship with them due to his human characteristics?	Put paper here	Personal
5	Which word means that God is not like humans and is unknowable?		Impersonal
6	What quotation from the Bible demonstrates that God is not like humans and is unknowable?	Put paper here	*"How great is God – beyond our understanding!"*
7	Which word means that God is within and involved in his creation (the universe)?		Immanent
8	Which word means that God is beyond and outside of his creation (the universe)?		Transcendent
9	How many names for God are there in Islam?	Put paper here	99
10	Give one reason why a general/special revelation may be important to a theist.		One from: it strengthens their belief in the divine / it brings them closer to the divine / it can help people to understand the divine better / it can show them how God wants them to live their lives

Previous questions

Now go back and use these questions to check your knowledge of previous topics.

Questions / Answers

	Questions		Answers
8	What is the strongest evidence for the existence of God in Islam?	Put paper here	The revelation of the Qur'an to Muhammad
9	Give a quotation from the Qur'an which demonstrates to Muslims that humans have the ability to deal with any suffering they might have in life.		*"God does not burden any soul with more than it can bear."*
10	What phrase means that humans can choose how they behave (without interference from God)?	Put paper here	Free will

Practice

Exam-style questions

01 Which **one** of these means that God is beyond and outside of his creation (the universe)?

Put a tick (✔) in the box next to the correct answer. **(1 mark)**

A	Omnipotent	☐
B	Omniscient	☐
C	Immanent	☐
D	Transcendent	☐

02 Which **one** of these means that God is all-powerful and almighty; he can do anything?

Put a tick (✔) in the box next to the correct answer. **(1 mark)**

A	Personal	☐
B	Transcendent	☐
C	Omniscient	☐
D	Omnipotent	☐

03 Give **two** religious beliefs about God. **(2 marks)**

04 Give **two** alternative explanations for visions. **(2 marks)**

05 Explain **two** similar religious beliefs about general revelation.

In your answer you must refer to one or more religious traditions. **(4 marks)**

> **EXAM TIP**
>
> A 4-mark question requires two developed points. Show the examiner you have done this by writing in two paragraphs.

06 Explain **two** religious beliefs about special revelation.

Refer to sacred writings or another source of religious belief and teaching in your answer. **(5 marks)**

> **EXAM TIP**
>
> Make sure you include religious teachings in your answer.

07 'The only explanation for visions is that they were caused by the divine.'

Evaluate this statement.

In your answer you:

- should give reasoned arguments in support of this statement
- should give reasoned arguments to support a different point of view
- should refer to religious arguments
- may refer to non-religious arguments
- should reach a justified conclusion. **(12 marks)**

(+ SPaG 3 marks)

Knowledge

32 D: Peace, justice, forgiveness, and reconciliation

Peace

† Christian views	☾ Muslim views

Whilst the Bible includes accounts of times when there was not peace, Jesus often promoted peace.
 	
   66 *Blessed are the peacemakers, for they will be called children of God.* 99   (Matthew 5:9)
	• One of the meanings of the Arabic word 'Islam' is peace.
	• Muslims often greet each other by saying 'as-salamu alaikum', meaning 'peace be with you'.
	
	   66 *The servants of the Lord of Mercy are those who walk humbly on the earth, and who, when aggressive people address them, reply with words of peace.* 99 (Qur'an 25:63)

Justice

† Christian views	☾ Muslim views

God is just and expects humans to also be just in their treatment of each other.
 	
   66 *But let justice roll on like a river, righteousness like a never-failing stream!* 99   (Amos 5:24)
	• God is just and will treat people fairly on the Day of Judgement.
	• We should also treat others justly.
	
	   66 *Do not let hatred of others lead you away from justice, but adhere to justice, for that is closer to awareness of God.* 99 (Qur'an 5:8)

Forgiveness

† Christian views	☾ Muslim views

• Forgiveness (showing grace and mercy and pardoning someone for what they have done wrong) is an important part of being a Christian.
• Jesus died on the cross so that human sins can be forgiven by God.
• Jesus also told people that they should forgive others.
 	
   66 *Then Peter came to Jesus and asked, 'Lord, how many times shall I forgive my brother or sister who sins against me? Up to seven times?' Jesus answered, 'I tell you, not seven times, but seventy-seven* times.* 99   (Matthew 18:21–22)
 	
*Note: some translations use 'seventy times seven'.
	• Forgiveness is important as God is all-forgiving and all-merciful.
	• The Qur'an says we should pardon someone for what they've done wrong.
	
	   66 *...ask forgiveness of God: He is most forgiving and merciful.* 99 (Qur'an 2:199)

Knowledge

32 D: Peace, justice, forgiveness, and reconciliation

Reconciliation

✝ Christian views	☪ Muslim views
• Christianity is based on reconciliation between humans and God, following their separation due to the Fall and their personal sin. • Christians are encouraged to 'Love your neighbour', and Jesus said: ❝ *Love your enemies and pray for those that persecute you.* ❞ (Matthew 5:44) • For Catholics the sacrament of reconciliation (Confession) allows humans to ask God for forgiveness and for them to reconcile with God.	• The Qur'an and Hadith support the idea that humans should reconcile with one another if they have fallen out. • If a couple want to divorce, there is a period of time to wait to see if they can reconcile. ❝ *Shall I tell you of something that is better than fasting, prayer, and charity? [It is] reconciling between two people.* ❞ (Hadith)

Violence

- **Violence** may be used for:
  - retaliation
  - defence
  - protesting against something.
- It may be justified by some Christians who believe in 'an eye for an eye' and by Muslims as part of the **Lesser Jihad** (defending threats to faith, family, and community).
- Others will be against violence as Christians believe that Jesus said to 'turn the other cheek,' and Muslims believe that there is a Hadith that says to 'Hate your enemy mildly'.

Terrorism

Terrorism is the unlawful use of violence, usually against innocent civilians, to achieve a political goal. Both Christianity and Islam have teachings that show that terrorism is not acceptable:

✝ Christianity – Jesus said:

❝ *Love your enemies and pray for those that persecute you.* ❞ (Matthew 5:44)

☪ Islam – terrorism doesn't follow the rules for a Holy War. Muslims are against the killing of innocent people:

❝ *Whoever kills a human is as if he has killed the whole of mankind* ❞ (Qur'an 5:32)

 Key terms Make sure you can write a definition for these key terms

violence   Lesser Jihad   terrorism

Retrieval

Learn the answers to the questions below, then cover the answers column with a piece of paper and write as many as you can. Check and repeat.

Questions

Answers

	Questions	Answers
1	True or false: one of the meanings of the Arabic word 'Islam' is peace.	True
2	Which quotation from the Qur'an shows Muslims that they should treat people fairly?	"Do not let hatred of others lead you away from justice, but adhere to justice, for that is closer to awareness of God."
3	What did Jesus do so that human sins can be forgiven by God?	He died on the cross
4	Christianity is based on reconciliation between humans and God, following their separation for what two reasons?	The Fall, personal sin
5	Give a quotation from the Bible where Jesus promotes peace.	"Blessed are the peacemakers, for they will be called children of God."
6	What is the Arabic phrase for 'peace be with you'?	As-salamu alaikum
7	According to Islam, when will God judge us fairly?	On the Day of Judgement
8	How many times did Jesus say someone should forgive?	77 (or seventy times seven)
9	What does this quotation from the Bible tell Christians? "But let justice roll on like a river, righteousness like a never-failing stream!"	God is just and expects humans to be just in their treatment of each other
10	What is the sacrament of reconciliation in Catholic Christianity also known as?	Confession
11	Give a quotation that encourages Christians to reconcile with one another.	"Love your enemies and pray for those that persecute you."
12	In the Hadith, what does Muhammad say is more important than fasting, prayer, and giving to charity?	Reconciliation between two people
13	Give a quotation from the Qur'an which shows Muslims that killing of innocent people us wrong.	"Whoever kills a human is as if he has killed the whole of mankind"
14	Give one situation in which the use of violence might be acceptable to Christians and Muslims.	One from: retaliation / defence / protesting against something

Put paper here

Practice

Exam-style questions

01 Which **one** of these means showing grace and mercy and pardoning someone for what they have done wrong?

Put a tick (✓) in the box next to the correct answer. **(1 mark)**

A	Peace	☐
B	Justice	☐
C	Forgiveness	☐
D	Reconciliation	☐

02 Which **one** of these is unlawful use of violence, usually against innocent civilians, to achieve a political goal? **(1 mark)**

A	Terrorism	☐
B	Protest	☐
C	War	☐
D	Pacifism	☐

03 Give **two** religious beliefs about forgiveness. **(2 marks)**

04 Give **two** religious beliefs about justice. **(2 marks)**

05 Explain **two** similar religious beliefs on peace.

In your answer you must refer to one or more religious traditions. **(4 marks)**

> **EXAM TIP** ⌖
> Develop two points to make two paragraphs.

06 Explain **two** religious beliefs about reconciliation.

Refer to sacred writings or another source of religious belief and teaching in your answer. **(5 marks)**

> **EXAM TIP** ⌖
> Remember, you must name a sacred writing or source of authority in your answer, for example, the Bible. If you are quoting, you don't need to state the exact chapter or verse.

07 'If you fall out with someone you should always reconcile with them afterwards.'

Evaluate this statement.

In your answer you:

- should give reasoned arguments in support of this statement
- should give reasoned arguments to support a different point of view
- should refer to religious arguments
- may refer to non-religious arguments
- should reach a justified conclusion. **(12 marks)**

(+ SPaG 3 marks)

33 D: War

Reasons for war

Greed (e.g., acquisition of land, oil, assets)

† Christian views	☾★ Muslim views
Some Christians may be against war if it is for reasons of greed because: ❝ *For the love of money is a root of all kinds of evil. Some people, eager for money, have wandered from the faith and pierced themselves with many griefs.* ❞ (1 Timothy 6:10)	Some Muslims would be against war if it is for greed: ❝ *God does not like arrogant, boastful people, who are miserly and order other people to be the same, hiding the bounty God has given them.* ❞ (Qur'an 4:36–37)

Self-defence

† Christian views	☾★ Muslim views
Some Christians may accept war if it is to help those who are being persecuted: ❝ *Defend the weak and the fatherless; uphold the cause of the poor and the oppressed.* *Rescue the weak and the needy; deliver them from the hand of the wicked.* ❞ (Psalm 82:3–4)	Some Muslims may agree with war for reasons of self-defence because: ❝ *Those who have been attacked are permitted to take up arms because they have been wronged – God has the power to help them.* ❞ (Qur'an 22:39)

Retaliation (getting back at someone for something they have done to you)

† Christian views	☾★ Muslim views
Some Christians may not agree with retaliation because: ❝ *Do not repay anyone evil for evil. ... If it is possible, as far as it depends on you, live at peace with everyone.* ❞ (Romans 12:17–19) ❝ *If anyone slaps you on the right cheek, turn to them the other cheek also.* ❞ (Matthew 5:39) Some Christians may refer to the Old Testament 'an eye for an eye' to support proportionate retaliation.	Some Muslims may agree with retaliation because: ❝ *If you [believers] have to respond to an attack, make your response proportionate, but it is best to stand fast.* ❞ (Qur'an 16:126) ❝ *...there is cause to act against those who oppress people and transgress in the land against all justice ... though if a person is patient and forgives, this is one of the greatest things.* ❞ (Qur'an 42:43) However, Islam teaches that retaliation in war must be measured, and that forgiveness is always the best response to avoid war.

REVISION TIP

There are many reasons for war but they will generally come under these three headings so concentrate on these.

✿ Knowledge

33 D: War

The just war theory

- The **just war** theory gives criteria for when war can be justified and therefore can be seen as an ethical war.
- It is generally considered to be based on Christian beliefs, so can be used to justify war by some Christians.

Criteria for a just war:

- Just cause
- The intention must be to defeat wrongdoing and promote good
- Reasonable chance of success
- Declared by a recognised authority
- Last resort – all other ways of resolving the issue, such as diplomacy, must have been attempted before war can be declared
- Proportional methods – no excessive force and innocent civilians not harmed.

✝ Christian views	☾ Muslim views
☑ Some Christians would agree with the just war criteria as it allows for war to be the last resort and might be used to protect the weak. ☒ Some Christians do not accept the just war theory because, particularly in modern times, it often causes unnecessary death, and it is almost impossible to fulfil all the criteria in real-life conflicts.	☑ Many Muslims would agree with the conditions for a just war if the recognised authority was Islamic. The criteria are very similar to those for Lesser Jihad that can be used in defence. ☒ Some Muslims would say that the conditions can never be met so it will never be just.

Holy war

- A **holy war** is a war that is fought 'for God', in the name of a religion.
- It is often thought to give those involved religious benefits, such as removal of sins or access to heaven.

✝ Holy war in Christianity

In Christianity, a holy war is one that is started by a leading Christian authority and has the purpose of defending Christianity. There are spiritual rewards for those who fight.

The Crusades (1095–1291)

- Christians travelled to Jerusalem in the Holy Land to claim the land from Muslim groups.
- Both sides believed that they were fighting for God.

✝ The Christian Crusaders were told by the ruling Pope that their sins would be forgiven, so even if they died along the way, they could access heaven.	☾ The Muslims would have considered it a Lesser Jihad as they were fighting in the defence of Islam.

☾ Holy war in Islam

A holy war in Islam is often linked to the concept of the Lesser Jihad.

Last resort – negotiations have failed.

A religious concept so the decision to fight should be made by a community leader.

Attack on an Islamic community – Muslims are allowed to join a conflict to help another Muslim community.

No women, children, or elderly to be killed.

Conditions for Lesser Jihad

Self-defence – only defence and protection are allowed, not attacking.

Just cause – not started for gain but only to defend or protect.

Protection – allowed to fight in support of other Muslims who are being persecuted.

No crops or trees to be damaged.

- Muhammad 'struggled' to defend Islam in Makkah, so Muslims believe fighting is sometimes acceptable.

- As with a just war, the Lesser Jihad has specific conditions that must be fulfilled for it to be allowed, and then once the war has started, conditions that need to be met. Modern weapons make this more difficult.

- Shi'a Muslims believe that the offensive Jihad can only be led and declared by the Imam, who is chosen by God.

- Islam teaches that fighting for God will be rewarded:

> **66** *Let those of you who are willing to trade the life of this world for the life to come, fight in God's way. To anyone who fights in God's way, whether killed or victorious, We shall give a great reward.* **99** (Qur'an 4:74)

- Some Muslims believe that the conditions for Lesser Jihad are rarely met.

- Some Muslims believe that these conditions no longer apply today, when war is more complex and weapons are very different. Also, they think that the conditions were created for the time when Muhammad and the Muslims were under attack. Muhammad told the Muslims when they returned from war:

> **66** *We have finished the Lesser Jihad, let us now focus on the* **Greater Jihad.** **99** (Hadith)

> **REVISION TIP** ☑
>
> Some of the conditions for Lesser Jihad are similar to the just war criteria.
>
> Make a chart with 3 headings: same; similar; different. Write the conditions for Lesser Jihad and the just war criteria in the correct column to help you remember them.

Pacifism

- A pacifist believes that we should not fight or use violence to resolve issues.
- Pacifists are against war.
- The arguments in favour of **pacifism** are often those given against war and vice versa.

 # Knowledge

33 D: War

Arguments for and against pacifism

Arguments in favour of pacifism (against war)	**Arguments against pacifism**
☑ In war, people are killed unnecessarily, and often innocent civilians are injured or killed.	☒ Other countries may see you as weak if you don't defend yourself.
☑ We can use diplomacy and negotiation to resolve issues.	☒ In the past, it has taken wars to stop injustice and remove tyrannical leaders.
☑ Weapons today (e.g., nuclear weapons) can harm large areas and cause damage way beyond their initial target.	☒ We should defend the weak and those who are being treated unfairly.

REVISION TIP

Be careful using 'You shall not murder' when talking about war. Is killing in war classed as murder? Many would say it isn't.

Christian and Muslim views on pacifism

✝ Christian views

☒ Some Christians use the Old Testament 'eye for an eye' to justify retaliation.

☑ However, this can be countered by Jesus saying,

> 66 *You have heard that it was said, 'Eye for eye, and tooth for tooth.' But I tell you, do not resist an evil person. If anyone slaps you on the right cheek, turn to them the other cheek also.* 99   (Matthew 5:38)

☒ Other Christians say that when Jesus turned over the tables in the temple (Matthew 21:12), it shows that he accepted violent protest.

☑ Some Christians argue that Jesus was a pacifist. Jesus told people:

> 66 *For all who draw the sword will die by the sword.* 99   (Matthew 26:52)

Some Christians take this to mean they shouldn't fight.

☾ Muslim views

☒ Many Muslims do not agree with pacifism as:
- Muhammad fought in wars
- the Lesser Jihad allows wars as long as they meet certain conditions.

☑ Muhammad said,

> 66 *We have finished the Lesser Jihad, let us now focus on the Greater Jihad.* 99   (Hadith)

Some Muslims believe this shows that he wanted Muslims to stop the fighting and focus on their inner struggle.

☑ Some Muslims might also say that war has changed so much since early Islamic times that the conditions aren't appropriate for today, and so we shouldn't fight to resolve issues.

 Key terms Make sure you can write a definition for these key terms

just war   holy war   Greater Jihad   pacifism

Learn the answers to the questions below, then cover the answers column with a piece of paper and write as many as you can. Check and repeat.

Questions	Answers
1 Give one reason for war.	One from: greed / retaliation / self-defence
2 Give a quotation where Jesus encourages Christians not to retaliate.	One from: *"Do not repay anyone evil for evil. ... If it is possible, as far as it depends on you, live at peace with everyone."* / *"If anyone slaps you on the right cheek, turn to them the other cheek also."*
3 True or false: the just war theory is not considered to be based on Christian principles.	False - the just war theory is generally considered to be based on Christian principles.
4 Give one criteria for a just war.	One from: the war must have a just cause / it must be declared by a recognised authority / the intention of the war has to be to defeat wrongdoing and promote good / fighting must be a last resort / there must be a reasonable chance of success / proportional methods used / innocent civilians should not be harmed
5 What is a war that is fought 'for God' or for a religion?	Holy war
6 What did Muhammad tell Muslims to do when they returned from war?	*"We have finished the Lesser Jihad, let us now focus on the Greater Jihad."*
7 What is the word for a person who believes we should not fight or use violence to resolve issues?	Pacifist
8 What did Jesus do that some Christians may say shows he supported violent protest?	Turned the tables in the temple
9 Which of Jesus's words do some Christians take to mean they should not fight?	*"For all who draw the sword will die by the sword."*

Put paper here

Previous questions

Now go back and use these questions to check your knowledge of previous topics.

Questions	Answers
10 Give a quotation from the Bible where Jesus promotes peace.	*"Blessed are the peacemakers, for they will be called children of God."*
11 What is the Arabic phrase for 'peace be with you'?	As-salamu alaikum
12 According to Islam, when will God judge us fairly?	On the Day of Judgement
13 How many times did Jesus say someone should forgive?	77 (or seventy times seven)

Put paper here

Practice

Exam-style questions

01 Which **one** of these is a theory that follows a set of criteria to make war fair and ethical?

Put a tick (✓) in the box next to the correct answer.   **(1 mark)**

A   Pacifism   ☐

B   Jihad   ☐

C   Just war   ☐

D   Holy war   ☐

02 Which **one** of these is the meaning of pacifism?

Put a tick (✓) in the box next to the correct answer.   **(1 mark)**

A   A war fought for God   ☐

B   A war fought for the right reasons   ☐

C   Forgiving those who fight with you   ☐

D   Not fighting or using violence to resolve issues   ☐

03 Give **two** reasons for war.   **(2 marks)**

04 Give **two** of the criteria for a just war.   **(2 marks)**

> **EXAM TIP**
> 'Contrasting' just means 'different' in these questions.

05 Explain **two** contrasting religious beliefs about pacifism in contemporary British society.

In your answer you should refer to the main religious tradition of Great Britain and one or more other religious traditions.   **(4 marks)**

> **EXAM TIP**
> A 4-mark question requires two developed points. Show the examiner you have done this by writing in two paragraphs.

06 Explain **two** religious beliefs about holy wars.

Refer to sacred writings or another source of religious belief and teaching in your answer.   **(5 marks)**

> **EXAM TIP**
> Make sure you have clearly evaluated in your answer.

07 'No religious person should be pacifist.'

Evaluate this statement.

In your answer you:

- should give reasoned arguments in support of this statement
- should give reasoned arguments to support a different point of view
- should refer to religious arguments
- may refer to non-religious arguments
- should reach a justified conclusion.   **(12 marks)**

          (+ SPaG 3 marks)

34 D: Religion and belief in 21st century conflict

Religion and belief as a cause of war and violence

Whilst not all wars and violence are caused by religion, there are conflicts and acts of violence in recent history that claim to be rooted in religious beliefs (although they often have other causes including political differences).

In many cases the perpetrators believe that they:

- are defending their religion
- are fighting for God
- will be rewarded by God.

Islamic state of Iraq and Syria (ISIS) invasion of Iraq and Syria

The Troubles in Northern Ireland 1968–1998

Conflicts and violence linked to religious belief

The Israeli–Palestinian conflict

Charlie Hebdo attack in Paris, 2015

Ariana Grande concert bombing in Manchester, 2017

Religion and peace-making in the contemporary world

The Peace People

The Peace People organisation was started in 1976 by Mairead Corrigan, Betty Williams, and Ciaran McKeown. They worked for peace in Northern Ireland.

They held **peace-making** activities such as marches to help people see that fighting and killing weren't necessary.

Corrigan and Williams won the Nobel Peace prize in 1976 for their work.

> **REVISION TIP** ☑
>
> You can study the examples here or others, but you must ensure that the people or organisation you write about has recently worked for peace.

Malala Yousafzai

Malala spoke out against the Taliban when she was a schoolgirl in Pakistan. She was targeted and shot in the head, surviving her injuries after treatment in England. She is a Muslim and has talked about her beliefs being important in her work. She received the Nobel Peace Prize in 2014, and has worked for peace-making by:

- speaking against terrorism and war
- asking Muslims to come together and follow the true message of Islam in the struggle for peace
- promoting education to overcome war and violence
- meeting with world leaders to encourage them to support peaceful methods of resolving conflict and support the education of girls.

34 D: Religion and belief in 21st century conflict

Religious responses to the victims of war

Religious groups and individuals may not be able to prevent war, but they can work to help the victims of war. They can do this by:

- giving shelter to those who have been displaced
- ensuring people have access to clean water
- helping to rebuild communities
- providing short- and long-term support to rebuild lives

- giving medicine and medical help
- supplying food to those in need
- giving emotional and mental health support to people who have had life-changing experiences
- arranging opportunities for education.

Christian Aid

Christian Aid is a religious organisation that helps victims of war. It was established in 1945 to help refugees from World War II.

What they do	Examples of where they have worked	Religious principles that support their work
<ul><li>Humanitarian relief.</li><li>Long-term development support for poor communities worldwide.</li><li>Tackling injustice.</li></ul>	<ul><li>Haiti earthquake.</li><li>Afghanistan crisis.</li><li>East Africa hunger crisis appeal.</li><li>Ukraine humanitarian appeal.</li></ul>	<ul><li>Christian Aid believe that everyone is equal in the sight of God and so they aim to end poverty around the world.</li></ul> christian **aid**

Islamic Relief

Islamic Relief is a religious organisation that helps victims of war. It was set up in 1984 by a group of medical doctors and activists.

What they do	Examples of where they have worked	Religious principles that support their work
<ul><li>Disaster and emergency response.</li><li>Promote sustainable economic and social development.</li></ul>	<ul><li>Pakistan flood.</li><li>Afghanistan crisis.</li><li>East Africa hunger crisis.</li><li>Save a Life in Gaza appeal.</li></ul>	Islamic Relief is guided by values and teachings of the Qur'an and the prophetic example (Sunnah). One of their focuses is social justice (Adl). Islamic Relief Worldwide

 Key terms Make sure you can write a definition for these key terms

peace-making

REVISION TIP

Check which organisations you are studying. If they are not mentioned above, set yourself a task to put what you've learnt into some bullet points like these.

Learn the answers to the questions below, then cover the answers column with a piece of paper and write as many as you can. Check and repeat.

Questions | Answers

#	Questions	Answers
1	Give one reason why people may believe that they should go to war for their religion.	One from: they are defending their religion / they are fighting for God / they will be rewarded by God
2	Give one example of conflicts/violence in recent history that are rooted in religious beliefs.	One from: Islamic state of Iraq and Syria (ISIS) invasion of Iraq and Syria / The Israeli–Palestinian conflict / The Troubles in Northern Ireland 1968–1998 / Charlie Hebdo attack in Paris, 2015 / Ariana Grande concert bombing in Manchester, 2017
3	Name one place and event where Christian Aid have provided support.	One from: Haiti earthquake / Afghanistan crisis / East Africa hunger crisis / Ukraine humanitarian appeal
4	How can religious groups and individuals respond to war?	By working to help victims
5	Name one place and event where Islamic Relief have provided support.	One from: Pakistan flood / Afghanistan crisis / East Africa hunger crisis / Save a Life in Gaza appeal
6	Where does the organisation 'The Peace People' work for peace?	Northern Ireland
7	Give one way in which Malala Yousafzai has worked for peace-making.	One from: speaking against terrorism and war / asking Muslims to come together and follow the true message of Islam in the struggle for peace / promoting education to overcome war and violence / meeting with world leaders to encourage them to support peaceful methods of resolving conflict and support the education of girls

Put paper here (repeated in the centre divider)

Previous questions

Now go back and use these questions to check your knowledge of previous topics.

Questions | Answers

#	Questions	Answers
8	What did Muhammad tell Muslims to do when they returned from war?	*"We have finished the Lesser Jihad, let us now focus on the Greater Jihad."*
9	Give one reason for war.	One from: greed / retaliation / self-defence
10	What is the word for a person who believes we should not fight or use violence to resolve issues?	Pacifist
11	What is a war that is fought 'for God' or for a religion?	Holy war
12	What did Jesus do that some Christians may say shows he supported violent protest?	Turned the tables in the temple

Put paper here (repeated in the centre divider)

Exam-style questions

01 Which **one** of these is a main religious benefit for a person to fight in a holy war?

Put a tick (✓) in the box next to the correct answer. **(1 mark)**

A They will be rewarded by God ☐

B To gain land ☐

C They will get money ☐

D To be more powerful ☐

02 Which **one** of these is **not** an example of something that a religious organisation might do to help victims of war?

Put a tick (✓) in the box next to the correct answer. **(1 mark)**

A Give medicine ☐

B Give shelter ☐

C Get involved in the fighting ☐

D Give access to clean water ☐

03 Name **two** places where there have been conflict and violence due to religious belief in recent history. **(2 marks)**

04 Give **two** examples of things that a religious organisation might do to help victims of war. **(2 marks)**

05 Explain **two** ways the work of one present-day religious organisation helps victims of war.

In your answer you must refer to one or more religious traditions. **(4 marks)**

EXAM TIP
Use the key words from the question in your answer.

06 Explain **two** similar religious responses to victims of war.

Refer to sacred writings or another source of religious belief and teaching in your answer. **(5 marks)**

07 'Religious people should visit war zones to help victims of war.'

Evaluate this statement.

In your answer you:

- should give reasoned arguments in support of this statement
- should give reasoned arguments to support a different point of view
- should refer to religious arguments
- may refer to non-religious arguments
- should reach a justified conclusion. **(12 marks)**

(+ SPaG 3 marks)

EXAM TIP
Make sure you come to a judgement in your answer. This can be at the start, throughout, or at the end of your argument.

35 D: Nuclear weapons and weapons of mass destruction

Weapons of mass destruction

Weapons of mass destruction (WMDs) can be used far away from the intended target and attack large areas.

Biological weapons	Chemical weapons	Nuclear weapons
Weapons that have living organisms or infective material that can lead to disease or death, for example, a germ or virus that poisons humans.	Weapons that use chemicals to poison, burn, or paralyse humans and destroy the natural environment.	Weapons that work by a nuclear reaction that devastate huge areas and kill large numbers of people.

⬇

Nuclear weapons

- Countries around the world make and stockpile nuclear weapons.

- Possessing nuclear weapons is considered a **nuclear deterrent**. This means that they can discourage other countries from attacking.

- A country might be seen as more powerful if it has a stockpile of nuclear weapons.

Hiroshima and Nagasaki, Japan - August 1945

During World War II, the USA dropped a nuclear bomb on the city of Hiroshima and another on the city of Nagasaki, Japan. ➡ The explosions caused over 100 000 deaths and hundreds of thousands more were harmed. ➡ This brought World War II to an end as Japan surrendered a few days later.

Knowledge

35 D: Nuclear weapons and weapons of mass destruction

Arguments for and against WMDs

 Arguments for WMDs

- ☑ They can prevent wars by acting as a deterrent.
- ☑ It makes people feel safer having them, if other countries also have them.

 Arguments against WMDs

- ☒ They are indiscriminate and can kill many people, including innocent civilians.
- ☒ They cause widespread environmental damage for many years.

Christian and Muslim arguments for WMDs

- ☑ A minority of Christians and Muslims may accept that countries need WMDs to be able to defend themselves.
- ☑ Some might use 'an eye for an eye' (both in the Bible and in the Qur'an) to justify having and potentially using WMDs when enemies are doing the same.

REVISION TIP

No religion teaches that using weapons of mass destruction is a good thing. Most arguments are based on nuclear deterrence.

Christian and Muslim arguments against WMDs

- ☒ Some Christians and Muslims believe that WMDs are not acceptable because they cause large numbers of deaths and long-term damage.

 † *66 Do not repay anyone evil for evil. ... If it is possible, as far as it depends on you, live at peace with everyone. 99* (Romans 12:17–19)

 ☪ *66 Do not contribute to your destruction with your own hands, but do good, for God loves those who do good. 99* (Qur'an 2:195)

REVISION TIP

Look back at the criteria for a just war and the conditions for a Lesser Jihad. Which of them would not be met if WMDs are used? Why?

 Key terms Make sure you can write a definition for these key terms

weapons of mass destruction biological weapon
chemical weapon nuclear weapon nuclear deterrent

Learn the answers to the questions below, then cover the answers column with a piece of paper and write as many as you can. Check and repeat.

Questions / Answers

#	Questions	Answers
1	Which type of weapons have living organisms or infective material that can lead to disease or death, for example, a germ or virus that poisons humans?	Biological weapons
2	Which type of weapons use chemicals to poison, burn, or paralyse humans, and destroy the natural environment?	Chemical weapons
3	Give one argument for having weapons of mass destruction.	One from: they can prevent wars by acting as a deterrent / people feel safer having them if other countries also have them
4	Give one argument against having weapons of mass destruction.	One from: they cause large numbers of deaths / they cause long-term damage
5	What does 'nuclear deterrent' mean?	Having nuclear weapons to deter other countries from attacking
6	Where did the USA drop nuclear bombs in 1945?	Hiroshima and Nagasaki, Japan
7	Give a quotation from the Qur'an which supports the argument against WMDs.	*"Do not contribute to your destruction with your own hands, but do good, for God loves those who do good."*
8	Give a quotation from the Bible which supports the argument against WMDs.	*"Do not repay anyone evil for evil. … If it is possible, as far as it depends on you, live at peace with everyone."*

Put paper here (repeated)

Previous questions

Now go back and use these questions to check your knowledge of previous topics.

Questions / Answers

#	Questions	Answers
9	Give a quotation that encourages Muslims to reconcile with one another.	*"Shall I tell you of something that is better than fasting, prayer, and charity? [It is] reconciling between two people."* (Hadith)
10	Give one reason why people may believe that they should go to war for their religion.	One from: they are defending their religion / they are fighting for God / they will be rewarded by God
11	How can religious groups and individuals respond to war?	By working to help victims
12	What is the word for a person who believes we should not fight or use violence to resolve issues?	Pacifist
13	Give one reason why people may believe that they should go to war for their religion.	One from: they are defending their religion / they believe they are fighting for God / they believe they will be rewarded by God

Put paper here (repeated)

Practice

Exam-style questions

01   Which **one** of these are weapons that poison, burn, or paralyse humans, and destroy the natural environment?

Put a tick (✓) in the box next to the correct answer.   **(1 mark)**

A   Nuclear weapons   ☐

B   Biological weapons   ☐

C   Chemical weapons   ☐

D   Artillery   ☐

02   Which **one** of these is a weapon of mass destruction (WMD)?

Put a tick (✓) in the box next to the correct answer.   **(1 mark)**

A   Hand grenade   ☐

B   Nuclear weapons   ☐

C   Assault rifle   ☐

D   Submachine gun   ☐

03   Name **two** types of weapons of mass destruction.   **(2 marks)**

04   Give **two** arguments against the use of weapons of mass destruction.   **(2 marks)**

05   Explain **two** contrasting religious beliefs on weapons of mass destruction.

In your answer you must refer to one or more religious traditions.   **(4 marks)**

> **EXAM TIP**
> Name the religion that you are writing about so the examiner can check what you've written is correct.

06   Explain **two** religious beliefs about nuclear weapons.

Refer to sacred writings or another source of religious belief and teaching in your answer.   **(5 marks)**

> **EXAM TIP**
> Remember, you must name the sacred writings or source in your answer to get the fifth mark, for example, the Bible.

07   'No country should have nuclear weapons.'

Evaluate this statement.

In your answer you:

• should give reasoned arguments in support of this statement

• should give reasoned arguments to support a different point of view

• should refer to religious arguments

• may refer to non-religious arguments

• should reach a justified conclusion.   **(12 marks)**

(+ SPaG 3 marks)

36 E: Good and evil intentions and actions

Intentions and actions

Sometimes people act in a way where the **intention** is **good** but the action itself could be considered to be bad or **evil**. In these cases, what is more important: the intention or the action itself?

REVISION TIP

Remember that someone's intention is the reason or the plan behind doing something.

Example	Intention	Action
A person lies to their friend about something to avoid upsetting them.	To avoid upset	Lying to a friend
To stop people being persecuted by a ruthless dictator a person sends an army to find and kill the dictator.	To stop persecution	Killing
Someone steals food from a supermarket to feed their children.	To feed children	Stealing
A person helps someone that is ill and **suffering** to end their life.	To stop suffering	Ending a life

Can it ever be acceptable to cause suffering?

When considering their intentions and actions, most people will try to avoid causing suffering. However, there may be times when it may be acceptable to cause suffering, for example:

- to learn lessons from the suffering
- doing something that God requires you to do, even though it causes suffering, for example, telling the truth about who committed a crime

- as a punishment to show criminals that what they have done is not acceptable
- if the benefit outweighs the suffering the action causes.

✝ Christianity	☪ Islam
• We should take strength from suffering: ❝ *We also glory in our sufferings, because we know that suffering produces perseverance; perseverance, character; and character, hope.* ❞ (Romans 5:3–4) • Jesus suffered for humans to be saved: ❝ *For Christ also suffered once for sins, the righteous for the unrighteous, that he might bring us to God.* ❞ (1 Peter 3:18)	• We should stay strong through our suffering: ❝ *… you are sure to be tested through your possessions and persons; you are sure to hear much that is hurtful … If you are steadfast and mindful of God, that is the best course.* ❞ (Qur'an 3:186) • However, some suffering might be a test from God or as a result of giving into temptation: ❝ *God does not burden any soul with more than it can bear: each gains whatever good it has done, and suffers its bad.* ❞ (Qur'an 2:286)

Key terms — Make sure you can write a definition for these key terms

| intention | good | evil | suffering | sin | halal | haram | niyyah |

 # Knowledge

36 E: Good and evil intentions and actions

✝ Christian responses to good and evil intentions and actions

- Evil actions might be considered to be those that go against God's teachings in the Bible, for example, murder, adultery, lying. This is called **sin**.

- The Bible emphasises that what you do is linked to your inner thoughts:

> ❝ He [Jesus] went on: 'What comes out of a person is what defiles them. For it is from within, out of a person's heart, that evil thoughts come – sexual immorality, theft, murder, adultery, greed, malice, deceit, lewdness, envy, slander, arrogance, and folly. All these evils come from inside and defile a person. ❞
>
> (Mark 7:20–23)

- As a guide for life, Jesus said:

> ❝ … in everything, do to others what you would have them do to you. ❞
>
> (Matthew 7:12)

This emphasises considering your actions.

☪ Muslim responses to good and evil intentions and actions

- Good actions (**halal** – allowed) and evil actions (**haram** – forbidden) are described in the Qur'an and in the Hadith.

- Intention (**niyyah**) is important in Islam as it will be taken into consideration at Judgement by God:

> ❝ All actions are judged by motives, and each person will be rewarded according to their intention. ❞
>
> (Hadith)

- Muhammad outlines how our intentions and actions will be judged:

> ❝ Whosoever intended to perform a good deed, but did not do it, then Allah writes it down with Himself as a complete good deed. And if he intended to perform it and then did perform it, then Allah writes it down with Himself as from ten good deeds up to seven hundred times, up to many times multiplied. And if he intended to perform an evil deed, but did not do it, then Allah writes it down with Himself as a complete good deed. And if he intended it [i.e. the evil deed] and then performed it, then Allah writes it down as one evil deed. ❞
>
> (Hadith)

- Some believe that our actions and intentions will then be 'weighed' by Allah like scales of justice, as the Qur'an says:

> ❝ On that Day the weighing of deeds will be true and just: those whose good deeds are heavy on the scales will be the ones to prosper, and those whose good deeds are light will be the ones who have lost their souls through their wrongful rejection of Our messages. ❞
>
> (Qur'an 7:8–9)

> **REVISION TIP**
>
> You may know that meat in Islam is also classed as 'halal' or 'haram': the terms come from the core belief of what is allowed/ not allowed throughout life. Make a list of halal and haram actions in Islam to help you remember these.

 # Retrieval

Learn the answers to the questions below, then cover the answers column with a piece of paper and write as many as you can. Check and repeat.

Questions	Answers
1. Give one example of something that the Bible considers to be a sin against God.	One from: murder / adultery / lying
2. Where does the Bible say evil thoughts come from?	A person's heart
3. What did Jesus say to urge Christians to consider their actions?	"…in everything, do to others what you would have them do to you."
4. What does 'niyyah' mean in Islam?	Intention
5. What does 'halal' mean in Islam?	Allowed
6. What does 'haram' mean in Islam?	Forbidden
7. What does this quotation from the Bible tell Christians? *"We also glory in our sufferings, because we know that suffering produces perseverance; perseverance, character; and character, hope."*	That they should take strength from suffering
8. According to the Hadith, how will God judge the intention to do a good action but not doing it?	As one good deed
9. According to the Hadith, how will God judge intending to do a good action and doing it?	As multiple good deeds
10. According to the Hadith, how will God judge intending to do a bad action but not doing it?	As one good deed
11. According to the Hadith, how will God judge intending to do a bad action and doing it?	As one bad deed
12. In Christianity, who suffered to save humans from their sins?	Jesus

Put paper here

Practice

Exam-style questions

01   Which **one** of these would be classed as an evil action in Christianity?
Put a tick (✓) in the box next to the correct answer.   **(1 mark)**

A   Giving to charity   ☐

B   Committing murder   ☐

C   Helping the homeless   ☐

D   Prayer   ☐

02   Which **one** of these means 'intention' in Islam?
Put a tick (✓) in the box next to the correct answer.   **(1 mark)**

A   Niyyah   ☐

B   Halal   ☐

C   Haram   ☐

D   Jihad   ☐

03   Give **two** examples of when killing may have good intentions.   **(2 marks)**

04   Give **two** examples of when it may be considered acceptable
for some people to cause suffering.   **(2 marks)**

> **EXAM TIP** 🎯
> You can write using one or more religions but you should name them so the examiner knows which you are writing about.

05   Explain **two** similar religious beliefs about causing suffering.
In your answer you must refer to one or more religious traditions.   **(4 marks)**

06   Explain **two** religious beliefs about good and evil intentions.
Refer to sacred writings or another source of religious belief
and teaching in your answer.   **(5 marks)**

> **EXAM TIP** 🎯
> You don't need to quote the sources word for word but you must name the source of authority that they are from.

07   'Sometimes suffering can be good for a person.'
Evaluate this statement. In your answer you:
- should give reasoned arguments in support of this statement
- should give reasoned arguments to support a different point of view
- should refer to religious arguments
- may refer to non-religious arguments
- should reach a justified conclusion.   **(12 marks)**
                                                                      (+ SPaG 3 marks)

37 E: Reasons for crime

Why people commit crime

There are many different reasons why people commit crimes.

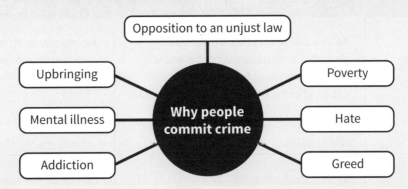

† Christian views about people who break the law for these reasons

- Christians believe that whilst we all sin and do wrong, we should help those who struggle in life and commit crimes.

- Christianity is based on the idea of reformation – that we are all sinners and can be saved. Therefore people who break the law should be helped to change.

- Whilst Jesus was dying on the cross, he told the criminal to his right:

> **"** *... today you will be with me in paradise.* **"**
> (Luke 23:43)

This demonstrates that, until death, a criminal can be forgiven for their sins and enter heaven.

☪ Muslim views about people who break the law for these reasons

- Muslims believe that in Islamic societies, these reasons for crime should not exist. The poor can receive **Zakah** (charity), and laws should be fair so that people don't need to commit crimes to oppose unjust laws.

- People should not be tempted to be greedy, and the Hadith condemns hating others:

> **"** *Hate your enemy mildly.* **"** (Hadith)

- However, the Qur'an is clear on specific punishments for certain crimes and **Shari'ah law** outlines how someone should have a fair trial for any accusation made. However, Shari'ah law doesn't apply in Great Britain or any other non-Muslim country, and Qur'anic punishments should not be carried out.

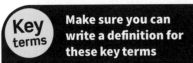 **Key terms** Make sure you can write a definition for these key terms

Zakah   Shari'ah law   hate crime

37 E: Reasons for crime

Views about different types of crime

Crime	✝ Christianity	☪ Islam
Hate crime (Crime motivated by prejudice on the basis of race, religion, sexuality, disability, or gender or other protected characteristic.)	*Anyone who hates a brother or sister* is a murderer, and you know that no murderer has eternal life residing in him.* (1 John 3:15) (*This means anyone, not just your actual brother/sister.)	*Hate your enemy mildly, he may become your friend one day.* (Hadith)
Theft	*You shall not steal.* (Exodus 20:15) (From the Ten Commandments.)	*Cut off the hands of thieves, whether they are man or woman, as punishment for what they have done – a deterrent from God.* (Qur'an 5:38)
Murder	*You shall not murder.* (Exodus 20:13) (From the Ten Commandments.)	*Do not kill each other, for God is merciful to you.* (Qur'an 4:29)

Forgiveness

- Forgiveness is showing grace and mercy, and pardoning someone for what they have done wrong.
- Both Christianity and Islam teach that forgiveness is an important aspect of life between humans and with God.

> **REVISION TIP**
>
> Knowing The Lord's prayer is useful here and you need to know it for the Christianity exam paper.

✝ Christianity	☪ Islam
Jesus died on the cross so that human sins can be forgiven by God. Jesus also told people that they should forgive: *Then Peter came to Jesus and asked, 'Lord, how many times shall I forgive my brother or sister who sins against me? Up to seven times?' Jesus answered, 'I tell you, not seven times, but seventy-seven times.'* (Matthew 18:21–22) Christians often ask God for forgiveness of their sins: *Forgive us our sins, as we forgive those who sin against us.* (The Lord's prayer)	Forgiveness is important as God is all-forgiving and all-merciful: *...ask forgiveness of God: He is most forgiving and merciful.* (Qur'an 2:199) The Qur'an also says we should pardon someone for what they've done wrong: *A kind word and forgiveness is better than a charitable deed followed by hurtful [words].* (Qur'an 2:263)

Learn the answers to the questions below, then cover the answers column with a piece of paper and write as many as you can. Check and repeat.

Questions | Answers

#	Question	Answer
1	Give three reasons for crime.	Three from: poverty / upbringing / mental illness / addiction / greed / hate / opposition to an unjust law
2	True or false: Shari'ah law doesn't apply in Great Britain and Qur'anic punishments should not be carried out.	True
3	Which quotation from the Qur'an tells Muslims that God is all-forgiving and all-merciful?	"...ask forgiveness of God: He is most forgiving and merciful."
4	What are crimes, often including violence, which are usually targeted at a person because of their race, religion, sexuality, disability, or gender called?	Hate crimes
5	What does the Qur'an say should happen to "thieves, whether they are man or woman." (Qur'an 5:38)?	Cut off their hand
6	Which of the Ten Commandments says not to deliberately kill someone?	"You shall not murder."
7	How many times did Jesus say we should forgive?	Seventy-seven
8	In which line in the Lord's prayer do Christians ask for God's forgiveness?	"Forgive us our sins, as we forgive those who sin against us."
9	What word means showing grace and mercy, and pardoning someone for what they have done wrong?	Forgiveness
10	Which quotation from the Qur'an urges Muslims to forgive others?	"A kind word and forgiveness is better than a charitable deed followed by hurtful [words]."

Put paper here

Previous questions

Now go back and use these questions to check your knowledge of previous topics.

Questions | Answers

#	Question	Answer
11	Give one example of something that the Bible considers to be a sin against God.	One from: murder / adultery / lying
12	Where does the Bible say evil thoughts come from?	A person's heart
13	What does 'halal' mean in Islam?	Allowed
14	What does 'haram' mean in Islam?	Forbidden
15	According to the Hadith, how will God judge the intention to do a good action but not doing it?	As one good deed

Put paper here

Practice

01 Which of these is **not** a common reason for crime?

Put a tick (✓) in the box next to the correct answer. **(1 mark)**

A Greed ☐

B Hate ☐

C Upbringing ☐

D Happiness ☐

02 Which **one** of these is a crime motivated by prejudice on the basis of race, religion, sexuality, disability, or gender or other protected characteristic?

Put a tick (✓) in the box next to the correct answer. **(1 mark)**

A Theft ☐

B Hate crime ☐

C Murder ☐

D Greed ☐

03 Give **two** reasons for crime. **(2 marks)**

04 Give **two** religious beliefs about those that commit crimes. **(2 marks)**

05 Explain **two** contrasting religious views in contemporary British society about forgiveness.

In your answer you should refer to the main religious tradition of Great Britain and one or more other religious traditions. **(4 marks)**

> **EXAM TIP**
> Make sure you answer the question exactly.

06 Explain **two** religious beliefs about people who commit hate crime.

Refer to sacred writings or another source of religious belief and teaching in your answer. **(5 marks)**

07 Explain **two** religious beliefs about people who commit theft.

Refer to sacred writings or another source of religious belief and teaching in your answer. **(5 marks)**

08 'We should always forgive others when they do wrong.'

Evaluate this statement.

In your answer you:

- should give reasoned arguments in support of this statement
- should give reasoned arguments to support a different point of view
- should refer to religious arguments
- may refer to non-religious arguments
- should reach a justified conclusion. **(12 marks)**

(+ SPaG 3 marks)

> **EXAM TIP**
> You can spend time planning for a 12-mark question but it needs to be quick as you won't have much time to plan and write.

38 E: The aims of punishment and the treatment of criminals

Retribution

Retribution means that the punishment should make the criminal pay for what they have done wrong.

✝ Christianity	☪ Islam

• Old Testament:
 	
  " *But if there is serious injury, you are to take life for life, eye for eye, tooth for tooth, hand for hand, foot for foot, burn for burn, wound for wound, bruise for bruise.* " (Exodus 21:23–25)
 	
• New Testament:
 	
  " *You have heard that it was said, 'Eye for eye, and tooth for tooth.' But I tell you, do not resist an evil person. If anyone slaps you on the right cheek, turn to them the other cheek also.* " (Matthew 5: 38–39)
 	
• Most Christians believe that the New Testament teaching clarifies the Old Testament teaching and any potential punishment should be God's decision.
	" *We prescribed for them a life for a life, an eye for an eye, a nose for a nose, an ear for an ear, a tooth for a tooth, an equal wound for a wound: if anyone forgoes this out of charity, it will serve as atonement for his bad deeds.* " (Qur'an 5:45)
	
	  " *Fair retribution saves life for you, people of understanding, so that you may guard yourselves against what is wrong.* " (Qur'an 2:179)
	
	• In some cases the victim or victim's family family can grant mercy and can receive compensation instead.

Deterrence

Deterrence means that the likely punishment should put people off committing crime.

✝ Christianity	☪ Islam
• Whilst the Old Testament speaks of punishments that may act to deter criminals, the New Testament gives a message about love and forgiveness.	• In some Muslim countries punishments are carried out in public to try to deter others from committing the crime. " *…ensure that a group of believers witnesses the punishment.* " (Qur'an 24:2)

> **REVISION TIP**
>
> Remember that these are the purpose of punishments not actual punishments.

Knowledge

38 E: The aims of punishment and the treatment of criminals

Reformation

Reformation means that the punishment should change the criminal's behaviour for the better.

✝ Christianity	☾ Islam

• Christianity is based on the idea of reformation, that we are all sinners and can be saved. So, people who commit crimes should be helped to change. Whilst Jesus was dying on the cross, he told the criminal to his right:
 	
    ❝ *...today you will be with me in paradise.* ❞
    (Luke 23:43)
	• The Qur'an supports reformation if the person is repentant for some crimes:
	
	    ❝ *... if they repent and mend their ways, leave them alone – God is always ready to accept repentance, He is full of mercy.* ❞ (Qur'an 4:16)
	
	    ❝ *But if anyone repents after his wrongdoing and makes amends, God will accept his repentance: God is most forgiving, most merciful.* ❞ (Qur'an 5:39)

Prison

- In Great Britain, being sent to prison is a punishment used to deter people from committing crimes. It also offers protection for society from the criminal while they are inside prison.
- Prison aims to reform criminals so they stop re-offending.
- Depending on the crime, a criminal can be given up to a full life sentence in prison.
- Whilst in prison, criminals can be supported to reform with opportunities to gain qualifications, carry out meaningful work to gain new skills, and complete rehabilitation programmes.

✝ Christianity	☾ Islam
• Most Christians support reformation and so would agree that prison gives criminals the chance to change whilst keeping society safe.	• Many Muslims may agree with the role of prison in reforming the criminal, though the Qur'an gives other punishments for certain crimes. • Under Shari'ah law, prison is mostly used to protect society, whilst corporal or capital (execution) punishments are decided.

Corporal punishment

- **Corporal punishment** means punishing offenders by causing them physical pain, for example, by lashing, amputation of limbs, or caning.
- Examples of countries that use corporal punishment include Iran, Saudi Arabia, and Singapore. It is illegal in Great Britain.

> **REVISION TIP**
>
> Although the Qur'an says cutting off hands is a punishment for theft, this is not a commonly reported punishment.

† Christianity	☾ Islam
• Most Christians would not support corporal punishment for criminals as it causes physical harm, and Jesus taught 'pray for those that persecute' and instead of 'an eye for an eye' to 'turn the other cheek'. • However, the Bible says: ❝ *He who spares the rod hates their children, but the one who loves their children is careful to discipline them.* ❞ (Proverbs 13:24) So some Christians may argue that it is important to discipline a child, which may include corporal punishment.	• The Qur'an gives examples of when corporal punishment can be used. These can be seen as a deterrent to prevent people committing the crimes in the first place: ❝ *Cut off the hands of thieves, whether they are man or woman, as punishment for what they have done – a deterrent from God: God is almighty and wise. But if anyone repents after his wrongdoing and makes amends, God will accept his repentance: God is most forgiving, most merciful.* ❞ (Qur'an 5:38) • However, the Qur'an says that if someone is sorry and asks for forgiveness then the punishment does not need to be used. • This means it is better to refrain from using corporal punishment, and those that don't use it will be favoured by God.

Community service

- Punishing offenders by making them do unpaid work in the community, for example, cleaning litter from public spaces.

† Christianity	☾ Islam
• Most Christians would support **community service** as it gives a chance for the criminal to reform, and it contributes to society in a positive way. • Jesus taught: ❝ *Blessed are the merciful, for they will be shown mercy.* ❞ (Matthew 5:7)	• Muslims may believe that community service can be valuable, but Islam would emphasis the importance of deterrence in punishment.

 Key terms — Make sure you can write a definition for these key terms

retribution   deterrence   reformation   corporal punishment
community service

Retrieval

Learn the answers to the questions below, then cover the answers column with a piece of paper and write as many as you can. Check and repeat.

Questions	Answers
1 What does retribution mean?	Making a criminal pay for what they have done
2 Which aim of punishment is to put people off committing crimes?	Deterrence
3 Which aim of punishment is to change someone's behaviour for the better?	Reformation
4 Some Muslim countries carry out punishments in public. Why is this and which quotation supports it?	To deter others from committing the crime *"…ensure that a group of believers witnesses the punishment."*
5 What did Jesus say to counter and 'eye for an eye'?	Turn the other cheek
6 Give one example of opportunities that prisons in Great Britain may offer to try to reform criminals.	One from: gain qualifications / do meaningful work to gain new skills / complete rehabilitation programmes
7 What is corporal punishment?	Punishing an offender by causing them physical pain
8 Give one example of corporal punishment.	One from: lashing / amputation of limbs / caning
9 Which Bible quotation urges parents to discipline their children?	*"He who spares the rod hates their children, but the one who loves their children is careful to discipline them."*
10 Which type of punishment makes offenders do unpaid work in the community?	Community service

Put paper here

Previous questions

Now go back and use these questions to check your knowledge of previous topics.

Questions	Answers
11 According to the Hadith, how will God judge the intention to do a good action but not doing it?	As one good deed
12 According to the Hadith, how will God judge intending to do a bad action and doing it?	As one bad deed
13 Give three reasons for crime.	Three from: poverty / upbringing / mental illness / addiction / greed / hate / opposition to an unjust law
14 In which line in the Lord's prayer do Christians ask for God's forgiveness?	*"Forgive us our sins, as we forgive those who sin against us."*
15 How many times did Jesus say we should forgive?	Seventy-seven

Put paper here

38 The aims of punishment and the treatment of criminals

Exam-style questions

01 Which **one** of these means to make a criminal pay for what they have done wrong? **(1 mark)**

Put a tick (✓) in the box next to the correct answer.

A	Retribution	☐
B	Deterrence	☐
C	Protection	☐
D	Reformation	☐

02 Which **one** of these means to put people off committing crimes? **(1 mark)**

Put a tick (✓) in the box next to the correct answer.

A	Retribution	☐
B	Deterrence	☐
B	Protection	☐
C	Reformation	☐

03 Give **two** religious beliefs about using prison as a punishment. **(2 marks)**

04 Explain **two** similar religious beliefs about using deterrence to stop people committing crime.

In your answer you must refer to one or more religious traditions. **(4 marks)**

> **EXAM TIP** ⊚
> Remember to name the religion that you are writing about so the examiner is clear if your answer is correct.

05 Explain **two** religious beliefs on the use of corporal punishment.

Refer to sacred writings or another source of religious belief and teaching in your answer. **(5 marks)**

06 'We should always follow an "eye for an eye" when punishing criminals.'

Evaluate this statement.

In your answer you:

> **EXAM TIP** ⊚
> Remember to read the statement carefully and use the words from it in your answer to ensure you answer it fully.

- should give reasoned arguments in support of this statement
- should give reasoned arguments to support a different point of view
- should refer to religious arguments
- may refer to non-religious arguments
- should reach a justified conclusion. **(12 marks)**

(+ SPaG 3 marks)

Knowledge

39 E: The death penalty

Countries that use the death penalty

The **death penalty** is illegal in Great Britain today, but it is legal in some countries around the world. Different methods, such as lethal injection, hanging, and beheading, are used to carry out the death penalty.

Country	Example of crimes that may be punished with the death penalty
USA (some states)	Murder, large-scale drug trafficking
China	Murder, rape, robbery, drug trafficking
Iran	Murder, adultery, apostasy (turning away from Islam)
Saudi Arabia	Murder, rape, apostasy, drug smuggling

Ethical arguments related to the death penalty

Broadly, there are two ideas to consider when arguing for and against the death penalty:

The principle of utility

> An action is right if it promotes maximum happiness for the maximum number of people affected by it.

Sanctity of life

> All life is holy as it is created and loved by God.

Arguments to support the death penalty	Arguments against the death penalty
☑ It makes society safer and stops the criminal reoffending (protection).	☒ It ignores the rights of the criminals and prevents possible reformation.
☑ Murderers have taken away life and deserve their life to be taken (retribution).	☒ It's murder, which is always wrong.
☑ The **principle of utility** on the grounds of the protection of wider society.	☒ Risk of error - innocent people can (and have) been sentenced to death.
☑ It acts as a deterrent to prevent people committing crimes.	☒ Evidence shows it isn't effective as a deterrent.
☑ Sanctity of life: if you take away the life God has given, you deserve to have your life taken.	☒ Sanctity of life: if you take the life of a criminal you are playing God, which you should not do.

 Key terms Make sure you can write a definition for these key terms

death penalty   principle of utility

Christian and Muslim arguments for the death penalty

† Christianity	☪ Islam
• The death penalty is used as a punishment in the Bible, and it is justified in the Old Testament. ❝ *Whoever sheds human blood, by humans shall their blood be shed.* ❞ (Genesis 9:6) • Some Christians believe in retribution and that the death penalty gives justice to the criminal and to the victim's family. ❝ *Life for life, eye for eye, tooth for tooth.* ❞ (Exodus 21:23–24) • Christians believe in the sanctity of life so for some, this means that if you commit murder you should have your life taken away as life is sacred.	• The Qur'an supports the death penalty for certain crimes (e.g., adultery). • Shari'ah law allows the use of the death penalty for certain crimes such as murder. • Some Muslims believe in retribution and that the death penalty gives justice to the criminal and to the victim's family. ❝ *…do not take life, which God has made sacred, except by right [justice]. This is what He commands you to do: so that you may use your reason.* ❞ (Qur'an 6:151) • Muslims believe in the sanctity of life so for some, this means that if you commit murder you should have your life taken away as life is sacred.

 ## Christian and Muslim arguments against the death penalty

Christians and Muslims believe in the sanctity of life so for some this means the death penalty is playing the role of God – only God should take life away. These Christians and Muslims may support alternative punishments such as prison to help reform criminals and protect society. They may believe that final judgement should be left to God.

† Christianity	☪ Islam
• Murder is breaking one of the Ten Commandments. ❝ *You shall not murder.* ❞ (Exodus 20:13) • Jesus spoke against 'an eye for an eye' and said 'turn the other cheek'. • Some Church leaders have spoken against the death penalty. ❝ *This conviction (that human life and dignity should be protected) has led me, from the beginning of my ministry, to advocate at different levels for the global abolition of the death penalty. I am convinced that this way is the best, since every life is sacred, every human person is endowed with an inalienable dignity, and society can only benefit from the rehabilitation of those convicted of crimes.* ❞ (Pope Francis)	• The Qur'an says those who show mercy will be rewarded by God. ❝ *We prescribed for them a life for a life, an eye for an eye, a nose for a nose, an ear for an ear, a tooth for a tooth, an equal wound for a wound: if anyone forgoes this out of charity, it will serve as atonement for his bad deeds.* ❞ (Qur'an 5:45) • Some Muslims allow 'blood money' where the victim or their family receives money as compensation. ❝ *But if the culprit is pardoned by his aggrieved brother, this shall be adhered to fairly, and the culprit shall pay what is due in a good way. This is an alleviation from your Lord and an act of mercy.* ❞ (Qur'an 2:178)

⇄ Retrieval

Learn the answers to the questions below, then cover the answers column with a piece of paper and write as many as you can. Check and repeat.

Questions | Answers

#	Question	Answer
1	Name two ideas often considered in relation to the death penalty.	Sanctity of life, the principle of utility
2	What is the name for Islamic law, that allows the use of the death penalty for certain crimes, such as murder?	Shari'ah law
3	What does apostasy mean in Islam?	Turning away from the faith
4	What is the principle of utility?	An action is right if it promotes maximum happiness for the maximum number of people affected by it
5	What does the sanctity of life mean?	All life is holy as it is created and loved by God
6	Give an Old Testament Bible quotation which is often quoted in defence of the death penalty.	One from: *"Life for life, eye for eye, tooth for tooth."* / *"Whoever sheds human blood, by humans shall their blood be shed."*
7	Which of the Ten Commandments can be used to oppose the death penalty?	*"You shall not murder."*
8	In Islam and Christianity, who has final judgement on human behaviour?	God
9	True or false: Both Christians and Muslims believe in the sanctity of life.	True
10	What is 'blood money' in Islam?	Where a victim, or their family, receive money as compensation for the crime

Put paper here

Previous questions

Now go back and use these questions to check your knowledge of previous topics.

Questions | Answers

#	Question	Answer
11	According to the Hadith, how will God judge intending to do a bad action but not doing it?	As one good deed
12	What word means showing grace and mercy, and pardoning someone for what they have done wrong?	Forgiveness
13	In which line in the Lord's prayer do Christians ask for God's forgiveness?	*"Forgive us our sins, as we forgive those who sin against us."*
14	Which quotation from the Qur'an urges Muslims to forgive others?	*"A kind word and forgiveness is better than a charitable deed followed by hurtful [words]."*
15	Which type of punishment makes offenders do unpaid work in the community?	Community service

Put paper here

Exam-style questions

01 Which **one** of the following means that an action is right if it promotes maximum happiness for the maximum number of people?

Put a tick (✓) in the box next to the correct answer.　　　**(1 mark)**

A　Deterrence ☐

B　Reformation ☐

C　Sanctity of life ☐

D　Principle of utility ☐

02 Which **one** of the following means that all life is holy as it is created and loved by God?

Put a tick (✓) in the box next to the correct answer.　　　**(1 mark)**

A　Sanctity of life ☐

B　Principle of utility ☐

C　Deterrence ☐

D　Shari'ah law ☐

> **EXAM TIP**
> These questions are worth 1 mark only so do not spend a long time on them. However, it's important to read the question and answer options carefully so you do not make a silly mistake.

03 Give **two** arguments against the death penalty.　　　**(2 marks)**

04 Explain **two** contrasting religious beliefs in contemporary British society on the death penalty.

In your answer you should refer to the main religious tradition of Great Britain and one or more other religious traditions.　　　**(4 marks)**

> **EXAM TIP**
> Try to remember one quotation that supports, and one source that opposes, the death penalty.

05 Explain **two** religious beliefs about the death penalty.

Refer to sacred writings or another source of religious belief and teaching in your answer.　　　**(5 marks)**

06 'The death penalty should be made legal in Great Britain.'

Evaluate this statement.

In your answer you:

- should give reasoned arguments in support of this statement
- should give reasoned arguments to support a different point of view
- should refer to religious arguments
- may refer to non-religious arguments
- should reach a justified conclusion.　　　**(12 marks)**

(+ SPaG 3 marks)

> **EXAM TIP**
> Top-mark answers are those which have a well-argued response. Make sure your answer flows and follows a logical argument.

⚙ Knowledge

40 F: Prejudice and discrimination

Prejudice and discrimination

- **Prejudice** is judging someone unfairly before the facts are known. It also means holding biased opinions about an individual or group.
- Discrimination means actions or behaviour that result from prejudice.

REVISION TIP

A way to remember the difference between prejudice and discrimination is to think that prejudice is in someone's 'head' – it's what they think or believe. If they take action as a result of this prejudice, it becomes discrimination.

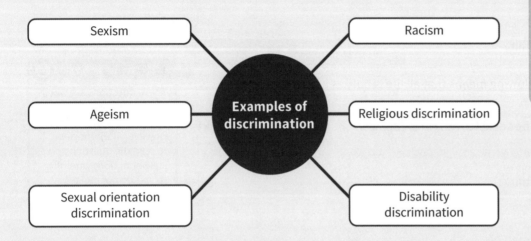

Sexism — Racism — Ageism — **Examples of discrimination** — Religious discrimination — Sexual orientation discrimination — Disability discrimination

Christian and Muslim teaching on prejudice and discrimination

Both religions teach that all humans are equal, and therefore that prejudice and discrimination are wrong.

† *There is neither Jew nor Gentile, neither slave nor free, nor is there male and female, for you are all one in Christ Jesus.* **»** (Galatians 3:28)

☾ *People are equal like the teeth of a comb.* **»** (Hadith)

The status and treatment of women

† Christianity	☾ Islam
• Christians believe that women are equal to men. • Traditional views are that a woman's role is that of a mother and a housekeeper. • Modern views say that women and men should share these roles and women can also work, as men do. • In most Christian communities, girls and women are free to get an education and work in a job.	• Women are equal to men in Islam. *Anyone, male or female, who does good works and is a believer, will enter paradise.* **»** (Qur'an 4:124) • Men and women have different roles and traditionally the woman's role is to be a mother, bring up the children in Islam, and to look after the house. • Modern views say that if the woman is fulfilling her role, then she may also work. • In some Muslim contexts, girls and women may be separated from boys and men, for example, at school, at social occasions such as weddings, on transport, or even whilst shopping.

Women in religious life

† Christianity	☾ Islam
• Some Christians do not allow women to take a role in the Church as Jesus was a male and he chose all male disciples. They may believe that St Paul's first letter to the Corinthians supports this. It says: *❝ Women should remain silent in the churches. They are not allowed to speak [...] for it is disgraceful for a woman to speak in the church. ❞* (1 Corinthians 14:34–35) • Some Christians allow women to lead in the Church. The Church of England has allowed women priests since 1993. These Christians use Galatians 3:28 to show that women are equal to men.	• All Muslims have a duty to worship God – however, the role of a woman as mother and housekeeper means that women are not obliged to attend the mosque for the daily and **Jummah** prayers. If they do attend, then they pray separately from men. • The majority of religious leaders in Islam are men, as women have their own duties to fulfil. There are a few examples of women **imams** around the world – however, these are not accepted by many Muslims.

†Christian views on homosexuality

There are different views within Christianity regarding homosexuality. These can broadly be divided into three different views – each view has a different interpretation of Bible references.

Some Christians accept homosexuality	Some Christians accept being homosexual but do not accept homosexual acts	Some Christians do not accept homosexuality
• Homosexuals are part of God's creation and everyone should be treated with respect. • Texts that forbid homosexuality have been misinterpreted as they are often contextual to the time of writing. • There are homosexual relationships in the Bible, for example, David and Jonathan. Some Christian Churches will marry same-sex couples, and some will bless a civil marriage.	• Being homosexual is accepted as we are all part of God's creation but taking part in homosexual acts is not acceptable. • God told humans to procreate ('be fruitful', Genesis 1:28) but homosexual couples are not able to do this naturally so they cannot fulfil God's command. • Catholic teachings say that sex is for procreation so homosexuals should remain chaste. • Bible texts that forbid homosexual acts support their view. These Christian Churches will not marry or bless homosexual couples.	• Heterosexuality is part of God's plan for humans and the Bible speaks about a man and a woman as husband and wife, for example, **Adam and Eve**. • The Bible speaks about procreation as a command from God ('be fruitful') and that only heterosexual couples can do this naturally. • Texts in the Bible that forbid homosexual acts are taken literally. *❝ Do not be deceived: Neither the sexually immoral nor idolaters nor adulterers nor men who have sex with men nor thieves nor the greedy nor drunkards nor slanderers nor swindlers will inherit the kingdom of God. ❞* (1 Corinthians 6:9–10) These Christian Churches will not marry or bless homosexual couples.

⚙ Knowledge

40 F: Prejudice and discrimination

☾ Muslim views on homosexuality

- Many Muslims see homosexuality as a choice that should be rejected as it is against God's natural law.

- The majority believe that it is against God's will – humans should marry someone of the opposite sex and have children, as Muhammad did.

- In Islam, homosexuals cannot marry, so all homosexual sex is viewed as sex outside marriage and sex outside marriage is not allowed in Islam.

- Some Muslim scholars state that it is not a sin to have feelings for someone of the same sex but once you act upon this, it becomes a sin.

- Homosexuality is illegal in many Islamic countries, with severe punishments under Shari'ah law.

- In Shari'ah law, to be convicted, a person must confess, or there must be four eyewitnesses to the act. Some Muslims believe that homosexual acts may be punished by God on the Day of Judgement.

> 66 *Must you, unlike [other] people, lust after males and abandon the wives that God has created for you? You are exceeding all bounds.* 99
> (Qur'an 26:165–166)

> 66 *If two men commit a lewd act, punish them both; if they repent and mend their ways, leave them alone – God is always ready to accept repentance, He is full of mercy.* 99 (Quran 4:16)

> 66 *How can you commit this outrage with your eyes wide open? How can you lust after men instead of women? What fools you are!* 99
> (Qur'an 27:54–55)

> 66 *Marry those who are single among you for [God] will develop their moral traits [through marriage].* 99 (Hadith)

Muslims who accept homosexuality

- A few Muslims believe that homosexuality is not a choice, and that God will judge people's actions.

- Some accept that homosexuality is part of British society and people have the right to make their own choices as society is different from the time of Muhammad and the Qur'an.

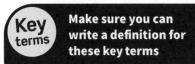
Key terms — **Make sure you can write a definition for these key terms**

prejudice   Jummah   imam   Adam and Eve

Equality and freedom of religion and belief

Equality

Both Christianity and Islam teach that all people are equal, and that God treats everyone fairly.

† 66 *For God does not show favouritism.* 99
(Romans 2:11)

☪ 66 *He created you all from a single being, from which He made its mate.* 99 (Qur'an 39:6)

Freedom of religion and belief

- Countries that sign up to the Universal Declaration of Human Rights should allow people to choose a religion (or none) and to practise it without persecution or discrimination.

- However, in countries that do not follow these principles, religious people can be, and are, discriminated against.

† Christian views on freedom of religion and belief

- Christianity teaches that people should be free to choose their beliefs. Jesus taught:

66 *Love your neighbour as yourself.* 99
(Matthew 22:39)

This includes people who may not be the same as us.

- Even if people are not Christian, Christians should be tolerant:

66 *(If it is possible, as far as it depends on you), live at peace with everyone.* 99
(Romans 12:18)

- Jesus taught religious freedom when he said:

66 *My Father's house has many rooms.* 99
(John 14:2)

Some Christians believe that this means that there are no limits to who can enter the Kingdom of Heaven.

REVISION TIP

Remember, the way in which religion is followed and practised around the world can differ from place to place. This is because followers differ in their interpretation of the sources of authority.

☪ Muslim views on freedom of religion and belief

- The Qur'an is clear that religion is a choice:

66 *There is no compulsion in religion.* 99
(Qur'an 2:256)

- The Qur'an emphasises that believing in Islam is the correct way to be sure of entering Heaven – other paths may lead to punishment from God:

66 *Do not try to justify yourselves; you have gone from belief to disbelief. We may forgive some of you, but We will punish others: they are evildoers.* 99 (Qur'an 9:66)

- The Qur'an mentions 'People of the Book' (Christians and Jews) but encourages Muslims to remember that, whilst they worship the same God, they should:

66 *. . . not go to excess in your religion, and do not say anything about God except the truth.* 99 (Qur'an 4:171)

- All 'People of the book' are protected in Islam and should not be discriminated against. This is why Muslim men can marry women who aren't Muslim.

- In some Muslim countries, religious freedom may be limited and people who follow other religions may be discriminated against.

Retrieval

Learn the answers to the questions below, then cover the answers column with a piece of paper and write as many as you can. Check and repeat.

Questions | Answers

#	Question	Answer
1	Tue or false: neither Christianity nor Islam teach that all humans are equal.	False – both Christianity and Islam teach that all humans are equal
2	Name three types of discrimination.	Three from: sexism / racism / ageism / religious discrimination / sexual orientation discrimination / disability discrimination
3	Which Hadith quotation promotes equality?	*"People are equal like the teeth of a comb."*
4	What is the traditional role of a woman in Islam?	Mother and housekeeper
5	Who in the Bible said, *"Women should remain silent in the churches"*?	St Paul (in 1 Corinthians 14:34–35)
6	In what year did the Church of England first allow women priests?	1993
7	Give one reason why some Christians might not allow women leaders in church.	One from: Jesus was male / Jesus chose male disciples / St Paul spoke against women speaking in church
8	Name one reason why some Muslims might accept homosexuality.	One from: some Muslims believe that homosexuality is not a choice, and that God will judge people's actions / some accept that homosexuality is part of British society and people have the right to make their own choices as society is different from the time of Muhammad and the Qur'an
9	Give one reason why some Christians do not accept homosexual relationships.	One from: homosexual couples cannot procreate naturally through sex / the Bible supports heterosexuality (e.g., Adam and Eve) / the Bible condemns homosexual acts
10	Which Bible quotation teaches Christians to love other people, including those who might not be the same as them?	*"Love your neighbour as yourself."*
11	Who are the 'People of the Book' mentioned in the Qur'an?	Jews and Christians
12	Which quotation from the Qur'an makes it clear that religion is a choice?	*"There is no compulsion in religion."*

Put paper here

Exam-style questions

01 Which **one** of these means behaviour or actions that result from prejudice?

Put a tick (✓) in the box next to the correct answer. **(1 mark)**

A Violence ☐

B Freedom of religion ☐

C Procreation ☐

D Discrimination ☐

02 Which **one** of these means judging someone unfairly before the facts are known or holding biased opinions about an individual or group?

Put a tick (✓) in the box next to the correct answer. **(1 mark)**

A Prejudice ☐

B Reconciliation ☐

C Persecution ☐

D Equality ☐

03 Give **two** religious beliefs about women in religion. **(2 marks)**

04 Explain **two** contrasting religious beliefs on the freedom of religious expression.

In your answer you must refer to one or more religious traditions. **(4 marks)**

> **EXAM TIP**
>
> When you use religious views, use 'Some' and 'Others' if you are unsure of specific groups within a religion.

05 Explain **two** religious beliefs about the status and treatment of homosexuals.

Refer to sacred writings or another source of religious belief and teaching in your answer. **(5 marks)**

> **EXAM TIP**
>
> Make sure your reference to the sacred writing or source of authority is clear to the examiner.

06 Explain **two** religious beliefs about prejudice.

Refer to sacred writings or another source of religious belief and teaching in your answer. **(5 marks)**

07 'A woman's place is in the home.'

Evaluate this statement.

In your answer you:

- should give reasoned arguments in support of this statement
- should give reasoned arguments to support a different point of view
- should refer to religious arguments
- may refer to non-religious arguments
- should reach a justified conclusion. **(12 marks)**

(+ SPaG 3 marks)

⚙ Knowledge

41 F: Social justice, racial prejudice, and discrimination

Social justice

- **Social justice** means ensuring that society treats people fairly, and protects people's **human rights**.
- Governments can support social justice by making laws, and funding programmes that attempt to reduce inequality in society.

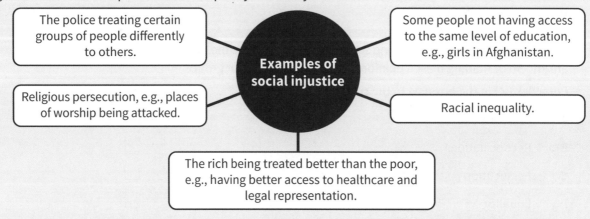

The police treating certain groups of people differently to others.

Religious persecution, e.g., places of worship being attacked.

Examples of social injustice

Some people not having access to the same level of education, e.g., girls in Afghanistan.

Racial inequality.

The rich being treated better than the poor, e.g., having better access to healthcare and legal representation.

Christian and Muslim views on social justice

- Both Christianity and Islam support social justice.
- Their sources of wisdom and authority give their followers clear guidance on how society should support all people.

† Christianity

> ❝ *Let justice roll on like a river, righteousness like a never-failing stream!* ❞
> (Amos 5:24)

> ❝ *The righteous care about justice for the poor, but the wicked have no such concern.* ❞
> (Proverbs 29:7)

☪ Islam

> ❝ *God commands justice, doing good, and generosity towards relatives, and He forbids what is shameful, blameworthy, and oppressive.* ❞
> (Qur'an 16:90)

> ❝ *Adhere to justice, for that is closer to awareness of God … God has promised forgiveness and a rich reward to those who have faith and do good works.* ❞
> (Qur'an 5:8–9)

41

Racial prejudice and discrimination

- **Racial prejudice** and **discrimination** are often known as racism.
- Racism is showing prejudice against someone because of their ethnic group or nationality, but sometimes it is used when referring to religion as well.
- It is illegal in the UK, and laws have been passed to ensure that those who speak or behave in a racist way are punished.

Positive discrimination

- **Positive discrimination** is where a particular group is given special privileges to overcome possible discrimination.
- Examples of positive discrimination based on race include:
  - reserving school places for students from certain ethnic groups
  - organisations setting recruitment targets for employees from minority ethnic groups.
- UK law does not allow positive discrimination and only allows positive action. This is where people can act to reduce disadvantage or underrepresentation of a certain group, for example, minority ethnic groups.
- For example, if an employer had two equally qualified candidates for a job, they could give the role to the candidate who has a protected characteristic that is under-represented in the workplace.
- However, positive action does not allow an employer to give the job to a less suitable candidate just because that candidate has a protected characteristic.
- The purpose of taking action is to counter inequality and make things fair (just) for people who have not been treated fairly in the past.

REVISION TIP

For each of the following types of discrimination, write one example of behaviour that would show negative discrimination, and one example of positive action: racism, sexism, disability discrimination, ageism.

Christian and Muslim views on racial prejudice and discrimination

- Both Christians and Muslims are against racial prejudice and discrimination.
- Both religions have followers from all races – they are not limited or exclusive to one race.
- Their sources of wisdom and authority support equality and justice.

† Christianity

> 66 *There is neither Jew nor Gentile, neither slave nor free, nor is there male and female, for you are all one in Christ Jesus.* 99   (Galatians 3:28)

> 66 *Stop judging by mere appearances, but instead judge correctly.* 99   (John 7:24)

☾ Islam

> 66 *People, We created you all from a single man and a single woman, and made you into races and tribes so that you should get to know one another.* 99   (Qur'an 49:13)

> 66 *People are equal like the teeth of a comb.* 99   (Hadith)

Knowledge

41 F: Social justice, racial prejudice, and discrimination

Human rights and responsibilities

- Human rights are the basic freedoms to which all human beings should be entitled.
- The Universal Declaration of Human Rights (UDHR) was adopted by the United Nations General Assembly in 1948.
- The UDHR set out 30 articles which uphold the fundamental human rights to be universally protected:

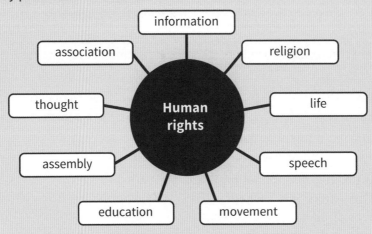

- Not all countries have signed up to uphold the UDHR.
- The UK also passed the Human Rights Act (HRA) in 1998. This means that public organisations, for example, the NHS, must respect and protect an individual's rights when dealing with them.

The responsibilities that come with rights

- Your human rights are balanced by your responsibility to consider other people's human rights and to obey the law.
- Sometimes people's rights may be limited. For example, people serving prison sentences have had their liberty and right to freedom of movement taken away.

Article from UDHR	Human right	Responsibility to uphold that right
Article 4	No one shall be held in slavery or servitude.	The responsibility to ensure that people are not forced to work against their will, and to pay people fairly for the work they do.
Article 18	Everyone has the right to freedom of thought, conscience, and religion.	The responsibility to ensure that all religions are treated fairly.
Article 19	Everyone has the right to freedom of opinion and expression.	The responsibility to ensure that what we express does not incite hatred or damage, or break any other law.

† Christian views on human rights and responsibilities

- Most Christians agree that we should support all of the human rights in the UDHR.

- As part of 'loving your neighbour' and following the Golden Rule, 'Treat others as you wish to be treated', Christians aim to ensure that everybody is treated fairly.

- Galatians 3:28 reminds Christians about equality:

> ❝ *There is neither Jew nor Gentile, neither slave nor free, nor is there male and female, for you are all one in Christ Jesus.* ❞

- Proverbs 31:8–9 is clear that Christians should stand up for other people's rights:

> ❝ *Speak up for those who cannot speak for themselves for the rights of all who are destitute. Speak up and judge fairly; defend the rights of the poor and needy.* ❞

☾ Muslim views on human rights and responsibilities

- Not all Muslim countries agree with the UDHR as Shari'ah law already covers protecting human rights.

- The Cairo Declaration on Human Rights (CDHR) in 1990 used Islamic teachings to create a similar set of rights.

- Article one of the CDHR states:

"All human beings form one family whose members are united by their subordination to Allah and descent from Adam. All men are equal in terms of basic human dignity and basic obligations and responsibilities, without any discrimination on the basis of race, colour, language, belief, sex, religion, political affiliation, social status or other considerations."

- The Qur'an teaches to:

> ❝ *... help one another to do what is right and good ...* ❞   (Qur'an 5:2)

- In his farewell sermon the Prophet Muhammad said:

> ❝ *So regard the life and property as a sacred trust. Return the goods entrusted to you to their rightful owners. Hurt no one so that no one may hurt you. Remember that you will indeed meet your Lord and that He will indeed reckon your deeds.* ❞

Key terms	Make sure you can write a definition for these key terms	social justice human rights racial prejudice discrimination positive discrimination

⮂ Retrieval

Learn the answers to the questions below, then cover the answers column with a piece of paper and write as many as you can. Check and repeat.

Questions / Answers

	Questions	Answers
1	Give one example of social injustice.	One from: the rich being treated better than the poor / some people not having access to education / the police treating certain groups of people badly / racial inequality / religious persecution
2	Name one of the main types of human rights that the Universal Declaration of Human Rights outlined.	One from: association / information / religion / life / speech / education / movement / thought / assembly
3	Article 4 of the Universal Declaration of Human Rights says 'No one shall be held in slavery or servitude'. Give one possible responsibility from this.	One from: to pay people fairly for the work that they do / to ensure people are not made to work against their will
4	Give a quotation from the Bible which supports equality.	*"There is neither Jew nor Gentile, neither slave nor free, nor is there male and female, for you are all one."*
5	Why do some Islamic countries not agree with the Universal Declaration of Human Rights?	They believe that Shari'ah law already protects human rights
6	What does positive discrimination mean?	Giving a particular group special privileges to overcome possible discrimination
7	What phrase means treating someone unfairly due to their ethnic group or nationality?	Racial discrimination or racism

Put paper here

Previous questions

Now go back and use these questions to check your knowledge of previous topics.

Questions / Answers

	Questions	Answers
8	True or false: neither Christianity nor Islam teach that all humans are equal.	False – both Christianity and Islam teach that all humans are equal
9	Who in the Bible said, *"Women should remain silent in the churches"*?	St Paul (in 1 Corinthians 14:34–35)
10	Which Hadith quotation promotes equality?	*"People are equal like the teeth of a comb."*
11	In what year did the Church of England first allow women priests?	1993
12	What is the traditional role of a woman in Islam?	Mother and housekeeper

Put paper here

Practice

Exam-style questions

01 Which **one** of these is showing prejudice against someone because of their ethnic group or nationality?

Put a tick (✓) in the box next to the correct answer. **(1 mark)**

A	Violence	☐
B	Ageism	☐
C	Racism	☐
D	Sexism	☐

02 Which **one** of these means ensuring that society treats people fairly and protects people's human rights?

Put a tick (✓) in the box next to the correct answer. **(1 mark)**

A	Social justice	☐
B	Prejudice	☐
C	Positive discrimination	☐
D	Discrimination	☐

03 Give **two** religious beliefs about social justice. **(2 marks)**

04 Name **two** forms of discrimination. **(2 marks)**

05 Explain **two** similar religious beliefs on racial prejudice.

In your answer you must refer to one or more religious traditions. **(4 marks)**

> **EXAM TIP**
>
> You can develop your points by giving more detail, or you could use an example to illustrate your point.

06 Explain **two** religious beliefs about the responsibilities people have to uphold human rights.

Refer to sacred writings or another source of religious belief and teaching in your answer. **(5 marks)**

07 'It is easy to ensure that there is social justice.'

Evaluate this statement.

In your answer you:

- should give reasoned arguments in support of this statement
- should give reasoned arguments to support a different point of view
- should refer to religious arguments
- may refer to non-religious arguments
- should reach a justified conclusion. **(12 marks)**

(+ SPaG 3 marks)

> **EXAM TIP**
>
> Check your spelling as much as possible in your 12-mark answer as it will contribute to your SPaG (spelling, punctuation, and grammar) mark.

⚙ Knowledge

42 F: Wealth and exploitation of the poor

The right attitude to wealth

- Being wealthy means having a great deal of money, resources, or assets.
- In 2021, there were over 2000 billionaires around the world and over 50 million millionaires.
- Some very wealthy individuals, such as Bill Gates, the billionaire founder of Microsoft, donate a significant proportion of their wealth to charity, and encourage others to do the same.
- Some people believe that if you are wealthy, you have a duty to help others.

Use of wealth

Help those who cannot afford basics such as clothing, food, water, and healthcare.

Help support people to raise themselves out of poverty.

Sharing wealth

Provide people with training to improve their skills so they can find work.

Provide education so everyone has a basic level of literacy/numeracy.

Provide shelter for people who don't have a safe place to live.

The causes of poverty

- **Poverty** means not having enough money for food or other basic needs of life.
- There are many causes of poverty, and levels of poverty may depend on where a person lives.
- In less economically developed countries (LEDC) many people live in poverty.
- People also live in poverty in more economically developed countries (MEDC), including in the UK. Research suggests that 90 000 people die in poverty each year in the UK.

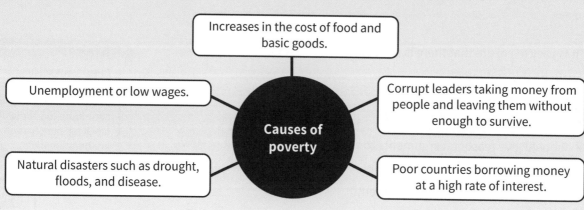

Increases in the cost of food and basic goods.

Unemployment or low wages.

Corrupt leaders taking money from people and leaving them without enough to survive.

Causes of poverty

Natural disasters such as drought, floods, and disease.

Poor countries borrowing money at a high rate of interest.

† Christian views on wealth and poverty

- In the Old Testament **wealth** was seen as a blessing from God:

> 66 *But remember the Lord your God, for it is he who gives you the ability to produce wealth.* 99
> (Deuteronomy 8:18)

- In the New Testament Jesus warned people not to become greedy and selfish as wealth can take you away from focusing on God:

> 66 *It is easier for a camel to go through the eye of a needle than for someone who is rich to enter the kingdom of God.* 99
> (Mark 10:25)

> 66 *Jesus said, 'No one can serve two masters [...] You cannot serve both God and money.* 99
> (Matthew 6:24)

- Christian teachings support sharing wealth to help tackle poverty as a form of Christian love (agape). This may include giving to a Christian charity.

☾ Muslim views on wealth and poverty

- Islam teaches that wealth is a blessing from God but that it should be used for the benefit of everyone and not stockpiled:

> 66 *Tell those who hoard gold and silver instead of giving in God's cause that they will have a grievous punishment.* 99
> (Qur'an 9:34)

- The core practice of almsgiving (Zakah/Khums) means that Muslims help those who are living in poverty.
- They will be rewarded by God on Judgement Day for sharing what they have with others.
- Muslims should not gain wealth through things such as gambling or receiving interest payments on loans:

> 66 *Intoxicants and gambling, idolatrous practices, and [divining with] arrows are repugnant acts – Satan's doing – shun them so that you may prosper.* 99
> (Qur'an 5:90)

Exploitation of the poor

- Some people exploit people living in poverty.
- This means they misuse power or money to get people to do things for little or unfair reward.
- People living in poverty often feel that they have no other options, so they are pressured into being exploited.

Fair pay	• Some companies do not pay their workers a fair wage for the country that they live in. • The companies know the workers may find it difficult to find work elsewhere, so pay them very little. • Some countries have no laws to enforce a minimum wage. • The UK has a national minimum wage, and companies can be prosecuted for paying workers less than this.
Excessive interest on loans	• If someone living in poverty doesn't have enough money for basic necessities, they might need to take out a loan. • Some companies and individuals offer to lend money, but at excessive interest rates. • For example, someone borrows £100 but the excessive interest rates means that they end up owing £5000. • People are never able to pay back the loan due to the excessive interest, so the debt keeps increasing. • People take out a loan because they are in poverty, but the excessive interest charged means that they are driven further into poverty.
People trafficking	• People traffickers profit from controlling and exploiting people, often those living in poverty. • They may offer people living in poverty work, which often appears to be well-paid and a route out of poverty. • They then force them to work away from home for little or no pay. • This may be in another country that they don't know, and they may not know where they are or speak the language. • People traffickers often tell people that they will earn a good wage, but they often work in poor conditions and without the money promised. • Some are forced to be slaves or prostitutes. • Other people are kidnapped by people traffickers and forced to work with no pay. • People traffickers often threaten or use violence. • The victims can be too afraid to escape or to notify the authorities, so stay where they are.

Key terms — Make sure you can write a definition for these key terms

> poverty   wealth   fair pay   people trafficking

✝ Christian teachings on the exploitation of the poor

- Christianity teaches that we should look after people living in poverty and not exploit their situation, so would agree with fair pay:

> ❝ *Do not exploit the poor because they are poor.* ❞ (Proverbs 22:22)

- In the Old Testament of the Bible it is forbidden to charge interest. Christians today may believe that the Old Testament teachings were for a specific time and context, and it is acceptable to charge interest if it is a reasonable amount and does not create further poverty:

> ❝ *Do not charge your brother interest, whether on money or food or anything else that may earn interest.* ❞ (Deuteronomy 23:19)

- The teachings of Christianity lead Christians to believe that slavery is wrong. People trafficking does not respect victims and so goes against key teachings of 'Love your neighbour as yourself' and the Christian belief of 'agape' (unconditional love for all humans):

> ❝ *Truly I tell you, whatever you did for one of the least of these brothers and sisters of mine, you did for me.* ❞ (Matthew 25:40)

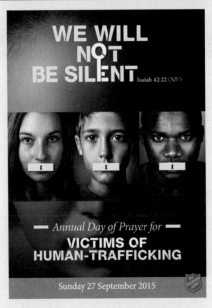

▲ *Salvation Army poster promoting a day of prayer for victims of human trafficking*

☪ Muslim teachings on the exploitation of the poor

- Islam teaches that you should pay people fairly for the work that they have done:

> ❝ *Give the worker his wages before his sweat dries.* ❞ (Hadith)

- Islam forbids charging interest on loans (usury), and there are Islamic banks that allow people to borrow money without paying interest:

> ❝ *God has allowed trade and forbidden usury. Whoever, on receiving God's warning, stops taking usury may keep his past gains – God will be his judge – but whoever goes back to usury will be an inhabitant of the Fire, there to remain. God blights usury, but blesses charitable deeds with multiple increase.* ❞ (Qur'an 2:276)

- Slavery was common at the time of Muhammad, and he did not stop it. However, the Qur'an and Hadith are clear that slaves should have rights and also be able to be freed. However, Muslims would not agree with people trafficking as it exploits people, and Islam does not allow this:

> ❝ *Your slaves are your brothers and Allah has put them under your command. So whoever has a brother under his command should feed him of what he eats and dress him of what he wears. Do not ask them (slaves) to do things beyond their capacity (power) and if you do so, then help them.* ❞ (Hadith)

REVISION TIP ☑

Consider the following situations and write down how you think a Muslim and Christian might respond, based on the relevant teachings.

1 A person wins 1 million pounds on the lottery.
2 A person is given a pay bonus of £500.
3 A person lends their friend £10, but asks the friend to pay them back £20 instead of £10.

Retrieval

Learn the answers to the questions below, then cover the answers column with a piece of paper and write as many as you can. Check and repeat.

Questions		Answers
1	Give one way that wealth can help others.	One from: money for basics such as clothing, food, water, and health care / help people raise themselves out of poverty / train people so they can find work / provide education / provide shelter
2	Give one reason for poverty.	One from: unemployment / natural disasters (drought, floods, and disease) / corrupt leadership / countries borrowing at a high rate of interest / increases in the cost of food and basic goods
3	Which quotation from the Bible warns people not to become greedy and selfish?	*"It is easier for a camel to go through the eye of a needle than for someone who is rich to enter the kingdom of God."*
4	Which quotation from the Qur'an warns against stockpiling money and encourages Muslims to share their wealth?	*"Tell those who hoard gold and silver instead of giving in God's cause that they will have a grievous punishment."*
5	What is it forbidden to do if money is lent to someone, according to Islam?	Charge interest
6	Name two types of almsgiving in Islam.	Zakah, Khums
7	What is the word for Christian unconditional love for all humans?	Agape

(Put paper here)

Previous questions

Now go back and use these questions to check your knowledge of previous topics.

Questions		Answers
8	Give one reason why some Christians might not allow women leaders in church.	One from: Jesus was male / Jesus chose male disciples / St Paul spoke against women speaking in church
9	Why do some Islamic countries not agree with the Universal Declaration of Human Rights?	They believed that Shari'ah law already protects human rights
10	What does positive discrimination mean?	Giving a particular group special privileges to overcome possible discrimination
11	What phrase means treating someone unfairly due to their ethnic group or nationality?	Racial discrimination or racism

(Put paper here)

42 Wealth and exploitation of the poor

Exam-style questions

01 Which **one** of these means paying someone a proper amount for the work that they do?

Put a tick (✓) in the box next to the correct answer. **(1 mark)**

A   Fair pay ☐

B   Interest ☐

C   Slavery ☐

D   Bonus pay ☐

02 Give **two** reasons for poverty. **(2 marks)**

> **EXAM TIP**
> Keep your answers as short as possible to save yourself time for longer answers later.

03 Give **two** ways that religious believers can help the poor. **(2 marks)**

04 Explain **two** similar religious beliefs about the uses of wealth.

In your answer you must refer to one or more religious traditions. **(4 marks)**

05 Explain **two** religious beliefs on fair pay.

Refer to sacred writings or another source of religious belief and teaching in your answer. **(5 marks)**

> **EXAM TIP**
> Remember that you must name the source of authority when you refer to it, for example, the Bible, the Qur'an.

06 Explain **two** religious beliefs about excessive interest on loans.

Refer to sacred writings or another source of religious belief and teaching in your answer. **(5 marks)**

07 'Religious people should give away their wealth.'

Evaluate this statement.

In your answer you:

- should give reasoned arguments in support of this statement
- should give reasoned arguments to support a different point of view
- should refer to religious arguments
- may refer to non-religious arguments
- should reach a justified conclusion. **(12 marks)**

(+ SPaG 3 marks)

⚙ Knowledge

43 F: People in poverty helping themselves, and charity

The responsibilities of those living in poverty to help themselves

Depending on the reason for poverty, some believe that those living in poverty have a responsibility to help themselves.

✝ Christianity	☪ Islam
• Christians will encourage those living in poverty to help themselves out of it. This may mean finding work: ❝ *The one who is unwilling to work shall not eat.* ❞ (2 Thessalonians 3:10)	• Whilst the poor may receive the benefit of Zakah, they are encouraged to manage their money wisely as it will mean they won't get into poverty: ❝ *I guarantee that those who economise will never fall poor.* ❞ (Hadith)
• If the cause of poverty can be addressed, then people should try to deal with the cause: ❝ *...for drunkards and gluttons become poor, and drowsiness clothes them in rags.* ❞ (Proverbs 23:22)	• Muslims are warned not to overspend on things: ❝ *...do not be extravagant: God does not like extravagant people.* ❞ (Qur'an 7:31)

Charity

- Many people give money and goods, or fundraise for charities to help those who are in need.

- Some people prefer not to give money directly to those in need as it may be misused, for example, the money might be used to buy alcohol or drugs. Instead they give via a charity that they know will use the money in the area of most need. For example, instead of giving money to homeless people they will donate to a charity that helps the homeless.

> **REVISION TIP** ✅
>
> Look back at the Christianity practices section to remind yourself what some of these charities do.

† Christianity and charity

- Many Christians share their wealth by giving money in a collection in church on a Sunday, paying a **tithe** (10% of their earnings), or by giving to charities that help others.

- This shows Christian love (agape) to people that they do not know, and it can help to tackle poverty.

- The Parable of the Sheep and Goats (Matthew 25:31–46) shows that people that help those in poverty will go to God's 'right side' in heaven.

- Christian charities such as Christian Aid and CAFOD use donations to help those living in poverty.

REVISION TIP

The Parable of the Sheep and Goats (Matthew 25:31–46) is useful here and also for other topics such as life after death.

☾ Islam and charity

- The practice of **almsgiving** is a core practice for all Muslims.

  - Zakah: giving 2.5% of wealth over a certain amount (Sunni Pillar of Islam and Shi'a Obligatory Act).

  - **Khums**: giving 20% of wealth (Shi'a Obligatory Act).

- Muslims will be rewarded by God at Judgement for giving to charity:

> 66 …those who perform the prayers, pay the prescribed alms, and believe in God and the Last Day – to them We shall give a great reward. 99
>
> (Qur'an 4:162)

- Muslims can also give additional charity (**Sadaqah**) which may include money, clothing, food, and their time.

- Muslim charities such as Islamic Relief and Muslim Aid use donations to try to reduce poverty around the world.

REVISION TIP

Look back at the Islam practices section to remind yourself about Zakah and Khums.

Islamic Relief Worldwide

Key terms — Make sure you can write a definition for these key terms

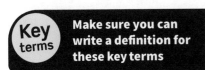

tithe   almsgiving   Khums   Sadaqah

Retrieval

Learn the answers to the questions below, then cover the answers column with a piece of paper and write as many as you can. Check and repeat.

Questions / Answers

#	Questions	Answers
1	Give the Bible quotation from 2 Thessalonians 3:10: which supports the idea that those in poverty should try to help themselves.	*"The one who is unwilling to work shall not eat."*
2	Which quotation from the Qur'an warns Muslims not to spend too much?	*"...do not be extravagant: God does not like extravagant people."*
3	What percentage of their wealth do some Christians give as tithe?	10%
4	Why might some people prefer not to give money directly to those in need, but prefer to give to a charity?	The money could be misused, for example, to buy alcohol or drugs
5	Muslims can also give Sadaqah. What is this?	Additional charity, which may include money, clothing, food, and their time
6	Which Hadith reassures Muslims that they will not be poor if they manage their money wisely?	*"I guarantee that those who economise will never fall poor."*
7	What percentage of their wealth should Muslims pay in Zakah?	2.5%
8	True or false: Shi'a Muslims should pay 10% of their wealth in Khums.	False – they should pay 20% of their wealth in Khums
9	In which parable in the Bible does it show that people who help those in poverty will go to God's 'right side' in heaven?	The Parable of the Sheep and Goats

Put paper here

Previous questions

Now go back and use these questions to check your knowledge of previous topics.

Questions / Answers

#	Questions	Answers
10	What is the word for Christian unconditional love for all humans?	Agape
11	Name one of the main types of human rights that the Universal Declaration of Human Rights outlined.	One from: association / information / religion / life / speech / education / movement / thought / assembly
12	What phrase means treating someone unfairly due to their ethnic group or nationality?	Racial discrimination or racism
13	Which Bible quotation teaches Christians to love other people, including those who might not be the same as them?	*"Love your neighbour as yourself."*
14	What is it forbidden to do if money is lent to someone, according to Islam?	Charge interest

Put paper here

43 People in poverty helping themselves, and charity

Exam-style questions

01 Which **one** of these is not an act of charity?

Put a tick (✓) in the box next to the correct answer. **(1 mark)**

   A   Volunteering to help victims of war   ☐

   B   Giving clothing to refugees   ☐

   C   Giving money to the homeless   ☐

   D   Buying new clothes for yourself   ☐

02 Which **one** of these is the correct percentage for Khums?

Put a tick (✓) in the box next to the correct answer. **(1 mark)**

   A   2.5   ☐

   B   5   ☐

   C   10   ☐

   D   20   ☐

EXAM TIP

In the exam, make sure you clearly write the correct answer's letter. You can use capital letters to help the examiner see your answer clearly.

03 Name **two** ways religious people can give to charity. **(2 marks)**

04 Give **two** reasons why religious people give to charity. **(2 marks)**

05 Explain **two** similar religious beliefs about the responsibilities of those living in poverty to help themselves overcome the difficulties they face.

In your answer you must refer to one or more religious traditions. **(4 marks)**

06 Explain **two** religious beliefs about giving to charity.

Refer to sacred writings or another source of religious belief and teaching in your answer. **(5 marks)**

07 'Everyone should give money to charity.'

Evaluate this statement.

In your answer you:

- should give reasoned arguments in support of this statement
- should give reasoned arguments to support a different point of view
- should refer to religious arguments
- may refer to non-religious arguments
- should reach a justified conclusion. **(12 marks)**

(+ SPaG 3 marks)

EXAM TIP

In a 12-mark question you don't have to write arguments 'against' the statement. You must present a different view which doesn't have to be the opposite of the statement.